Microsoft®
Flight Simulator
for Windows® 95
inside
moves

Microsoft *Press*

Gary M. Meredith

PUBLISHED BY
Microsoft Press
A Division of Microsoft Corporation
One Microsoft Way
Redmond, Washington 98052-6399

Library of Congress Cataloging-in-Publication Data
Meredith, Gary M., 1951–
    Microsoft flight simulator   :   inside moves / Gary M. Meredith.
        p.   cm.
    Indexes.
    ISBN 1-57231-362-5
    1. Microsoft flight simulator (Computer file)   2. Computer flight
games.   I. Title.
    TL712.8.M47   1996
    794.8'753--dc20   96-36333
                                                                    CIP

Printed and bound in the United States of America.

    3 4 5 6 7 8 9   QMQM   1 0 9 8 7

Distributed to the book trade in Canada by Macmillan of Canada, a division of Canada Publishing Corporation.

A CIP catalogue record for this book is available from the British Library.

Microsoft Press books are available through booksellers and distributors worldwide. For further information about international editions, contact your local Microsoft Corporation office. Or contact Microsoft Press International directly at fax (206) 936-7329.

The aeronautical charts used throughout this book are from the Ames Navigation Maps CD software system (copyright 1993–1996, Ames Maps LLC), and are reprinted with their kind permission.

The original aerobatics images (Bucker Jungmeister, Yak 18P, Zlin 50 and Cap-20) used in this book were provided to us through the courtesy of Sport Aerobics Magazine and the International Aerobatic Club, and are reproduced with their permission.

The approach charts, for the San Francisco International Airport in Chapter Six, are generated with the software package Final Approach by Georges Lorsche and are included with his permission.

Acquisitions Editors: Kim Fryer, Steve Guty, Lucinda Rowley
Project Editor: Stuart J. Stuple

Dedication

To my wife, Mari, and to my family and friends:
thanks for believing that eccentricity is an endearing quality.

Gary Meredith

Acknowledgments

In addition to Gary Meredith, I would like to thank the
many people who assisted in the creation of this book, including
the staff and associates of The PC Press, Inc.:
Richard Mansfield, Project Editor; Kim Davis, Art Director;
Kathleen Ingram, Book Coordinator; Phill Powell, Associate Editor;
Leslie Mizell, Associate Editor; and Sylvia Graham, Copy Editor.

Thanks are also due our many colleagues at Microsoft, including
Stuart Stuple, Microsoft Press, and Lynn Guthrie at Microsoft Games.
Special thanks to the many people who assisted us in other ways,
including Rodney Mazour and Michael Normandeau at AmesMaps,
Karen Diamond, Sport Aerobatics Magazine;
Guenther Eichorn at the International Aerobatics Club
and Georges Lorsche, Final Approach.

Robert C. Lock,
President and Editor-in-Chief, The PC Press, Inc.

Contents

Introduction

FLIGHT SIMULATOR HISTORY

Given the large number of flying accidents, it's a wonder that it took so long for effective flight simulators to be developed. To be sure, World War I saw a number of "interesting" experiments in flight simulation. One was a sort of hobby horse affair where the prospective pilot sat and fiddled with a stick while a couple of guys tilted him back and forth. A more common early simulator involved obsolete aircraft with their wings bobbed. The pilots-in-training taxied these around an airfield, safe in the knowledge that, no matter how fast they went, the only maneuver they'd be likely to perform would be a ground loop.

It would be a quarter century after the Wright's first flight before a really effective flight trainer would appear. Ed Link developed the Link Trainer in 1928, and flight instruction has never been the same. Like the Link Trainers still made today, the original featured an enclosed capsule with flight controls connected to various servos which would move the capsule relative to the control inputs. Every effort was made to produce a true feeling of flight, although the stubby little wings and empennage affixed to the outside of the capsule were more comical than anything else. The Link Trainer, and others, remained pretty much the same until the early sixties, when the power of mainframe computers was harnessed to bring even more realism to flight simulation. The Defense Department quite naturally saw flight simulation as a way to increase pilot proficiency in the midst of the escalating costs of actually flying the new high-performance jets. And with the introduction of computers a simulator could do more than just bob around in response to the stick and pedals. All sorts of situations could be set up for the pilot to react to, with the benefit that, when it came down to the real flying, a serious mechanical problem or a fatal combat situation didn't mean loss of either the pilot or the plane.

The Link Trainer.

Which brings us to the early 1980s and IBM's new baby, the PC. With computing power the Pentagon would have envied only a few years previously, the PC opened up new opportunities in many areas, not the least of which was simulation. For the first time, the performance envelopes of cars; ships; and, of course, aircraft could be calculated and modified on the fly, and the results viewed in real time.

Computer flight simulators are usually classified as either a flight combat simulator or as a realistic flight simulator. Flight combat simulators usually, though not always, emphasize the combat aspect over an attempt to replicate highly realistic flight. Even the sweetest flying combat jet is a real handful to fly in the real world. There are, after all, several very good reasons why military combat pilots don't do their basic training in F-16s. If a simulation were to make the same demands on the computer pilot as a real fighter plane makes, most people would give up almost immediately. The primary mission of combat flight simulators is entertainment, as in blasting the enemy from the sky, so there's usually quite a bit of buffering done to the aircraft flight envelopes to allow would-be aces to concentrate on running up big mission scores.

The other kind of simulator is represented by the original Microsoft Flight Simulator. These sims attempt to come as close to real flying as is possible within the confines of a computer screen. Every effort is made to model the flight envelopes of the sim planes after those of the genuine articles, and the degree to which a flight simulation program is successful is in direct proportion to how close the modeling comes. And with more and more actual pilots turning to flight simulators for entertainment, it's getting harder and harder for the software designer to get away with shipping a poorly modeled simulation.

Microsoft Flight Simulator appeared

In today's Flight Simulator, you can safely buzz Beijing's Forbidden City.

not long after the first IBM PCs were rolling off the assembly lines, and it has been an integral part of computer entertainment ever since. With each new iteration the essence of flight has been more fully realized, and with this newest version, harnessing the power of 32-bit computing offered by Windows 95, Microsoft Flight Simulator for Windows 95 comes closer than ever to putting the computer user up among the clouds.

We're starting the book, in Chapter One, by jumping directly into a "first" flight. If you'd like a bit more background in aviation basics, Chapter Two takes you through the extensive resources found in Microsoft Flight Simulator for Windows 95.

Chapter One

GETTING STARTED

Before going up for our first flight, let's take an overview of the major options and features you should know about before taking off. As with many other programs upgraded to Windows 95, Microsoft Flight Simulator for Windows 95 setup has been greatly simplified. With Windows 95 in charge of determining hardware and operating system configuration, your main concern is just how you want Flight Simulator to perform. While setup within Flight Simulator is easy, there are a few points worth highlighting.

Fly Now!

Once you've installed and started the program, you'll see an opening screen displaying options for accessing Flight Simulator. In later chapters we'll explore various additional options, but for your first flight we'll just click on Fly Now! and proceed to the program's main screen. By the way, even though you've already

Microsoft Flight Simulator for Windows 95: Opening Screen.

installed Flight Simulator, you'll need to keep the game CD in your drive to access files such as performance boosters and video files that are not transferred to your hard drive during installation.

Create Flight...	
Select **F**light...	
Reset Flight	CTRL-;
Save Flight...	;
S**u**rprise Flight	
Lessons...	
C**h**allenges...	
A**d**ventures...	
Show Opening Screen	
E**x**it	CTRL-C

Flights Menu.

Create Flight Menu.

Starting or Resuming a Flight

To load and save flights in Flight Simulator, click on the File heading at the far left on the menu bar. Here you have the option to create a new flight, load a previously saved flight, reset an already loaded flight, (which takes you back to the beginning of the flight) and save a flight, along with all its parameters (aircraft type, weather, control settings, and so on).

If you choose Create Flight from the Flight Menu, you can specify the type of aircraft, your location (usually an airfield near the city of your choice), the general weather conditions (clear, cloudy, or otherwise), and the time of day. You can control the conditions of flight in greater detail (see below), but the only way to get into the air more quickly is to go with Chicago's Meigs Field, the default flight.

The Select Flight option on the Flight

menu brings up a secondary menu with a listing of previously saved flights. Depending on the options you chose in the Preferences menu regarding flight parameters to be saved, Select Flight lets you resume a flight at exactly the spot where you left it, and with the same aircraft, weather, control, and view settings restored.

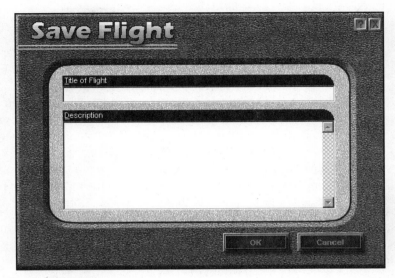

Save Flight Menu.

Stumble into a flat spin too near the ground or misread a chart and end up cruising over Death Valley with half a gallon of fuel left in a real airplane, and the last anyone will see of you is a faded photo behind the bar at the local airfield's watering hole, la Pancho's of Edwards Air Force Base (and *The Right Stuff*) fame. Flight Simulator lets you walk away from fatal mistakes by using the Reset Flight option on the Flight menu. This takes you back to where your flight started, but be aware that, unless you've saved the flight prior to your misstep, you'll go back to the default flight, sitting in the Cessna on the runway at Meigs. Also, don't be surprised when, after resetting a night flight, you find yourself back in broad daylight, no matter what the actual time is.

The Save Flight option allows you to save all the parameters of your flight, a handy feature when you're undertaking a cross-country flight but it's time for dinner. The menu that appears not only lets you give the flight a unique name but also provides space for a more detailed description of the flight, useful when you're experimenting with the same general flight (flying from Paris to London, for example), but under different conditions or with a variety of aircraft.

In addition, there's a Surprise Flight option for those times when you're seeking an adventure into the unknown. When you select Surprise Flight, Flight

Simulator chooses the parameters. Below the flight options are menu items that will take you to the Lessons section, to the Challenges (where you're thrust into flying situations that usually feature one or more adverse conditions for you to overcome), and to the Adventures section, which provides longer, more structured flights than the situations you encounter in Challenges. You can also go back to the opening screen from the Flight menu as well as exit completely from the program. Incidentally, you'll notice that the names of many of the options within the Flight menu and the other menus have a letter underlined. This lets you use the keyboard rather than the mouse to choose an item. Just press the underlined letter. A few items have an additional key combination listed to the right, which indicates that this particular item can be activated by pressing that key combination without having to go through the menu.

Keyboard Hot Keys

Reset Flight	CTRL-;	Maximize Current Window	W
Save Flight	;	Window 1	[(press twice to deselect)
Land Me (182 only)	X	Window 2	] (press twice to deselect)
Slew Control	Y	Map Window Numlock (press twice to deselect)	
Pause Flight	P	Instrument Panel	SHIFT - [
Simulation Rate	R	Display Flight Information	Z
Smoke System	I	Toggle Views (Cockpit—Tower—Spot Plane)	S
Sound	Q		

Yet another way to access some menu items quickly is to click the right mouse button. This brings up a small floating menu with entries to select Cockpit, Tower, or Spot Plane Views; maximize the current window; close the main window and instrument display; and the Mouse As Yoke option. (See below in the Controller section.)   There's also a What's This item for whenever you just can't remember whether a gauge is relaying altitude or speed or whether you're listening to AM or FM.

Aircraft Settings

Your first flight in Flight Simulator, unless you choose otherwise, is from Meigs Field near Chicago, Illinois, in a Cessna 182RG, already idling on the runway.

This is a good place to start, given the open airspace and interesting scenery. However, the default settings for your aircraft and for the views will almost certainly need some modification.

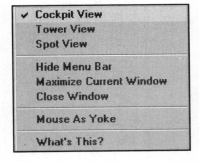

We'll assume you're going to stick with the Cessna for the first flight, but let's just take a quick look at the Select Aircraft menu. All six Flight Simulator planes are listed here, along with an animated thumbnail graphic, a brief description, and a rundown of essential aircraft specifications. You'll find these specifications explained in Chapter Three.

Menu—Right Mouse Click.

Having chosen the Cessna, let's establish just how we want the plane to react, what views we want to see, and what information we want relayed to us by the instruments. This setting up actually takes place under two different menus—Aircraft Settings in the Aircraft menu and Preferences in the Options menu. We'll work with the Aircraft Settings menu first. Click on any of the subheadings in the third section of the menu—Realism & Reliability, Crash & Damage, Engines & Fuel, or Instrument Display— and the menu for adjusting all these parameters appears.

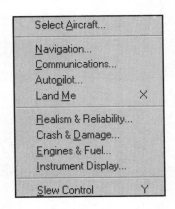

Select Aircraft.

Clicking on the Realism tab displays a set of parameters that determine how closely your Flight Simulator craft mimics its real-life counterpart. A slider control adjusts the amount of authenticity for overall control of the plane. The more you slide the control toward the Difficult setting, the more the craft responds like a real airplane. For your first few flights it's best to leave the control on its default setting of Easy so that you don't "overcontrol" your plane. As you become more experienced, you'll want a more responsive airplane and so will want to increase the difficulty level here, as well as in the Controls menu under Preferences. (See below).

Below the slider control are buttons for enabling other reality settings. Auto-coordination links a plane's rudder and aileron controls so that, when you make a turn, you only have to worry about one control input. There have actually been aircraft through the years where auto-coordination was a real-life feature, so this isn't totally a simulation oddity. Activating the Elevator Trim

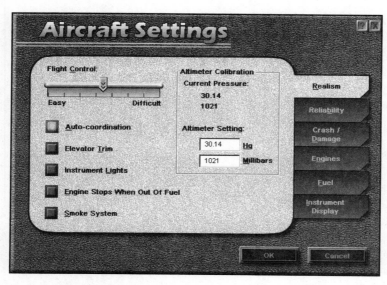

Aircraft Settings: Realism Menu.

Aircraft Settings: Reliability Menu.

button lets you adjust, from the instrument panel, whether a plane climbs, dives, or is neutral in a "hands off" situation. Instrument Lights is pretty obvious, turning on the instrument panel's lights whenever there's a perceived low-light condition. You'd think Engine Stops When Out of Fuel would be the default, but Flight Simulator's designers have chosen to give you a break on mileage, at least while you're learning. So you'll need to click on this button to experience the real thrill of dead-stick landing a 737. The Smoke System option causes the plane to trail smoke as do aerobatic aircraft. This is great if you're flying the Extra 300S but not a realistic, or popular, option at the local flying field. Since the Smoke System does

provide a continuous record of a plane's flight path, it can be a useful tool for perfecting your basic maneuvers, no matter what plane you're flying. Finally, there are entry windows for resetting your altimeter, with values expressed both in inches of mercury (Hg) and millibars. You should change these values only after you've learned a bit about the influence of atmospheric pressure since you can render your altimeter useless with an uninformed adjustment.

The adjustments on the next tab, Reliability, can turn your plane into either a lemon or a creampuff. There's an overall reliability slider control that acts to randomly impose the ravages of time and use on your plane. Additionally you can specify whether you'd like instrument lights to burn out on a random basis, as well as inflict gyro drift on your instrumentation. In a nutshell, a spinning gyro creates a resistance to force which can be measured, in the case of an airplane by the Artificial Horizon Indicator (AHI), the Turn and Bank Indicator (TBI), and the Heading Indicator (HI), all of which sense changes in a plane's atitude. Unfortunately, gyro drift also results from the unique forces of a quickly spinning object, namely precession. Precession affects the Heading Indicator most radically so that a pilot must compensate for gyro drift periodically by realigning the HI with the magnetic compass.

Crashes are, unfortunately, another inevitable fact of life, especially during those first few landing approaches you'll be making. Exactly how much damage you want a mishap to inflict can be set by clicking the Crash/Damage tab. You can, of course, choose the Ignore Crash option, but what sort of object lesson would that provide? If you do decide to experience the consequences of messing around with Newton's first and

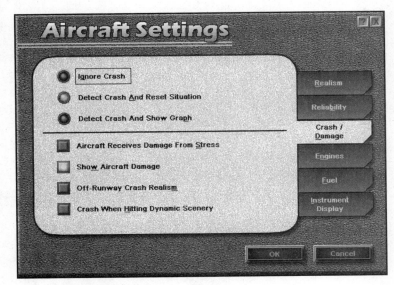

Aircraft Settings: Crash/Damage Menu.

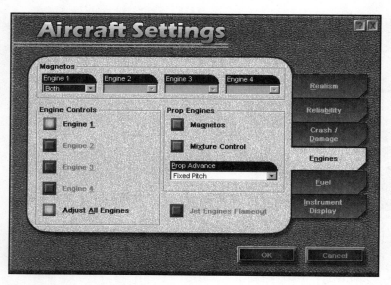

Aircraft Settings: Engines Menu.

second laws of motion you can either take your lumps and reset the flight (Detect Crash And Reset Situation) or get a graphic display of the forces and the damage involved (Detect Crash And Show Graph), as if seeing your precious plane shatter into several pieces wasn't enough graphic reinforcement!

Damage can occur to a plane in situations other than in a crash. Most planes are rated for a certain level of stress, beyond which structural damage can occur. An aerobatic plane like the Extra 300S will obviously be able to withstand stress—both aerodynamic and gravity-induced—better than a Cessna 182, but even stunt planes have their limits. Click on Aircraft Receives Damage from Stress will quickly underline the fact that high-speed outside loops are a no-no in a four-place light plane. Show Aircraft Damage is self-explanatory, while clicking Off-Runway Crash Realism and Crash When Hitting Dynamic Scenery keep you from either driving your plane anywhere you please around the airfield or buzzing the blimp flying over Chicago too closely.

The Engines tab simply gives you basic control over your powerplant(s). Depending on the plane you're flying, there will be buttons to activate the instrument panel controls. There are provisions for up to four engines, although none of the planes included with Flight Simulator have more than two. If you're flying the piston-engined Cessna, Extra, or Sopwith, you'll be able to select whether you want control over your magnetos (the ignition system), fuel mixture, and propeller settings. The latter two can be especially tricky to modulate, so it's better if you leave these options off for your first flight. Later

on you'll probably prefer to have control over at least the Prop Advance. The turbine power of the Boeing and the Learjet means fewer parameters under your control, but you can choose the Jet Engines Flame Out button to add a little excitement.

There's a great moment in the film *Spirit of St. Louis* where Jimmy Stewart, as Charles Lindbergh, finds his engine misfiring as if it's out of fuel. After a few moments of panic, he realizes that he's just forgotten to switch to another fuel tank. Don't you forget, however, should you choose to be in charge of fuel management by activating the Fuel Tank Selector button under the Fuel tab. Nearly all aircraft have multiple fuel tanks, and one of a pilot's most important secondary duties is to

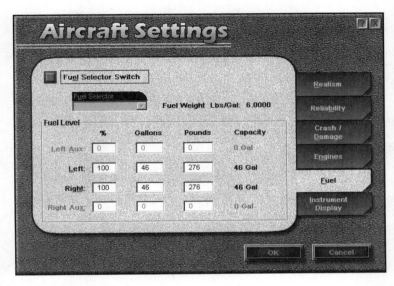

Aircraft Settings: Fuel Menu.

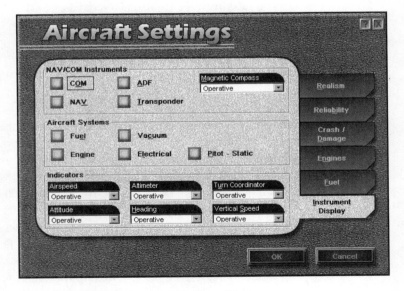

Aircraft Settings: Instrument Displays Menu.

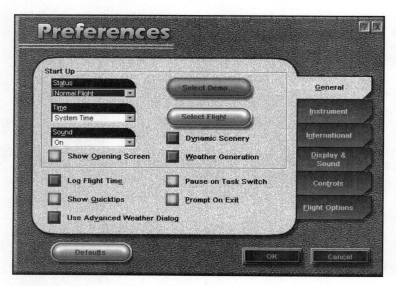

Preferences: General Menu.

make sure those tanks empty evenly. This is particularly true in a light plane like the Cessna where the fuel tanks are in the wings, and therefore any drastic imbalance can have dire consequences. In this section you can also allot yourself more fuel, although care needs to be taken here because too much fuel will result in a performance penalty.

The final tab, Instrument Displays, activates or deactivates your flight instruments. The default setting is "all on," and it would be a strange situation indeed willfully to disable an instrument, unless you're trying to simulate the loss of a particular gauge and don't want to wait for the randomness of the Reliability setting to cause that to happen. There are buttons for all your radios—Communication, Navigation, ADF (Automatic Direction Finder), and Transponder—as well as for the actual aircraft operations systems (fuel, electrical, engine values, and velocity measurement). Finally you can control the status of the indicators for most of the plane's functions. Again, unless you have a compelling reason for doing otherwise, you should leave all the buttons On and all the windows showing Operative.

To continue setting up the plane, we must move over to the Options menu and choose Preferences. Within the Preferences menu we'll first go to the General tab and modify the startup configuration. The windows for Status, Time, and Sound should remain at the default settings. The Time window, in particular, should remain set to System Time so that it's synchronized with your computer's internal clock. Later on, if you don't fancy the darkness of a 11:00 p.m. flight, you can always override the Time & Season settings from within the World menu.

Whether you want to invoke the Dynamic Scenery and Weather Generation options depends partly on how much you want to be distracted during a flight, but more importantly, on how much of a penalty you want to pay in computer performance. We'll have more to say about computer performance shortly, but if you're running Flight Simulator with what could be

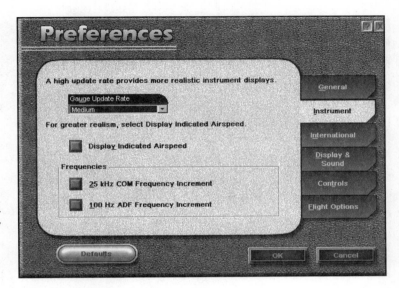

Preferences: Instrument Menu.

considered a marginal system, that is, a 486 with 8MB of RAM, you'll want to avoid options that tax your computer's processor. Unfortunately, any setting that either adds more graphical objects to the display or requires the computer to do additional computations, as these options do, will slow things down, perhaps unacceptably.

Within this menu you can also choose to log your flight time, an essential if you're going to run Flight Simulator "by the book," that is, following the basic procedures every pilot learns in Ground School. And if you feel you'd like to go it on your own, you can also disable the Quicktips option. Just don't come crying to anyone after you've managed to convert a Learjet into a John Deere in some Iowa cornfield for want of a helpful tip on the vagaries of flap management. By the way, don't disable the Prompt On Exit button unless you like starting over from scratch each time you boot up Flight Simulator, since this option gives you one last chance to save things.

Customizing the Instrument Panel

Buttons and windows in the Instrument tab allow customization of the instrument panel. The most critical parameter here is Gauge Update

Microsoft
Flight Simulator
for Windows 95

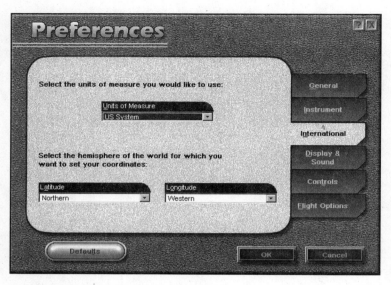

Preferences: International Menu.

Rate, which should always be set to high unless you discover that this setting appreciably degrades Flight Simulator's performance. And in almost all circumstances you'll want to be reading Indicated Air Speed, so activate this button, too. Unless you enjoy surrealistic shapes for your instrumentation, leave the panel stretching option off. Frequency increments for the Automatic Direction Finder and Communications radios are a matter of personal taste. It's advisable to select the smallest increment for most situations, so you'll want to activate both Frequency buttons.

The International tab just lets you establish your position on the globe, so to speak, for when you get down to some really serious navigation. Also, you have the option here of changing your units of measure, in case you're one of those forward-looking folks who can't figure out why metrics hasn't yet taken over.

There are as many different kinds of computers as there are different kinds of airplanes, and like airplanes, computers have strengths and weaknesses that must be taken into account. That's especially true with flight simulators, where so much is asked of the computer as a whole and also of each component. :There are hardware modifications you can add to your computer to achieve smoother, more realistic flight, but just getting the initial setup for your computer's display optimized can make Flight Simulator a more enjoyable experience.

You adjust the parameters of Flight Simulator, based in part on the relative performance of your computer, by using the options found under the Display & Sound tab. It goes without saying that you can't expect Pentium performance

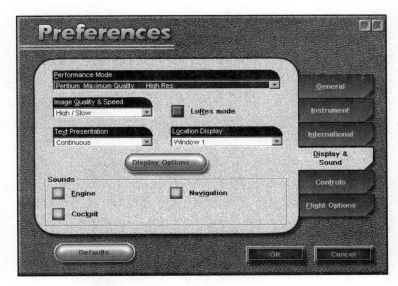

Preferences: Display & Sound Menu.

from a 486 computer, or even from one of the early 60 MHz or 66 MHz Pentiums. Yet many DX2-66 owners will wonder why simulator performance is so choppy and the aircraft so uncontrollable, especially if they've set everything up for highest graphic quality and densest detail. Unless you've got at least a 133 MHz Pentium with 24 MB of RAM (Random Access Memory), you simply won't be happy with the quality settings set to their maximums. Sure, it's tougher to tell whether that really is Helsinki you're flying over when the quality and detail settings are at mid range or lower, but it will be a lot easier to *land* in Helsinki if you've lowered those settings to a level your computer can handle. Flying even a Cessna at the highest graphic quality Pentium settings on even one of the first generation 60 MHz or 66 MHz Pentiums is akin to piloting one of the Consolidated PBY Catalina amphibians. These lumbering albatrosses, it was said, were so unresponsive to control input that, when turning, a pilot was directed (only slightly tongue in cheek) to apply full rudder and aileron, and then sing three verses of "Anchors Aweigh" while waiting for the old thing to respond. Trying to run Flight Simulator with settings above your computer's performance is just such an exercise in frustration.

Since even nominally identical computers can perform differently because of variations in memory, disk space, access times, or video configuration, you should play around with the settings to get the best balance between graphics quality and performance. The options list under the Performance Mode window runs from a minimally configured 486 to the latest fire-breathing Pentium, with enough intermediate configurations to cover just about any computer setup.

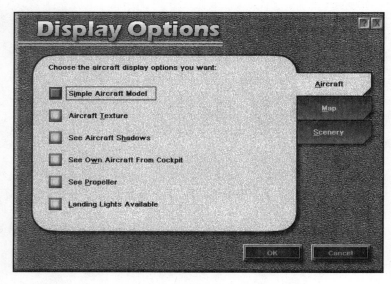

Display Options control. How you see your plane...

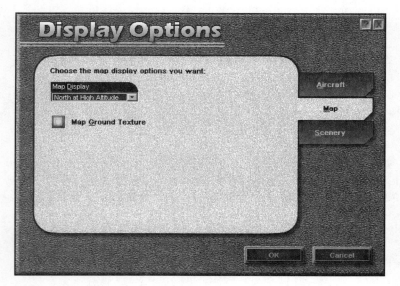

...and how maps will be presented.

Once you've specified the type of computer you're using, you can fine-tune the setup further by determining the balance you'd like between performance (that is, the smoothness and speed of the simulation) and appearance (the fineness of detail in the graphics). As mentioned above, if you have at least a 133 MHz Pentium with plenty of memory (24 MB or more), there's no reason not to select the High/Slow option here. That's a bit of a misnomer in this case, as you'll get the highest quality graphics that move smoothly and realistically as well. There is a button for low resolution which will make even the most marginally configured computer perform adequately, but the graphics suffer so much at this

setting that nearly all the illusion of flight is destroyed.

The tweaking process can get even more involved by clicking on the Display Options button. Here, three tabbed menus let you control the amount of detail you see in Aircraft (mainly in the Tower and Spot Plane views), Maps, and Scenery. Activating all the buttons in these menus does bring the utmost realism to Flight Simulator, but at the price of reduced

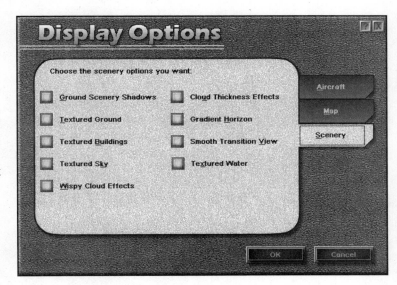

Display Options also lets you control how your surroundings will appear.

performance. Again, it's a personal decision as to where you set the balance between graphics and performance.

Flight Options

The Controls tab setup is covered below in the section on controllers, so we'll move on to the last tab, Flight Options. This section offers choices for parameters to be included whenever you save a flight. If you want to start with exactly the same setup each time you open a flight, click all of these buttons to the On position.

As you adjust the overall computer settings, you might also try varying the settings for both Scenery Complexity and Dynamic Scenery, found under the World heading on the menu bar. You might be able to choose a higher overall graphics quality if you simply limit either the complexity of the static scenery (that is, the fineness of its detail and the number of distinct objects displayed) or

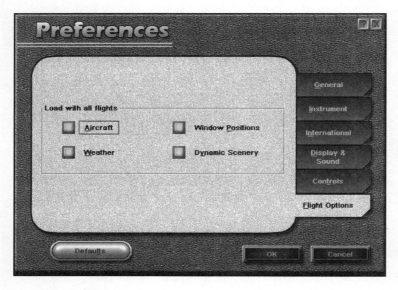

Preferences: Flight Options Menu.

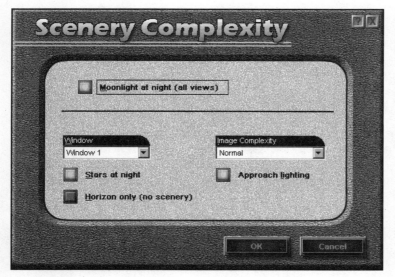

World: Scenery Complexity.

the density of the dynamic scenery, which includes planes and other moving objects.

Going back to the Aircraft heading on the menu bar, let's take a quick look at the other items listed there. An ellipsis (...) following any menu item means that clicking on the item will bring up a submenu. Changing values in the Navigation, Communication, and Autopilot menus is probably better left until you understand more about the complexities of these subjects, all of which we'll cover in later chapters. You won't need the services of any of these features for your first flights, so we'll leave them alone for now. You'll probably want to remember the Land Me command. (Press the X key.) It's a

handy item whenever you find yourself hopelessly lost. It can, however, make for some surprises because it doesn't always set you down exactly where you expect. That is, you may be in the vicinity of what you perceive to be an airfield, but Flight Simulator doesn't recognize it as such and sends you off on a joyride to its idea of the nearest airfield. Hope you had those fuel tanks topped off at your last stop!

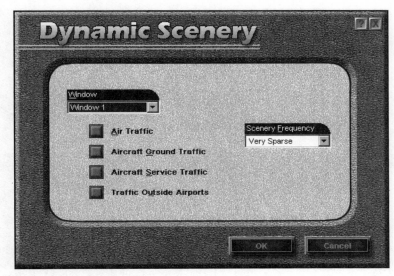

World: Dynamic Scenery.

At the very bottom of the menu is a nifty little item, the Slew Control. Can't be bothered with such insignificant concerns as taking off? Just click on the Slew Control (or press the Y key), move your plane up to 15,000 feet using the keystrokes listed below, and there you are. Admittedly this is not the most realistic way to gain altitude, but slewing is a real bonus when you're sitting in the cockpit of the Schweizer and discover that the tow plane pilots' union has just gone on strike. Slewing is also a lifesaver if you're cruising around sightseeing and want to pass quickly over a boring patch of farmland and get to something fascinating that you can see on the horizon.

You can slew your plane horizontally, even across hundreds or thousands of miles. Perhaps, though, long-range slewing is best accomplished with either the Go To Airport or Set Exact Position options in the World menu. Remember to take into account differences in altitude when you slew horizontally so that you don't materialize at your new location with a negative altitude reading on your altimeter or in the middle of a mountain. So embarrassing when they have to get the crane in to pull you out of that hole, you know. Also make sure you know the service ceiling (the highest altitude at which a plane can safely

Slew Control On-Screen Data.

operate) of your plane (see Chapter Three) since slewing up to an altitude well above an aircraft's maximum service ceiling can have serious consequences, unless you don't think plummeting uncontrollably through 30,000 feet of airspace is neither serious nor consequential. Using the Slew control can have some hilarious consequences, such as enabling a Cessna to fly at escape velocity, but it is a handy option when you don't have a lot of time to get where you want to be.

You may also slew an aircraft's position horizontally with the mouse. Again, press the Y key to place your plane in slew mode, and then click on the right mouse button and select Mouse as Yoke from the menu. A right or left drag of the mouse will yaw (turn the nose) the plane in the respective direction, with a forward or back drag actually moving the plane. Altitude adjustments are still entered with the keyboard commands.

Slew Control Keystrokes

Turn Slewing On	Y	Reduce Altitude Slowly	A
Slew Forward	K8 or Up Cursor	Halt Altitude Reduction	F2
Slew Backward	K2 or Down Cursor	Increase Altitude Quickly	F4
Slew Right	K6 or Right Cursor	Increase Altitude Slowly	Q
Slew Left	K4 or Left Cursor	Halt Altitude Increase	F3
Bank Right	K9 or PgUp	Attitude: Nose Up	F5
Bank Left	K7 or Home	Halt Nose Up	F6
Yaw Right	K3 or PgDn	Attitude: Nose Down	F8
Yaw Left	K1 or End	Halt Nose Down	F7
Stop Slewing	5	Aircraft Position Information	Z
Reduce Altitude Quickly	F1	Reset Aircraft Attitude and Orientation	Spacebar

The K prefix indicates a key on the numeric keypad. An F prefix indicates a function key. For example, to bank left, press 7 on the numeric keypad, or press Home.

The Control Panel

At first glance the cockpit of just about any aircraft seems a bewildering array of gauges and switches, only a few of which correspond to those found in a car. Nevertheless, in several respects a basic airplane like the Cessna 182 is simpler mechanically than many cars. So why all the bells and whistles? Well, partly because an airplane *is* simpler, there is more need for monitoring and intervention on the part of the pilot. While cars, for example, have had automatic chokes for decades now, many planes have manual chokes to adjust the fuel and air mixture. And even newer planes with fuel-injected engines still require the pilot to control fuel leanness or richness, depending on the situation.

The primary reason for the greater complexity and number of controls, however, is the greater number of parameters with which an aircraft operates. A pilot is responsible for an aircraft's velocity as well as its direction in three dimensions. In addition, control of attitude (an aircraft's orientation while moving through those three dimensions) is also a critical responsibility of the pilot. It's also necessary to monitor closely all aspects of an aircraft's mechanical well-being, to be aware of conditions outside the aircraft, to

Cessna 182RG Instrument Panel.

communicate with air traffic control, and to navigate accurately without benefit of a highway.

In Chapter Five we'll investigate aircraft instruments in more detail, but for that quick hop you're just dying to take, it's good to know at least the basic gauges and switches. For our example we'll use the panel from the Cessna 182RG, one of the most popular light planes of all time.

Altimeter.

Vertical Speed Indicator.

Right smack in the middle of the instrument panel where you'll be sure not to overlook it is the Altimeter. One of the first instruments to be included in early planes, it measures the aircraft's true altitude above sea level (sometimes referred to as MSL, or Mean Sea Level). This is not to be confused with *absolute* altitude, your actual height above the ground in a particular location. Making that mistake could be fatal. Notice that we're sitting on the runway at Meigs Field, near Chicago, Illinois, and yet, the altimeter is reading almost 600 feet. You'll need to take into account that, when your altimeter reads 800 feet, you're really only 200 feet above the ground, especially if you plan to buzz Wrigley Field on your first flight. For our first flight, which should stay well below 2,000 feet, we'll consider true altitude as a constant, although in practice it does vary as a function of temperature. The higher one goes the cooler the temperature and the more pessimistic the altimeter becomes. Later on we'll learn how to compensate for such variation.

Below the altimeter is the Vertical Speed Indicator (VSI). It measures the aircraft's speed along the vertical axis, its rate of climb or descent, in feet per minute (fpm). Most aircraft have a rate of climb that strikes the best balance between performance versus fuel consumption. Of course, you may find yourself in situations where you need to get up or down quickly (just ask the airline pilots who fly into Washington, DC) and must exceed optimal rates. For the Cessna 182, optimal rate of climb on takeoff is around 700 fpm while its maximum rate is 1140 fpm.

Attitude Indicator.

The round gauge to the left of the Altimeter is the Attitude Indicator (AI), also called the Artificial Horizon, a gauge ranking in importance with the neighboring Altimeter. Probably the most colorful gauge, it's divided into sky blue and ground brown sections, while in the center is a stylized image of your aircraft as seen from the rear. It displays climbing, diving, and banking (turning left or right). As you climb or dive, it shows the attitude of your plane (in degrees) relative to the horizon. It also conveys the angle of bank, how steeply you're tilting left or right. This gauge is especially useful when performing aerobatics or when flying blind, since it always provides you with a quick way to tell what's "up" and what's "down."

Control Surface Indicators.

Between the Altimeter and the AHI are three thin rectangular gauges. They display the positions of your main flight control surfaces: rudder, elevator, and ailerons. Make sure these are all centered before takeoff, or you may find yourself cruising the surface (or below) of Lake Michigan.

Left of the AHI is the Airspeed Indicator (ASI), which shows IAS, or Indicated Airspeed (your airspeed before factoring in the effects of atmospheric pressure or wind), as opposed to TAS, or True Airspeed, which is a calculated value. The distinction between IAS and TAS is important. Say your Indicated Airspeed is 60 knots (a knot, or nautical mile, being equal to about 1.15 miles per hour), but you're flying into a headwind of 60 knots. Simple math says your $90,000 Cessna has effectively become a $10,000,000 Harrier jet, hovering in place. Beyond that, understanding the effects of altitude on TAS is essential for accurate navigation.

Airspeed Indicator.

Directly below the IAS is the Turn Coordinator (TC), sometime known as the Turn and Bank Indicator, another gauge found in even

Turn Coordinator.

*Heading
Indicator.*

*Magnetic
Compass.*

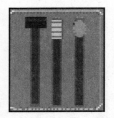

Throttle Control.

*Flaps and
Landing
Gear
Indicators.*

the earliest planes. While it would seem to relay information identical to the AHI, there's a bit more to it than that. A proper turn is a combination of yawing (turning the nose to the right or left along the horizontal plane) and banking (tilting the wings to the right or left). A good right turn, for example, requires depressing the right rudder pedal (which deflects the rudder, on the vertical stabilizer, to the right) and turning the yoke (or pushing the stick if you're in the Sopwith Camel or the Schweizer) to the right (which causes the right aileron to go up while the left aileron goes down). To perform this balancing act successfully, you must observe the turn and bank indicator. The stylized wings in this gauge show you the degree of bank, while the bubble (similar to that in a carpenter's level) indicates whether the aircraft is skidding (slipping towards the outside of the turn) or sliding (slipping towards the inside of the turn).

To the right of the Turn Coordinator is the Heading Indicator (HI), which uses a gyroscope to sense changes in the plane's horizontal attitude and display them as changes in heading or aircraft direction. The HI is usually synchronized with the Magnetic Compass, which shows the true magnetic heading and can be found to the left of the Fuel Gauges. In the real world the HI has to be re-synched at regular intervals during a flight because gyros drift. Unless you've selected Gyro Drift (and if you have, just how long have you had these masochistic tendencies?) from the Aircraft Settings-Reliability menu, you won't have to worry about resetting the HI during your flights.

The reason for using the HI instead of relying solely on the Magnetic Compass is that the HI displays more exact information about direction changes and is less susceptible to the effects of a plane's movements (acceleration/deceleration along all three axes) and variations in the Earth's magnetic field.

For this first familiarization flight we won't worry about the majority of the other gauges. They are covered in detail in Chapter Five. Most of them either monitor engine condition or are part of the navigation or communication systems. There are a few switches, however, that are all-important to a successful flight (that is, one that you can walk away from).

Of the three vertical slide controls in the lower left corner of the right-hand instrument cluster, the slider on the far left, the throttle, is the most important. It's what makes the plane go. The throttle can be controlled by

sliding it up or down with the mouse cursor, although you might find it more convenient to use either the Page Up and Page Down keys on the keyboard or the throttle switch on your joystick. In the Cessna, all the way up is the full power setting. (This can differ slightly among different types of aircraft.)

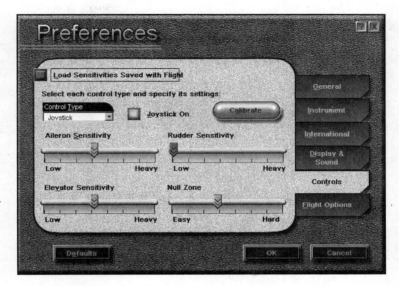

Preferences: Controls.

The small vertical gauge to the right displays aircraft trim settings, which we'll leave alone for now. Next to that are the indicators for the flaps and the landing gear. For landings (and sometimes for takeoffs) the flaps are usually partially lowered. Both these controls can be activated by the mouse cursor. Finally, to the far right are the magneto switches that control the plane's ignition system.

Input Devices

Flight Simulator for Windows 95, like its predecessors, features several options for controlling aircraft. And while some pilots will want to make the experience as real as possible by employing a joystick or yoke (often in concert with pedals), many find it more comfortable or expedient to use either the keyboard or the mouse. To select a control device, you must access the Preferences Menu under the Options heading on the menu bar, and then click on the Controls tab.

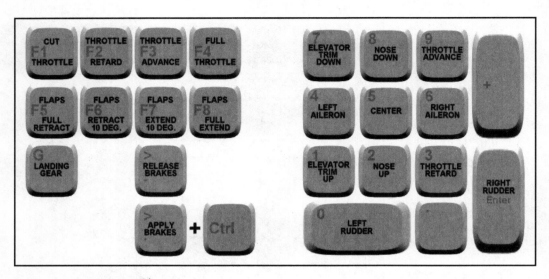

Function key and numeric keypad controls.

Keyboard Controls

The most basic control involves the keyboard or, more precisely, (excepting the brakes and landing gear) the numeric keypad (indicated in this table with a K prefix) and the function keys (an F prefix). Here are the keyboard commands for flight control:

Control Surface or Item	Desired Result	Command
Ailerons	Left Bank	K4 or Left Cursor
	Centered	K5
	Right Bank	K6 or Right Cursor
Elevator	Nose Up	K2 or Down Cursor
	Nose Down	K8 or Up Cursor
Rudder	Left Turn	K0 or Ins
	Centered	K5
	Right Turn	KEnter

continued

Control Surface or Item	Desired Result	Command
Flaps	Full Retraction	F5
	10° Extension	F6
	20° Extension	F6 twice
	30° Extension	F6 three times
	Full Extension	F8
Throttle	Slow Advance	K9 or PgUp
	Slow Retard	K3 or PgDn
	Cut Throttle	F1
	Retard	F2
	Advance	F3
	Full Throttle	F4
Brakes	Apply Brakes	Ctrl+. (period)
	Release Brakes	. (period)
Elevator Trim	Down Trim	K7 or Home
	Up Trim	K1 or End
Landing Gear	Retract and Lower	G

There are also some secondary keyboard commands to access several of the controls on the instrument panel of your plane. Pressing one of these keys lets you either toggle the control, or in the case of the various radios and the simulation rate, enter a new value:

Instrument Control	Command	Instrument Control	Command
VOR Settings	V	Carburetor Heat	H
Communication Radio	C	Lights	L
Navigation Radio	N	Strobes	O
DME Settings	F	Magnetos	M
Transponder	T	Simulation Rate	R

Mouse Control

In Flight Simulator the mouse functions in two modes, cursor mode and yoke mode. Use cursor mode (the default) to activate switches on the instrument panel. Yoke mode (activated by clicking the right mouse button, which brings

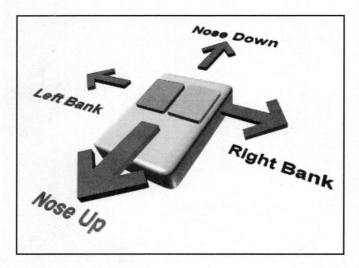

Mouse Control.

up a menu where you can select the Mouse As Yoke mode), is used for all maneuvering. Note that, in mouse mode, there is no provision for rudder control, so all turns will be aileron only unless you disable Auto-coordination and use the keyboard controls (K+Enter and K+0 for right and left rudder respectively). In the table below, "HL" means "hold down left mouse button" while "HR" instructs you to "hold down right mouse button."

Control Surface or Item	Desired Result	Command
Ailerons	Left Bank	Drag Left
	Right Bank	Drag Right
Elevator	Nose Up	Drag Back
	Nose Down	Drag Forward
Throttle	Retard	HL + Drag Back
	Advance	HL + Drag Forward
Brakes (only on ground)	Apply	HL + Drag Right
	Release	HL + Drag Left

Joystick Control

For complete joystick control in Flight Simulator you'll need either two joysticks, a four-button joystick along with a few keyboard commands, or a joystick (or yoke) and a set of pedals. Unlike the mouse and keyboard, joysticks must first be calibrated for proper performance. You'll have a chance to do this when you originally install Flight Simulator, but if for some reason you'd like to add a joystick after installation, you must set it up in the Options

and Preferences Menu. (Click on the "Controls" tab to reach these pull-down menus.) There you'll also be able to calibrate the stick. You may also find that you'll need to re-calibrate the stick occasionally since joystick settings can drift. Some joysticks allow you to adjust the trim of the horizontal and vertical axes, but even this won't provide enough adjustment to compensate for the drift in some sticks.

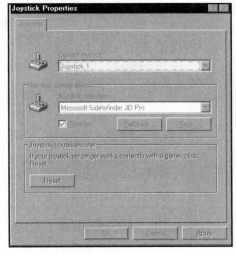

Joystick Preferences.

If you have only a basic joystick, the rudder and throttle and functions will revert to the keyboard. Since most joysticks have at least two buttons, you must stick control over the brakes and the landing gear. For these sticks, button 1 usually operates the brakes while button 2 retracts and lowers the landing gear.

Although it's a bit ungainly, the two-stick option does offer more freedom from the keyboard and so adds a measure of authenticity. It also adds a measure of complexity, but then, no one ever said flying, real or virtual, should be easy. One thing to note with this setup—you'll need a non-centering joystick for elevator and throttle control (Joystick 2), something that might be difficult to find since most joysticks are of the self-centering variety.

Command Control Surface or Item	Desired Result	Joystick 1	Joystick 2
Ailerons	Left Bank	Stick Left	
	Centered	Stick Center	
	Right Bank	Stick Right	
Elevator	Nose Up	Stick Back	
	Nose Down	Stick Forward	
Rudder	Left Turn		Stick Left
	Centered		Stick Center
	Right Turn		Stick Right
Throttle	Retard		Stick Back
	Advance		Stick Forward
Brakes (on ground only)	Apply		Stick Left
	Release		Stick Right

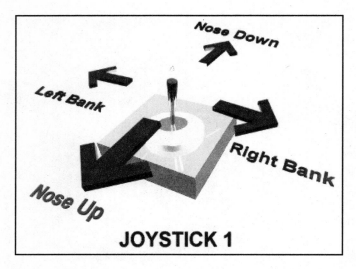

JOYSTICK 1

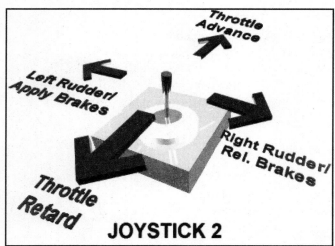

JOYSTICK 2

Joystick Control with Two Controllers.

Probably the most enjoyable of these choices, short of a dedicated yoke and pedal setup, is the four-button stick with throttle. This controller lets you control all the major aircraft functions from the stick, requiring you to venture to the keyboard only occasionally to operate the rudder. You'll actually rarely need to use the rudder, especially if you have your Control Preferences set to Auto Coordination (which automatically coordinates rudder and aileron movement, just like the old Ercoupe light plane). Even without Auto Coordination, rudder use is not absolutely necessary. While it's true that you can turn more tightly using the rudder, unless you're stunting with the Extra 300S, you simply won't need it. When a plane is banked, the natural aerodynamic tendency is to turn in the direction of the bank. To save weight and eliminate unnecessarily complex control systems, many radio-controlled model aircraft designers dispense with the rudder altogether. And beyond that, pilots of larger planes rarely use the rudder at all, preferring to make aileron-only turns. The only situation in normal flight where an independently actuated rudder is

essential is in a cross wind landing. Here you often need to yaw the aircraft, without banking, in the direction of the cross wind, to compensate for the wind pushing the plane away from its flight path.

Stick inputs are identical to the Joystick 1 layout above. The default button arrangement provides control for brakes (button 1), landing gear (button 2) and flaps (buttons 3 and 4). And of course you have the dedicated throttle.

Everyone Talks About the Weather, but...

You can inspect your plane, make sure your fluids are topped off and even triple-check your navigation—but controlling the weather is beyond even the most experienced and prepared pilot—unless, of course, the flying is done within Flight Simulator. The earliest versions of Flight Simulator paid little or no attention to weather, but with Flight Simulator for Windows 95, the effects and control of weather conditions have become major features.

For your first flights you'll almost certainly want to take advantage of the relative calm and good visibility of the default weather settings. You'll probably have enough problems keeping the wings level without having to worry about cloud layers, temperature inversions and atmospheric pressure variations. We'll study the effects of weather in Flight School, but for those adventurous souls, full control of these and many other parameters is available in the World pull-down menu.

You can change the weather in two ways, either locally or on a global basis. You fly through and out of

Default Weather values make for a smooth flight.

Weather Areas

Weather Area

Global

Global

Automatic Weather

- Clouds
- Winds

Beginning Lat: N000° 00' 00.0000"

Beginning Long: E000° 00' 00.0000"

Ending Lat: N000° 00' 00.0000"

Ending Long: E000° 00' 00.0000"

Width: 0000 Miles

Transition: 000 Miles

Course: 360.00 Degrees

Speed: 000 Kts

Note: Weather Area settings are saved with the current flight. If the flight is not saved, the weather area settings are discarded.

Add Area   Remove Area   Copy Weather...   OK   Cancel

Weather Setup Menu.

Advanced Weather

GLOBAL WEATHER

Cloud Layers

010003 011003 000000 Scattered 2/8   User Defined   Layer 1

Cloud Base: 010003 Feet MSL

Cloud Top: 011003 Feet MSL

Deviation: 000000 Feet MSL

Turbulence:

Light   Heavy

Icing

Cloud Type

User Defined

Coverage

Scattered 2/8

Clouds

Winds

Temperature

Visibility

Pressure

Add Layer   Remove Layer   OK   Cancel

Advanced Weather Menu.

local weather, say a thunderstorm or a low pressure area, but global weather remains consistent no matter where you go.

With local weather you set up one or more areas, adding areas for more complex and demanding weather conditions. The setup menu (see figure) under Weather Areas, lets you specify, with latitude and longitude values, the beginning and end of each area, its overall width, the size of the transition area from the previous weather area, and the speed and direction of the area. You can also simply define an area and let the program determine the weather.

For setting up Global Weather you'll need to access the Advanced Weather menu. First select Weather Generation from the Preferences Menu. The Advanced Weather Menu will

appear when you click on Weather. The values entered here affect the weather patterns throughout your entire flight. A wide range of cloud formations, wind and turbulence patterns, temperature and atmospheric pressure variations, and visibility values are possible, allowing you to create any sort of weather situation, up to and including hurricane-force winds and unpredictably deadly wind shear conditions.

Taking a Good Look at Things

The old chestnut about the advantages of seeing ourselves as others see us holds true in Flight Simulator. It's often a lot easier to see what you're doing wrong, or right, if you have an external view of your flight. Flight Simulator provides a couple of viewpoints to help you out.

The Tower View puts you in the control tower of the nearest airfield. Naturally, its usefulness diminishes as a function of distance, but for an overall view of how you're flying in the traffic pattern near the airfield, it can't be beat. You can increase the magnification of this or any other view from the View Options menu under the Views heading, although too much magnification with the Tower View can defeat the purpose of using it.

Possibly more informative overall is the Spot Plane View which affords a variable viewpoint from a chase aircraft. The Set Spot Plane menu provides flexible viewing, with graphic control for moving the spot plane in a 360-degree circle around your plane. Place the mouse cursor over the red asterisk (which

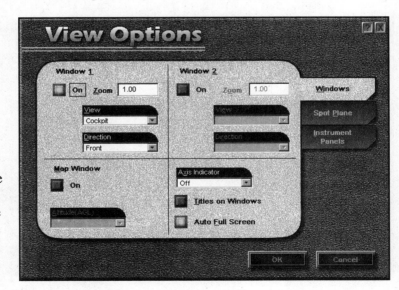

Set Spot Plane Menu.

represents the position of the spot plane), and then hold down the left mouse button to move the asterisk to a new position. The spot plane's altitude above or below your aircraft, as well as the distance from your plane, can be adjusted here, too, by entering new values in the appropriate windows. Even the transition from one view to another can be set up in this menu just by selecting a loop, a roll, or a straight shot, and whether you want a fast or slow transition.

You should note that, also under the View Options menu, are controls for setting up the viewing windows. Normally, Window 1 is the main cockpit view, but Window 2 could be a magnified version of the cockpit view or the Tower or Spot Plane views. This is also the menu to set up your Map Window and to adjust the way the instrument panel is displayed in the Cockpit View.

As with earlier versions of Flight Simulator, there are several ways for you to view your flights after the fact, for the instructional value or for the simple entertainment of reliving your ruthless attack on the blimp over Chicago.

If you're an experienced pilot or Flight Simmer, you may wish to go directly to Chapter Three. Flight Simulator's "hangar" features six aircraft, running the gamut of performance: from the aeronautical purity of the Schweizer sailplane to the rumbling power and all-business nature of the workhorse Boeing 737. In Chapter Three, we'll look at the aircraft in detail, including a bit of history on each plane, an orientation to their controls and gauges, and the unique flight characteristics of each plane.

For a good review of the basics, read on with Chapter Two.

Chapter Two

A BEGINNER'S GUIDE TO
FLIGHT SCHOOL RESOURCES

It's a dilemma. Which do you do first—jump right in and start flying (as we did in Chapter One) or start exploring Flight Simulator's vast training resources? Regardless of which activity you undertake first, you'll probably want to check out the program's extensive holdings at some time or another. The only problem is knowing where and how to initiate this process. There's so much information that can be studied and collected that it's somewhat difficult to know where you should start panning for gold.

Naturally, it all depends on what you're looking for—are you shopping for a full training course, or do you simply need the answer to a flight-pertinent question? Furthermore, how much time do you want to invest in this search for knowledge?

One from Five

The main fountains of information are the Flight School and the Lessons section. Other resources worth noting are those that allow you greatly to enrich your flight experience by using any number of national and international airports and varying the scenery you see during your flights. First, however, let's look at the major source of reference material for this software program—the Flight School.

Flight Simulator's Flight School is comprised of five different instructional departments. First and foremost is the Ground School, which provides a simulation of the type of classroom instruction a potential pilot might find in an actual flight school. In addition to the Ground School, there is also a Private Pilots course, which provides a heavy concentration of information about the plane, in this case the Cessna Skylane RG. A third part of the flight school is the Instrument Rating Course, and this relates to the added complexity of examinations for pilots' licenses, especially when instrument ratings are sought

by potential pilots, in addition to their standard license. The fourth component of Flight Simulator's Flight School is its Airline Transport Pilot Course, which lays out the regiments and requirements necessary to join that elite class of pilot—those men and women that control the massive jumbo jets. The final part of the Flight School is its Aerobatics Course, through which expert pilots can receive training and reference support materials on the dangerous and daring world of aerial acrobatics.

Training from the Ground Up

If you need flight instruction literally from the ground up, Flight Simulator's Ground School presents a flight curriculum largely comparable to that found in actual flight schools. Student pilots are expected to possess an estimable amount of aviation subjects both practical and theoretical. To that end, the Ground School contains 11 departments. They are Aerodynamics, Aircraft Controls, Engines, Flight Instruments, Fuel Systems, Electrical Systems, Navigation, Aviation Weather, the Flight Environment, Human Factors, and Rules and Regulations.

The Ground School presents selected topics in a variety of subject areas. The topics are dispersed through some 200 display screens. These serve as simple information digests designed to give you only the most essential information you need about a subject. Of course, more complex coverage of certain topics is sometimes warranted. The Ground School makes background information available by highlighting key words and changing their text color from black to green, signaling the student pilot that added information is available. For example, an aspiring pilot might wish to see a detailed explanation of Bernoulli's Principle, one of the central theories in physics, which explains, among other things, the way lift makes aviation possible. Should this student want to see a more thorough

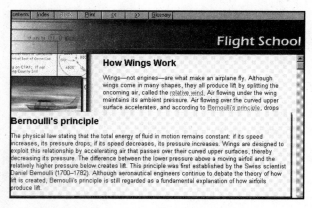

Ground School's display screens often contain highlighted text that leads you to more intensely detailed infomation.

statement explaining the principle, he or she can click on the green text reading "Bernoulli's Principle," and summon forth an information box specifically about Bernoulli and his theory.

The Setting of Priorities, 1-2-3

Ground School is a warehouse of aviation information, and sometimes it's easy to get overwhelmed by the amount of information that can be accessed, while it's equally difficult to know which display screens should be studied and which ones really *should* be studied.

So many Ground School subjects, so little time...

You can't always tell which topics are most important by the number of display screens that comprise them, either. The Rules and Regulations section, taken as a sum of three subsections, boasted 72 display screens, over a third of *all* the display screens. And yet, unless you're bound and determined to work toward an actual pilot's license, you probably won't miss out on anything if you don't see some of these arcane screens. On the other hand, some of the aircraft flown in this simulator are fussy about the various fuel mixtures they require at different altitudes, so it might benefit you greatly to spend a little time checking out the Fuel Systems screens, even though there are only a pair of them.

Level I: That Which You Need

In terms of defining which subject areas are most critical to both our short-term and long-term understandings of flight, perhaps we can try using a three-tier system. Within this system, subjects awarded Level I status would be considered the most useful, most integral subjects. Even casual users should be familiar with these Level I subjects, so basic are they to any discussion or practice of flight. Without some understanding of these subjects, your enjoyment of Flight Simulator might be greatly impaired. The first of these core subjects is Aerodynamics, the study of flight itself. This subject contains the building blocks of all other aspects of aviation. The next Level I subject would be Aircraft Controls, with a focus on those primary control surfaces that control devices like ailerons and rudders. This is where you're going to find your basic information about how flaps work, how the elevator can lift you up or bring

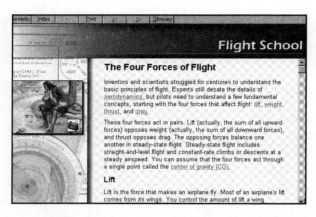

Flight School

The Four Forces of Flight

Inventors and scientists struggled for centuries to understand the basic principles of flight. Experts still debate the details of aerodynamics, but pilots need to understand a few fundamental concepts, starting with the four forces that affect flight: lift, weight, thrust, and drag.

These four forces act in pairs. Lift (actually, the sum of all upward forces) opposes weight (actually, the sum of all downward forces), and thrust opposes drag. The opposing forces balance one another in steady-state flight. Steady-state flight includes straight-and-level flight and constant-rate climbs or descents at a steady airspeed. You can assume that the four forces act through a single point called the center of gravity (CG).

Lift

Lift is the force that makes an airplane fly. Most of an airplane's lift comes from its wings. You control the amount of lift a wing

It's hard to imagine spending much time in the air without having some insight into the four forces that control all flight.

you down, and how to operate the airplane with the basic controlling devices. The category Navigation should also be worth your time and study because navigation has such far-ranging effects on your ability to get useful data from your communications equipment. Although it isn't necessary to memorize every thing the display screens show you, you're going to be seeing terms like VOR and DBE throughout your playing experience, so you may as well bite the bullet and learn them now. One last topic that any student pilot or virtual pilot should pay attention to is Aviation Weather. It covers 35 meteorological topics, everything from cloud formations to atmospheric pressure to understanding how different weather fronts affect flying conditions and the dangers of weather hazards such as icing and thunderstorms. This final area of discussion is particularly interesting since you can adjust the weather conditions yourself and pleasantly put yourself in the most adverse weather and the gravest circumstances possible.

Level II: Interesting, but Not Essential

These subjects are worth taking a look at, but don't break your neck hurrying about it. They'll keep indefinitely and be perfect for those occasions when you want to rummage around through the program's contents. The most worthwhile of this second tier of subjects is concerned with the various kinds of engines found in aircraft. The subject materials take you through the basic mechanics of how engines work—both piston engines and turbine-based jet engines. Ultimately, unless you're the most casual of users, this is going to be a subject you need to understand. Although it's true that you needn't understand everything about the engines to be able to fly the planes that use the engines, to fly well, you should know how your aircraft will react to various situations. Flight Instruments covers two separate standards of instrumentation: the Pitot Static System and Gyro Instruments. The Pitot Static System is certainly more

complex than the Gyro Instrument System, although understanding both will help to make you a double-threat pilot. Rounding out the Level II subjects should be the Flight Environment, a study in the procedures and processes of moving about airports and understanding things like runway markings and how approach lighting systems are laid out.

Sooner or later, you really ought to get to know the Pitot Static System of instrumentation.

Level III:
For Flight Freaks Only

Two of the subjects generating the least urgent study are Fuel Systems and Electrical Systems, each of which contains only two display screens. Neither screen's information is essential, particularly if you're eager to jump in the plane and roar off. The final two Level III subjects relate to pilot behavior. The first of the two, Human Factors, studies the effects of flight on human physiology. Topics studied within Human Factors include physical conditions such as motion sickness and night vision. Rules and Regulations, the final Level III subject, just happens to be the biggest of them all, at least in terms of its number of display screens. Taking its three sub-sections into account, topics within Rules and Regulations are profiled on 72 different display screens. For someone who is giving serious thought to pursuing an actual pilot's license, this subject could have great importance because its topics outline eligibility requirements of aspiring pilots and which aviation issues wind up as

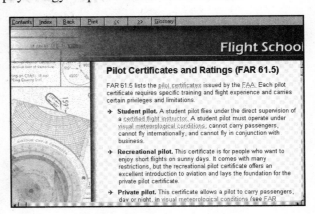

Unless you're an FAA lawyer (or getting ready to test for a pilot's license), you probably don't need to spend too much time in the Rules and Regulations section of Ground School.

test material when pilots go after added certificate ratings. For most of us, however, reading about FAA rules and regulations is apt to be considerably drier than might be enjoyable.

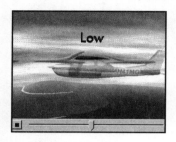

Need more than a definition? This animated sequence shows Bernoulli's Principle in action.

Ground School Bells and Whistles

Around 75 percent of each Ground School display screen is occupied by text related to the topic. The other 25 percent of each screen is reserved for graphics. Many of these graphic sections are only occupied by miscellaneous background images we associate with aviation (compasses, maps, aviator sunglasses, and so forth). At other times, however, a display screen's topic is bolstered by multimedia elements such as photographs and video clips. The most effective type of multimedia reinforcement comes from the animated sequences that are utilized to depict ordinarily invisible aeronautic processes, like the way wings slice through the slipstream, subsequently dividing air pressure and enabling lift. Through well-rendered clips, we are immediately able to grasp the way invisible air currents behave. Equally impressive are the animated clips demonstrating aerobatic maneuvers; these are considerably better at conveying the aerobatic experience than static diagrams.

Private Pilots Course

The Private Pilots Course presents a condensed version of Ground School, as well as specific airplane information, in this case the Cessna Skylane RG. The major topics necessary for an understanding of aviation are covered here: Aerodynamics, Aircraft Controls, Engines, Flight Instruments, Weather, Flight Environment, Human Factors, and Rules and Regulations. Private Pilots certificates are awarded based on the following criteria—at least 40 hours of flight time, made up of equal parts flight instruction and solo flight time. The course is designed for balance, so training includes a wide coverage of topics, all the way from basic maneuvers to long-distance navigation.

Airplane Handbooks

In order fully to convey the flight experience, Flight Simulator includes Airplane Handbooks so that you can comprehensively study the aircraft you

can fly in the program. In addition to showing you the location of instruments and discussing general performance issues about that particular aircraft, each handbook also provides a series of checklists like the ones actual pilots would use throughout the various stages of flight (from Pre-Start to After Landing and Shutdown.) If you really want to get to the heart of the matter of flying, Airplane Handbooks can give you an added frame of context. Each handbook varies in size, in accordance with the complexities of that particular plane. The handbook for the Boeing 737-400, for example, contains 25 different topics, while the handbook for the Schweitzer 2-32 sailplane only requires five topics to get its points across.

Preflight Briefings

Preflight Briefings provides an agenda for each structured flight featured in Flight Simulator. By studying these flight profiles, you will eliminate most, if not all, confusion about which bearings and maneuvers are necessary to make your flight successful. These briefings also include flying tips, easily visible since they're set apart with arrow icons. Like all display screens that make up Pilot's Help (the overall program category), the screens in Preflight Briefings suggest related topics and

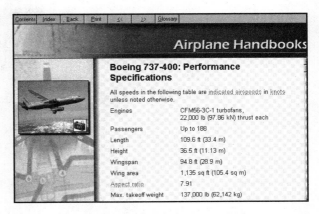

Before you try lifting this big bird off the ground, maybe you'd better get a little background on the subject through the Boeing 737-400 section.

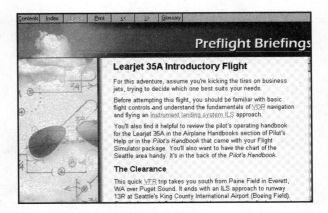

Check it out...Preflight Briefings show you the aeronautical moves you need to make, and in what sequence they fall.

often contain highlighted text that can lead interested parties to subscreens offering more concentrated study of a topic.

Ports of Call

One of the Flight Simulator's bonus qualities is the wide selection of airports that are available for your flights. Not only do certain lessons and adventures take you to these exotic locales, but you also are empowered to "move" a flight to another airport, should you so choose. For example, the Lessons section features several departures from Meigs Field in Chicago. If you want to fly one of those lessons but want a change of location, you can opt to take off from Las Vegas, Paris, or Africa. Four of the five continents are represented, so you're given plenty of choices about where you wish to fly. It should be noted, however, that changing airports can only be done before or between flights.

You change airports by choosing Go To Airport from the World menu. The airport selection screen holds added info about airports' precise geographic locations. There is also a convenient button that, once pressed, tunes your navigational radio to the airport's operating frequency. A related screen, entitled Set Exact Location lets you specify the altitude and heading of your aircraft at any given time, as well as giving you the location of an airport's control tower.

A reference tool that might aid you in picking new airports is found under the Help menu. It's called the Airport Facilities Directory, and if you select this directory, you'll see a flat map of the world with color-coded continents.

Clicking your cursor on any continent will prompt a list of all available airports. This scrollable list gives you necessary details about each airport (its location, identification letters, elevation, runway length, and so on).

Paris is nice this time of year. Want to see for yourself?

Stackable Scenery

Just as Flight Simulator lets you choose which airports you wish to visit, the program also allows you to customize the amount of scenery you see during your flights. The scenery is assigned to particular

flights via a prioritization scheme in which sections of scenery are assigned numerical values and then "stacked" one on top of another to make up the physical environment for your flight. Some categories are always essential (namely, Global), while Regional category scenery makes flying easier by filling in flight essentials like runways upon which to land. Regional scenery also includes the radio beacons set in place to help guide you through your flight. The final scenery category is designated as Local. This is where you derive, for example, the buildings that make a city's skyline or the natural attractions that add shape to landscapes. By using its numerical status system, Flight Simulator adds layers of scenery, as if it were building a movie set per your instructions. Further adjustments let you set the intensity of the scenery. This is a practical concern, too, since the level of graphics you choose to employ could well have a direct connection to the program's performance on your computer system. To manipulate scenery, you need only to pay a quick visit to the Scenery Library interface and search the available files. At the Scenery Library, you can also change the layering of scenery within a flight and add or delete scenery as you wish. This comes in handy because one of Flight Simulator's top strengths is the way add-on scenery is easily integrated. (For an exclusive look at Microsoft's new Southern California add-on scenery pack, check the Appendices section at the back of the book.)

Learning Your Lessons

The Lessons menu screen posts a backdrop of a plane buzzing a skyline, and there are two settings you can control before you select your lesson. One of them is Aircraft Control, where you decide whether you want to man the controls or whether you want the instructor to take the stick. If you man the controls, you'll be receiving the instruction, either hearing it or seeing it posted in a running band near the top of the cockpit view in red letters against a black background for added contrast. You'll still see that red text if the instructor flies, so either way you can take the lesson. It's just up to you in terms of if you feel ready to tackle the flying or if you're still tentative and want to get more feel of the subject before taking charge.

The other control that's posted in the top third of the screen is called Lessons in Sequence, which is self-explanatory. There are two other buttons at the bottom of the screen, one marked OK, indicating your acceptance of the

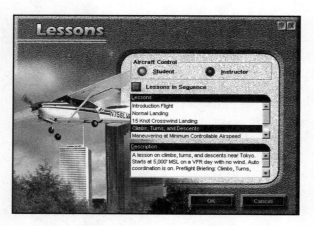

Lessons are selected here, although the airport and scenery can be customized before flights begin.

flight you've chosen and additional factors that you've preset. The other button is marked Cancel, which will take you out of the Lessons menu screen entirely.

If you've chosen to let the instructor fly, then the program is basically running a videotape of that flight, so those flights will always clock out the same, as opposed to those flights you control, which could vary infinitely depending on how closely you want to adhere to the instructor's suggestions. If the flights are the prerecorded videos (with the instructor taking control), then those videos range in length from 5 to 16 minutes, with much variance in between.

The Introduction Flight

"An introductory lesson on taking off, flying the traffic pattern and landing the Cessna 182RG at Chicago Meigs Field Runway 18. Day, VFR, no wind. Auto-coordination is on."

Duration (as flown by instructor): approximately 7 minutes.

The Introduction Flight, as you might expect, is the most basic of complete flights, paring down its pattern to a simple up-and-down cruise around Chicago's Meigs Field. The Introduction Flight encompasses only key activities, such as taking off, maintaining a steady-rate flight, banking a few turns, and lining up a descent and landing.

It's a sunny day, and you're flying a simple pattern along the shoreline of Lake Michigan. All you're really doing in the Introduction Flight is taking a plane up, getting it safely off the ground, flying it around, working on a few turns, learning to vary your speed control, getting familiar with the throttle, memorizing the landing sequence, learning how to blunt your wind speed by using your flaps correctly, and learning when to raise and lower your landing gear.

The fundamentals, maintaining a smooth, steady flight by using smooth, steady movements, are repeatedly stressed. The instructor illustrates a gradual curve on a crosswind leg and also reminds us that calculating altitude depends upon knowing the sea-level altitude of any present location.

The instructor stresses the importance of carefully preparing for descent, checking gauges, and keeping an eye out for other air traffic—small, common-sense ideas that still ring true. The instructor tells us which navigational moves he's going to make, and then we see our cursor become a hand that raises or lowers the thrusters and other controls, carrying out his commands.

At one point later in the flight, you appear to be headed straight into downtown Chi-town, your plane approaching from the lake. During this final descent preceding your landing, you'll see how essential the compass is in establishing navigational bearings. The instructor also spends a great deal of time on the importance of being able to brake your speed, through the considered use of flaps.

Normal Landing

"A lesson on normal landings in the Cessna Skylane RG at Meigs Field, Chicago. Starts at 1,527 feet MSL 6 NM east of the airport on a VFR day with no wind. Auto-coordination is on. Preflight Briefing: Normal Landings."

Duration (as flown by instructor): approximately 6 minutes.

As this lesson starts, we're six miles southeast of the airport and preparing the enter the traffic pattern. Several shifts in heading are enacted systematically to get us on course for our descent and landing. Like all these lessons, this lesson documents how flight is an exercise in geometry, connecting a series of angles that will become the bearings used in navigating a flight.

Our instructor works to foster good descent habits in us. He teaches us by his example of descending at 300 feet per minute, which is safely less than the 500 feet per second that the simulation recommends so that the ears of pilots and passengers can adjust to the quickly changing air pressure.

Fifteen-Knot Crosswind Landing

"A lesson on crosswind landings at Meigs Field, Chicago. Starts at 1000 feet AGL on a VFR day with 15-knot crosswind. Auto-coordination is off. Preflight Briefing: crosswind landings."

The longest lesson is Climbs, Turns, and Descents, which is over three times as long as the shortest lesson, Fifteen-Knot Crosswind Landing.

Duration (as flown by instructor): approximately five minutes.

Here's where things get more interesting. This lesson tosses something new into the mix—weather that offers a bit of challenge. In this case, there's some turbulence, with the occasional gusts strong enough to take you off course. If you're slow to recover when the wind sweeps you away, you could easily find yourself in a stall or a spin.

The rapidly jerking view from your cockpit shows what a bumpy ride you're taking. To counter the wind, the instructor works to stabilize conditions by adjusting the plane's nose and using the flaps to settle your speed down.

Landing the plane presents its own set of challenges. The instructor turns into the wind while making his final approach and withstands the dangerous gusts while setting the Cessna down safely, albeit a bit bumpily. First the aircraft lands on its left tire only before leveling off and taxiing to a halt.

Climbs, Turns, and Descents

"A lesson on climbs, turns, and descents near Tokyo. Starts at 5000 feet MSL on a VFR day with no wind. Auto-coordination is on. Preflight Briefing: climbs, turns, and descents."

Duration (as flown by instructor): approximately 16 minutes.

At over a quarter hour, this is by far the longest of the lessons as it focuses on the key maneuvers of aviation. The lesson begins in mid flight, with the instructor champing at the bit to take you through a succession of moves. The mini maneuvers clinic begins at high altitude (5000 feet +), so your plane will

have plenty of spare altitude to practice moves such as descending turns. The first maneuvers practiced are medium banked turns. The fundamentals are stressed—for example, being sure to counter a plane's natural tendencies to pulling up on the nose during turns. Descending turns are the next order of business and are performed to the left and right. Climbing turns are also studied in both directions, as is their dependence on power. The instructor wraps up the lesson by running through a set of steep turns, banking the plane at 45-degree angles, both at constant altitudes and during descents.

Maneuvering at Minimum Controllable Airspeed

"A lesson on maneuvers at minimum controllable airspeed. Starts at 3500 feet MSL near Bremerton, WA, on a VFR day with no wind. Auto-coordination is on. Preflight Briefing: flight at minimal controllable airspeed."

Duration (as flown by instructor): approximately 11 minutes.

The instructor points out (again) that it's wise to perform some turns at the beginning of the exercise to ensure that no other aircraft are dangerously near. It's a wobbly flight as the Instructor cuts the engine until it's barely puttering along. The point of all this is to get a better understanding of how your plane's general balance is affected by lower speeds. Pitch is used extensively as a means to control your airspeed, and the instructor even uses flaps to further cut his speed, already inching forward at a snail's pace. The angle of attack and athe tricky way it can trigger stalls is studied.

Other exercises challenge the instructor to hold a minimum controllable airspeed during descents and climbs.

Takeoff Stalls and Departure Stalls

"A lesson on arrival and departure stalls. Starts 10 nm west of Buchanan Field at Concord, CA, at 3500 feet MSL on a VFR day with no wind. Auto-coordination is on. Requires Concord 3.stn. Preflight Briefing: stalls."

Duration (as flown by instructor): approximately 9 minutes.

We're first shown an approach-to-landing stall, with the hope that we'll learn how to quickly recover from a stall by reestablishing a climb. Then the instructor shows how to maintain aeronautical integrity while holding a

20-degree bank during a stall. As in all of these lessons, we're repeatedly encouraged to make smooth moves, even when we fear that the stall we've fallen into will send us hurtling to earth in a lethal spin, ("Recover quickly...but come out smoothly.") A clearing turn is also performed, followed by a takeoff stall and turning stalls that send your plane to both left and right.

Chapter Three

THE FLIGHT SIMULATOR HANGAR

A hallmark of Microsoft Flight Simulator has always been its providing the full breadth of the flying experience, especially through the variety of aircraft featured in the program. Microsoft Flight Simulator for Windows 95 is no exception. Although only six aircraft are included, they still manage to encompass a large section of the flight performance range, low and slow to high and hot. From soaring like a hawk in the Schweizer 2-32 to buzzing about like a hummingbird in the Extra 300S, just about every performance envelope is available.

While you'll probably get to know the various aircraft while flying the simulation, you might like to have a little background on each before you begin your explorations.

Boeing 737-400

Boeing 737-400.

In the early 1930s the Boeing company really thought they had gotten it right. Their new Model 247 was such a quantum leap forward in the quality of commercial air travel that it seemed to have come from another planet. Compared with the other airliners of the day, particularly the Ford Trimotor and Junkers Ju52 (both of which looked as though they might have been designed, in part, by aluminum siding salesmen), the 247 was revolutionary. Among other features, its internally braced low-wing, retractable landing gear and comfortable cabin put Boeing at the top of a commercial aviation world used to externally braced biplanes or, at best, high-wing monoplanes with cumbersome cantilever bracing. It stayed there for only a very short time, however, due to the appearance in 1935 of the legendary Douglas DC-3, which forever changed commercial air travel. Boeing would have to wait until the 1960s to wrest the commercial mantle from Douglas (as well as a few others such as Lockheed and de Havilland) with its marvelous 7X7 series of aircraft, beginning with the 707.

By the mid-sixties Boeing management realized it had been slow out of the gate with a suitable short-haul airliner. Having just introduced the tri-motored 727 and wanting to cut tooling costs as much as possible with the new airliner, Boeing engineers decided simply to take a section of the 727's fuselage and graft a new nose, tail, and wings onto it. With the wide cross section of the older model but a much shorter fuselage, the new 737

The Boeing Company

The name Boeing has become so synonymous with commercial aviation that it's a surprise to many that, prior to the late 1950s and the introduction of the 707, the company was known almost exclusively for its military aircraft. Started in 1917 by William E. Boeing, the company immediately went after military contracts, first with the U.S. Navy. The long line of Boeing military aircraft, from the legendary B-17 Flying Fortress and B-29 Superfortress of World War II to the revolutionary B-47 Stratojet and long-lived B-52 Stratofortress, is testament to the company's success in defense. Though known for large planes, Boeing was also responsible in the early thirties for the tiny P-26 fighter, a monoplane that signaled the end to the biplane's reign in the Army Air Force. But Boeing was not without its commercial successes prior to the 707, most notably the innovative Monomail and 247 designs, as well as the last and greatest of the pre-WWII flying boats, the Model 314 Clipper. And as the millennium approaches, Boeing remains at the forefront of commercial aviation with its new 777, the first airliner designed completely by computer, and with its recently announced plans for a superliner that will dwarf even its gigantic 747 jumbo.

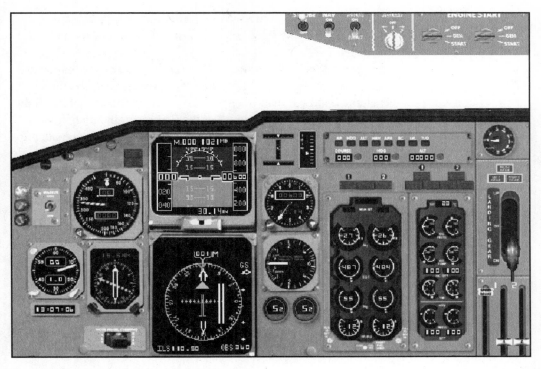

Control Panel Layout for the Boeing 737-400.

appeared decidedly portly next to its more svelte-looking siblings, but the airlines didn't care. They bought up the new airliner as quickly as Boeing could roll copies out the door in Seattle. Nearly 30 years after the 737's 1967 introduction, several versions of the plane are still being made, and the 737 has become the biggest selling jet airliner of all time with around 3000 units produced so far. The 737-400 you'll be flying is the big hauler of the series in terms of passenger-carrying capability, with advanced avionics and state-of-the-art turbofan engines.

While the temptation will be great to hop into the pilot's seat of the 737 right away, you might want to wait until you have a few flight hours under your belt in other planes; otherwise, it will be an unpleasant exercise in frustration. Unlike the Cessna or even the

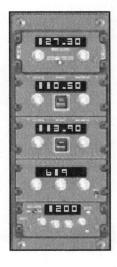

Learjet, the 737 won't lift itself off the runway. It requires considerable technique just to get the big plane into the air, and it's even harder to land in one piece.

A few minutes behind the yoke of the 737 will give you a new appreciation of why airline pilots get the big bucks. The main thing to remember is that control response is much slower than in any of the other craft featured in Flight Simulator. Furthermore, the default settings for the 737 mean the plane reacts less to a given amount of control input. That's just as well since it's considered poor form to subject passengers to 60-degree banks and outside loops (although aviation lore has it that the prototype of the 707 was actually looped once during one of its test flights in the late fifties).

Specifications for the Boeing 737-400

Length: 119' 7"
Height: 36' 6"
Wing Span: 94' 9"
Weight, Fully Loaded: 138,500 lbs.
Power plant: Two CFM-56 turbofans, 28,500 lbs. thrust each
Maximum Speed: 340 kts.
Range: 2,700 nm

Cessna 182RG Skylane

Next time you hear a small plane flying overhead, take a quick look. Chances are you'll see some sort of Cessna and, if it's a single-engine model, the chances are good that it will be a Cessna 182 Skylane. With Cessna building an average of over 600 Skylanes per year for 30 years, it would be surprising not to see a lot of them, especially considering Cessna's reputation for building sturdy, dependable planes. Possibly the only Cessna you'll see more often would be the Skylane's slightly older sibling, the 172 Skyhawk.

From 1956 until 1986 Cessna built nearly 20,000 Skylanes, and production is expected to resume in 1996. New legislation was passed to give more protection to light plane manufacturers such as Cessna, Piper, and Beech from the liability suits that caused production to end in the first place. There's good reason for the Skylane's popularity and longevity: it has sometimes been

Cessna 182RG Skylane.

described as a near-perfect airplane, a craft that does what it was designed to do with a minimum of trouble and expense.

From its earliest incarnation, the Skylane has been powered by a 230 hp Lycoming engine, and since the pairing has worked so well over the years, Cessna designers have seen no reason to change the basic specification. Other things have changed, however. The original 182 had a straight vertical stabilizer and a much smaller cabin. The familiar Cessna swept vertical stabilizer soon appeared, along with a larger cabin and revised landing gear. (The

Cessna Aircraft Company

Although it's difficult to imagine light commercial aviation without Cessna aircraft, the truth is that Cessna, along with the other big names of American light planes, Beech and Piper, just barely made it through the Great Depression. In Cessna's case, salvation came with World War II, as it manufactured thousands of small twin-engine planes and troop-carrying gliders. Founded in 1927 by Clyde Cessna, the company emerged from the war energized and ready to accomodate the demands of recently discharged military pilots who still wanted to fly. Along with a large number of war-surplus T-50 Bobcats, Cessna also offered the Model 120, the progenitor of the long line of high-wing, single-engine Cessnas that were soon to fill the flight lines of airfields not only around the U.S., but also around the world. The 170 was a direct development of the tiny 120, and from the 170 came a veritable horde of designs, including the 182 Skylane. As if the many pilots flying Cessna aircraft in the fifties and sixties didn't create sufficient ubiquity, Cessna also enjoyed a considerable marketing coup with the popular television show, Sky King. Every week millions watched Cessnas— first a T-50 Bobcat and later a Model 310—zoom "out of the blue of the western skies."

Control Panel Layout for the Cessna 182RG.

original gear gave the 182 a long-legged, almost storklike appearance.) The Skylane has for many years been made in fixed and retractable gear variants. The RG designation indicates that the plane in Flight Simulator is the retractable version.

The Skylane's greatest virtue has always been its forgiving nature, a trait that put it and the Skyhawk in good stead with flying schools for so much of its operational life. With the Skylane's large, high-mounted wing, the plane is so stable, in fact, that many flight instructors don't use it or its siblings as much these days because it does not provide the student pilot with enough experience actually controlling an aircraft. The high wing also reduces visibility considerably to the rear and above. Check out flying school, and you'll find more often than not that the basic trainer is a low-wing, bubble-canopied model like the Beech Skipper or the Piper Tomahawk.

Flying the Skylane, you'll need to remember that, with the default positive elevator trim, the plane is a natural climber. And there's so much lift in those big wings that the 182 can be a bit of a floater on landings. Because of the wing configuration, you'll probably need less flap than you might imagine for takeoffs and landings. (Flaps are sections of the wing's trailing edge which, when extended, provide extra lift.) Although newer 182s feature the usual 30 degrees maximum flap extension common on most light planes, the oldest models had flaps that could be lowered to 40 degrees, much more than would ever be needed with this plane.

Specifications for the Cessna 182RG

Length: 28′ 7.5″	
Height: 8′ 11″	
Wing Span: 35′ 10″	
Weight, Fully Loaded: 3,100 lbs.	
Power plant: 230 hp Lycoming	
Maximum Speed: 160 kts.	
Stall Speed: 54 kts.	
Service Ceiling: 14,300′	

Extra 300S

For nearly as long as people have been flying, there have been stunt pilots. Indeed, the barnstorming stunt pilots of the 1920s and 1930s did much to implant the romantic image of flying into the public mind. And almost from the beginning, designers have known what basic features are essential to a good stunt, or aerobatic, aircraft. A high power-to-weight ratio is essential because the plane must often power itself through maneuvers, especially those featuring vertical flight elements. Relatively short wingspan is also important; the longer the wingspan the more resistant a plane is to rolling (spinning on its front-to-back axis). Finally, good stunt planes are usually short-coupled; that is, their fuselages are also relatively short so that they can maneuver more quickly about their vertical and horizontal axes. The general principle

Extra Flugzeugbau GmbH

Something had to be done to stem the tide of Eastern Bloc aircraft flooding the aerobatic market in the late seventies and early eighties. Up until that time the amazing capabilities of these aircraft, especially the YAK 18, were known, but the aircraft themselves were kept for the most part safely behind the Iron Curtain. When less restrictive policies were instituted the planes started to fall into the hands of Western pilots, much to the chagrin of manufacturers such as Walter Extra. Extra, a pilot and designer, countered by producing in 1983 the innovative Model 230, a much-improved version of the Stephens Akro Laser aerobatic plane. Extra brought a much higher degree of precision to aerobatic plane manufacturing, the result being that the 230 and its descendant, the 300, are among the strongest and most able aerobatic aircraft ever made. Recently, Walter Extra added to his company's offering with the new and powerful Extra 400, one of the fastest piston-engined aircraft available today.

Extra 300S.

behind these last two points is to keep as much of the bulk of a plane as close to the center of gravity (the point at which the plane is balanced on all axes) as possible.

In the thirties the best aerobatic planes came from Germany and most notably from the Bücker company. Its Jungmeister biplane was the state of the art stunter for many years. In the fifties and sixties, Canada's de Havilland Chipmunk trainer was transformed into the Super Chipmunk aerobatic aircraft, while in the seventies and eighties, Eastern Bloc countries were producing what some say were the best stunt planes, period. Ships such as the Soviet YAK and the Czech Zlin were coveted by the top aerobatic pilots in the West. Other independent designers came up with a variety of designs, from the throwback Pitts/Christen biplane to the raw and powerful Laser. And now we've come full circle, with the latest stunt plane of choice, the Extra 300S, from Germany.

Control Panel Layout for the Extra 300S.

The Extra 300 is also produced in more commercially viable multi-seat editions, the 300 and 300L. But we're concerned with the single-seat 300S, first flown in 1992 and the weapon of choice for, among others, international aerobatics champion Patty Wagstaff (who provides the aerobatic lessons in Flight Simulator for Windows 95). As befits an aerobatic craft, the Extra 300S is no plane for a calm Sunday afternoon flight. From the moment you settle into the cockpit, you know this plane means business. The panel layout is no-nonsense and gives you information on flight parameters you weren't even aware of.

With all that power in such a light plane, throttle response is immediate and, much as with the Sopwith Camel, you'll have to be wary of engine torque, especially on takeoff. Even more important is realizing how sensitive the controls of the 300S are. Even at the lowest sensitivity settings, this craft is a handful. Unlike the Cessna, where you can make leisurely turns with little or no problem, turning the 300S smoothly is a real art. All those aerobatic design parameters we mentioned above make the Extra 300S a real nightmare for the unsuspecting pilot. Just remember that a little goes a long way with this plane, at least when you first fly it. Keep your control inputs light until you're experienced enough to take advantage of the 300S's phenomenal maneuverability.

Specifications for the Extra 300S

Length: 21' 10"	
Height: 8' 7"	
Wing Span: 24' 7"	
Weight, Fully Loaded: 1808 lbs. (aerobatic setup)	
	2028 lbs. (normal setup)
Power plant: 300 hp Lycoming	
Maximum Speed: 220 kts.	
Stall Speed: 55 kts.	
Service Ceiling: 16,000'	
Range: 415 miles	

Learjet 35A

Learjet 35A.

In the 1960s, Bill Lear became known for two innovations. One was the late and unlamented 8-track tape player. His other invention, and certainly the longer lasting of the two, was the Learjet. The original Learjet 23 (1963), wasn't the first private business jet (just ask Gulfstream or Rockwell), but it was the aircraft that took jet-powered flight from the domain of the airlines and placed it in private, if well-to-do, hands. It boasted near-fighter-jet performance, developed as it was from an unrealized European jet fighter project.

Unfortunately, its fighter heritage showed in its accommodations; it was tiny inside, with room for only about six passengers and virtually no headroom. Frequent fliers developed a pronounced Learjet crouch. Next came the Model 35, Lear's answer to the cry for a larger, more sophisticated airplane. It filled the bill, with a production run of nearly 700 (as of 1995, counting both the 35 and 35A models) in the past 25 years, high numbers for the business jet market.

The 35A is fairly sensitive to flap settings, so take care when either extending or retracting them in flight. You'll probably need 20 degrees of flap to reduce takeoff roll to a manageable distance, but just remember that the nose will really drop once you've retracted the flaps. Also, pay close attention to your speed. Much

Lear

Bill Lear liked to invent things. So far-ranging was his genius that, while most people associate his name with the line of eponymous business jets, his other inventions may be more influential. He managed to develop the first practical car radio, and beyond that, he gave the automotive public its first taste of portable music with the 8-track tape player. Beyond that, he created the Motorola Corporation which was eventually responsible for the microprocessors that went into every Macintosh computer. During one of his several "retirements," Lear moved to Switzerland in the early sixties, where he formed a company, the Swiss-American Aircraft Corporation, to develop a business jet out of the FFA (Flug and Fahrzeugwerke, A.G.) P-16 jet fighter plane, which first flew in 1955. He took this design back to the U.S. with him, settling down in Wichita, Kansas, to build the first Learjet Model 23. It was, of course, an immediate success, even though it had some rather tricky handling problems that resulted in a number of crashes. The Model 24 followed quickly, and soon the 35 and 36. But by 1969, Lear had "retired" again, only to reappear in the mid-seventies touting another revolutionary design, the Learfan, a sleek craft driven by a tail-mounted "fan" that promised quiet operation and greatly improved fuel economy. Lear died in 1978 before he could see the Learfan project to its completion, and although his wife eventually got the plane into the air, it was more or less a stillbirth.

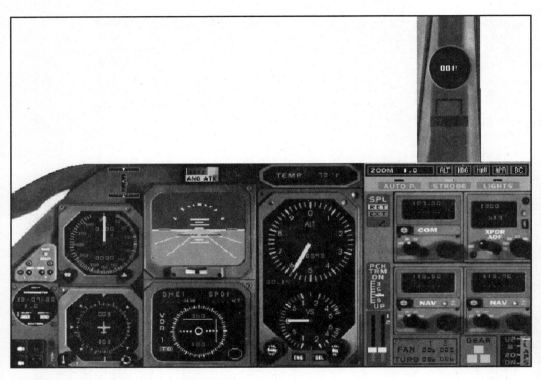

Control Panel Layout for the Learjet 35A.

like a high-performance touring car, the Learjet can reach its maximum speed without a lot of warning. Everything is so smooth you probably won't realize how fast you're going until you hear and see the Overspeed warning. With its efficient aerodynamics and engines, the 35A can cruise at very low power settings. You'll need to experiment to find the best settings for a given situation, but usually you should have power set and no higher than 35 percent.

Specifications for the Learjet 35A

Length: 48′ 9″	
Height: 12′ 3″	
Wing Span: 39′ 6″	
Weight, Fully Loaded: 18,300 lbs.	
Power plant: Two Allied Signal TFE731 turbofan jets	
Maximum Speed: .81 Mach	
Stall Speed: 96 kts.	

Schweizer 2-32

During World War I, the Germans ruled the skies of Europe with their Fokker and Albatross fighters, but after the Treaty of Versailles in 1919 officially ended the war, German aviation fell into a black hole. The country was prohibited from building warplanes (at least nominally), so Germans with a desire for the skies took to gliders, or more properly speaking, "sailplanes," creating a boom in soaring all over Europe and a renaissance in unpowered flight design. A glider is an aircraft with a high glide-to-sink ratio, which nonetheless progressively loses altitude (for example, the Horsa and Waco troop gliders used in WWII). A sailplane is a glider designed to make optimum use of thermals to stay aloft indefinitely.

Control Panel Layout for the Schweizer 2-32.

Schweizer 2-32.

Although the political situation was different across the Atlantic and war surplus aircraft like the Curtiss JN-4 "Jenny" were cheap and plentiful, soaring nonetheless "took off" in the U.S. as well. Today, with the cost of operating a light plane beyond the reach of many pilots, soaring has become more popular than ever. At the center of the sailplane revolution, as it has been for decades, is the Schweizer company, which has probably made more sailplanes than anyone. In particular, the 2-32 and 2-33 models are seen at airfields around the world, and with good reason. All Schweizers offer the relatively rare combination of performance and flying ease—relatively rare because the design of a sailplane's wing is critical to its performance. All sailplanes have high aspect ratio wings, so named because the wing span is very long relative to chord size (the distance from the front, or leading edge, of a wing to the back,

or trailing edge). The 2-32, for example, has an aspect ratio of a little over 18 to 1, which means that the wing span is 18 times longer than the wing's chord size. By way of comparison, the Extra 300S has relatively low aspect ratio wings, about 5 to 1, for two main reasons. Low aspect ratio wings allow the plane to roll more readily, and the shorter wings are easier to brace for the stresses involved in aerobatics.

The Schweizer 2-32 featured in Flight Simulator is perhaps as ubiquitous as a sailplane is likely to become. Many sailplane operators offer low-cost rides to the public, and should you decide to try one of these, chances are pretty good you'll find yourself in the passenger seat of a 2-32. And even though it exhibits gentle flying characteristics with none of the bad habits of other high-performance sailplanes, it has still managed to set many international records for both altitude and endurance. On top of that, the 2-32 is highly regarded for its aerobatic qualities.

Schweizer

In these days of corporate mergers and takeovers, any company that's been around for more than half a century has probably changed hands at least three or four times. Even some of the big names of the past, such as North American, Convair, or Douglas, have been changed so much as to be unrecognizeable from the original companies. So it is indeed strange that a small company in Elmira, New York, founded in the 1930s by three brothers, Ernest, Paul, and William Schweizer, is not only still doing business, but is also still run by that same family—and so successfully that to many people when you say "Schweizer," you might just as well have said "sailplane." That's how popular the company's designs have become over the years. There are sailplanes that are faster, or more efficient, or even more attractive, but very few manage to combine all the desireable qualities of a sailplane in such well-balanced packages as are Schweizers. In addition to the 2-32 that you'll be flying, there's the 2-33 two seater, and the single-seat I-36 sailplanes. Lest you think the company is nothing but a one-trick pony, you should know that Schweizer not only makes other types of fixed-wing aircraft, such as the Ag-Cat cropduster (developed from the original and very successful Grumman Ag-Cat first flown in the late 1950s), but helicopters as well. Schweizer bought the rights to the small Hughes 269 in 1983 and now manufactures it as the Schweizer 300C. In addition, it produces the Teal Amphibian and an interesting cross breeding of sailplane and powered craft, the SGM 2-37, which uses the same engine, a 112 hp Lycoming, as the Piper Tomahawk.

Flying the Schweizer in Flight Simulator, you should keep one word—*conserve*—in the back of your mind at all times. Conserve as in conserving speed and conserving altitude, especially the latter. Even with the 2-32's almost

phenomenal glide ratio (forward motion relative to vertical drop) you don't want to try maneuvers that radically reduce altitude, unless you have a convenient thermal (area of rising air usually found below cumulus clouds) or ridge lift area (the airspace above a ground ridge formation where the wind is deflected upward) in the neighborhood. Also note that the 2-32's controls, while not sensitive on the order of the Extra 300S, are still a bit twitchy compared to the Cessna or the Learjet.

Specifications for the Schweizer 2-32

Length: 26'9"
Height: 9'
Wing Span: 57'
Weight, Fully Loaded: 1340 lbs.
Maximum Speed: 172 mph
Stall Speed: 55 mph

Sopwith Camel

Sopwith Camel, Model F.1.

Ah, the romance of the fighter pilot. Forged in the skies over Europe in World War I, this image is etched in the psyche of every fan of aviation history. Manfred von Richtofen and Max Immelmann of Germany, Rene Fonck and Georges Guynemer of France, Albert Ball and Mick Mannock of Great Britain, Eddie Rickenbacker and Frank Luke of the United States, Billy Barker and Roy Brown of Canada—all added to the legend, as did their aircraft. Fokkers, Albatrosses, SPADs, and S.E. 5s were graceful yet deadly weapons in the hands of these masters. But no other plane of the era engenders so many memories, both good and bad, as the Sopwith Camel.

Actually, the plane was officially named the Sopwith F.1.; the nickname *Camel* came from the hump made by the machine gun breech covering just ahead of the cockpit. Whatever it's called, it was a great fighter for the same reasons it was a bad plane otherwise. With a short fuselage and wings and with most of the components (engine, fuel tank, gun, and pilot) bunched closely together, the Camel was wonderfully aerobatic, but a

Sopwith

Just what did old Thomas Octave Murdoch Sopwith think about his most famous creation being forever linked with a cartoon beagle? He certainly lived long enough to see the age of Peanuts, *but it's not clear whether anyone ever asked him his opinion of* Snoopy vs. the Red Baron. *What* is *clear is that he was one of the most influential of the early aviation pioneers, fostering a company that, in various guises, was an integral part of aviation history for nearly all of the twentieth century. And the Camel certainly wasn't his only, or to his mind, most successful design. His first real plane, the Tabloid, appeared in 1913 and was to provide the basic pattern for all his company's World War I designs, including the Pup, the Snipe, the Triplane, and, of course, the Camel. In some recollections he made in the eighties, just before his death, he actually felt the Pup, known as a real "pilot's plane," was his favorite early design. Indeed, the Pup, much like the French Nieuport, was a plane with no vices and it was a joy to fly, something that couldn't be said of the Camel. The Sopwith Triplane was a real innovation and, although not entirely successful itself, did provide inspiration for Anthony Fokker to design his own triplane (which, by the way, was the plane the aforementioned baron was flying when he met his death.) After the war Sopwith somewhat changed the name of his company to Hawker Aircraft, in honor of Sopwith's chief test pilot, the dashing though ill-fated Harry Hawker. Under this name, and later the Hawker-Siddeley name, Tom Sopwith's company went on to create some of the most memorable aircraft in aviation history, from Battle of Britain savior, the Hurricane fighter plane, to the still-unique (nearly 40 years after its first flight) Harrier vertical takeoff jet fighter.*

Control Panel Layout for the Sopwith Camel.

nightmare for the inexperienced pilot. Probably as many pilots were lost to snap rolls on takeoff as were lost in actual air combat, but it was just this incredible responsiveness that made the Camel so effective as a fighter. Experienced Camel pilots knew they could always out turn an opponent (except, perhaps, for a Fokker Triplane). The Camel was the great aerobatic plane of its day, allowing its pilots literally to "hang" the aircraft on its rotary engine, using the torque to enhance the Camel's already amazing turning ability.

The Sopwith Camel used a variety of engines throughout its relatively short lifespan (it was only operational from early 1917 until the end of the war in 1918), but they all had one thing in common. They were rotary engines, but not like the rotary engines used in some cars these days. In 1917, *rotary* meant that the propeller was actually attached to the engine's crankcase. The entire assembly—prop, crankcase, and cylinders—rotated. This arrangement had a high power-to-weight ratio unlike the radial and in-line engines of the period, but the rotary posed problems unique to its design, such as the difficulty of fitting a proper throttle. An even more basic problem was keeping oil inside the spinning engine. The rotating cylinders also created a pronounced gyroscopic effect which contributed a great deal to the Camel's notorious handling characteristics.

Fortunately you won't have to worry much about engine idiosyncrasies with Flight Simulator's version of the Camel. What you will have to watch out for, however, is the legendary Camel maneuverability. With full throttle at

takeoff, a real Camel will have a tendency to pull to the right so the pilot must compensate with a bit of left rudder, or at least a slight banking to the left, but the effect isn't much in evidence with Flight Simulator.

You can fly the Camel almost as crisply as the Extra 300S, keeping in mind that the older plane has less than half the horsepower of the aerobatic 300S. This means you'll have to set up your maneuvers more carefully rather than depending on the power of the engine to pull you through.

Specifications for the Sopwith Camel

Length: 18'9"
Height: 9'
Wing Span: 28'
Weight, Fully Loaded: 1482 lbs.
Power plant: 130 hp Clerget rotary
Maximum Speed: 117 mph
Stall Speed: 57 mph
Service Ceiling: 19,000'
Endurance: 2.5 hours

Now that we've had an overview of the planes you'll be flying, let's turn our attention in the following chapters to the flying characteristics of each plane, as well as to tips on aircraft behavior in general. First we'll check out the pussycat of the bunch, the Cessna 182, and take it up for a quick circuit or two around the airfield in Chapter Four.

LET'S GO FLYING

Many years ago a neat little book called *Eight Hours to Solo* could be found in many elementary school libraries. The title reflected the generally accepted idea of that period that a pilot should be ready for his or her first solo flight after eight hours of dual instruction. A thin volume, *Eight Hours to Solo* still managed in its relatively few pages to convey the exhilaration—and the tension—of those first few hours in a pilot's career. Following the progress of a student pilot and his instructor in an old Piper Cub, the book covered all the basics of learning to fly, at least as flying was in the early fifties, when this long-out-of-print book was written.

Flying, like many other things, was a lot simpler then. The Piper Cub in the book was as basic a plane as you could find, differing little from the first J-2 Cub of 1936. About the only concession to modernity was a simple communications radio. The little 65 hp engine, an improvement over the 40 hp of the earlier Cubs, did well enough in calm conditions, but even a moderate headwind could cause the little Cub to hover almost like a helicopter. The relatively large, slab-like wing, sometimes affectionately referred to as a "barn door," didn't help matters much. It generated a lot of drag (from friction with the air), but a lot of lift, too—too much lift, some said, making the plane a real "floater." And the seating was two uncomfortable seats, one behind the other and both very narrow. You even had to be a bit of a contortionist to get into the cockpit. The plane had dual controls for its flight-trainer role, but only one instrument panel for the front seat. This made for a comical situation when there was no passenger because the pilot had to sit in the rear seat to balance the plane. A pilot always needs good eyesight, but a solo Cub pilot might have needed a telescope as well just to check the altimeter.

Simplicity had its charms, however, for that was still a time (though already changing) when you could jump right into your plane and fly, often without filing a flight plan and usually with little more than a quick look around the

airfield pattern for traffic before taking off. Granted, there are a few airfields still around where that sort of devil-may-care flying can still be found, but for the most part, airspace regulations, sophisticated navigation equipment, and much more complex aircraft have made flying a far more serious business. Ah, so much for the romance of the skies...

Now you're about ready to take your first flight in a very different type of aircraft, but one that is nonetheless something of a descendant of that legendary Cub. The Cessna 172 and 182 models brought a new level of comfort and sophistication to the low end of the light plane spectrum. Your Flight Simulator 182 has been around, in one form or another, since 1956, although its original inspiration, the dainty little Cessna 120, appeared ten years earlier. Pilots are a discerning bunch, and no plane stays in production for over three decades without boasting at least a few redeeming features. As you're about to find out, the Skylane's most important asset is its rock-steady stability, good news for the novice pilot.

Another plus for the Skylane is its almost perfect match of structure with engine. That's not always the case with light planes. Their relatively small size results in a very narrow margin of error when a designer is mating power plant to plane. Piper Cub pilots, for example, rarely fly without wishing for a little more power at least once during the flight. On the other hand, many of the newer light planes—low-wing, sleek jobs with more than a little fighter plane in their heritage—often have too much horsepower stuffed into their cowlings in the quest for a few knots' advantage over the competition. Flight Simulator's Skylane 182 offers a nice balance—small wonder, then, that Cessna resumed production of both the 172 and 182 in 1996.

Preflight Check

While we won't have to actually do a preflight check, it's good to at least know a few of the main issues involved.

Most people wouldn't think it necessary to walk around their car and check everything before driving it away. But with an airplane, the consequences of even small mechanical problems are serious. Normally a preflight inspection involves checking all the control surfaces, moving them around a bit to feel for any binding or unusual play. The outer skin is also checked for damage, and the pilot verifies that the pitot-static ports (the ports that relay information about the air to various instruments such as the altimeter and airspeed indicator) are clear

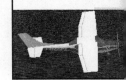

of obstructions. The fuel in the wing tanks is also measured—it's never a good idea to trust only the fuel gauge on the instrument panel. Of course, the wheels, tires, and landing gear struts are inspected, as is the engine (to make sure it has plenty of oil and that there are no leaks) and the propeller (for serious nicks or other damage to the blades or the pitch control mechanism).

Once inside the cockpit, the checkup continues by

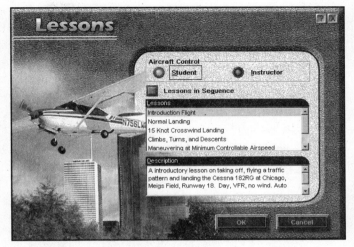

Flight Simulator provides a number of lessons with an instructor at your side.

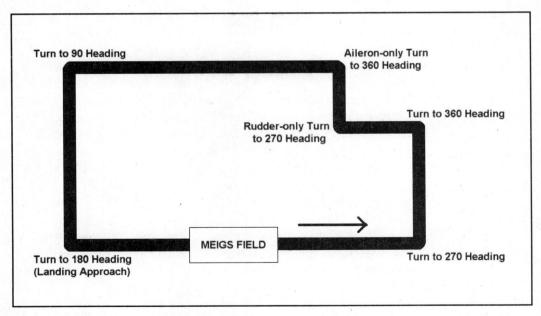

The Flight path.

trying out the controls and also making sure all the instruments are functioning. Much of this is done while the engine is run up to idle speed, since you'll need to make sure the oil and manifold pressures are reading correctly. Unless you've set your Reliability preferences for extreme unreliability (see Chapter One), everything should be reading to specs. If everything reads all right, we're ready to go.

There are several flight lessons included with Flight Simulator. Each is quite instructive and helps you learn to fly in small, easy-to-learn doses. You're under the tutelage of a knowledgeable, if not infinitely patient, instructor. If you are new to flight simulators, you should take all the lessons, but for this flight, because we're going to be experimenting with a few things, we'll fly on our own. Our flight plan here will be similar to the Introductory Flight in Lessons, starting at Meigs Field, but with a few differences. And we'll try not to be as snippy as Flight Simulator's instructor can get when you don't do things exactly his way. Hey, it's your plane and your airspace, after all, so let's just go up and have a little fun.

...and Just Before You Go

It's worth going over the instruments and controls one last time while you're sitting at the end of the runway with the engine turning over. The gauges you'll be using for this flight include the Altimeter (of course), the Airspeed Indicator (ASI), the Attitude Indicator (AI), the Turn Coordinator (TC), and the Heading Indicator (HI) or Magnetic Compass. (These should display identical readings unless you've selected Gyro Drift from the Reliability menu.) Remember to take into account the reading of the Altimeter, which tells you that, without leaving the ground, you're already some 600 feet above sea level. Also make sure you know where the throttle, flap, and landing gear indicators are, as well as how to read and control them.

Ground Handling

Before we take off, let's take a look at our flight path. We'll be taking off into the wind (well, what little wind there is—this is a calm day) on a heading of 180 degrees. We'll be climbing to an altitude of 1527 feet. Once at that altitude, we'll make a left turn to a heading of 90 degrees. After a minute or two on that course, we'll turn left again, a downwind leg at a heading of 360 degrees. It's on this leg that we'll deviate from the default Flight Simulator Introductory

Flight by trying a few maneuvers with and without Auto-coordination. Eventually we'll make another left turn, which places us perpendicular to the axis of the runway at Meigs Field. Finally, we'll make one last left turn, back to a heading of 180 degrees, so that we can make our approach and landing into the wind.

The Cessna 182 RG Skylane, as seen in the Pilot's Help. Complete specifications for this popular Cessna model are there as well.

Because the default flight puts you at the south end of the runway at Meigs, we'll have to do a little taxiing to place the plane at the north end for takeoff. That's okay, since it's good to get a feel for ground handling anyway. To be on the safe side, let's use the taxi strips rather than just cruise down the runway. With the default settings for Dynamic Scenery this would be no problem, but if you've activated

To taxi, advance the throttle up far enough to get the plane rolling.

Lined up on the runway.

Normal takeoff speed for the Cessna is around 60 knots.

all the buttons in the Dynamic Scenery menu, you might find another plane trying to land on the roof of the Cessna, should you take the shortcut. When taxiing, be very judicious in your throttle use, nudging the lever up slowly and only as much as needed to get the plane rolling. And be ready to tap the brakes should the plane accelerate too much.

If you'd prefer the quick route, you can switch on the Slew Control (press the Y key) and use your controller or the keyboard arrow keys to move to the other end of the runway. No matter which method you choose, once you're at the north end of the runway, turn the plane around so that the heading reads 180 degrees and place your nose gear on the runway centerline. (You can use the Slew Control again to nudge the plane right or left until you're lined up.)

Take a Deep Breath...

Okay, let's go. In the Introductory Flight included with Flight Simulator, flaps are not used for takeoff, and indeed, the Skylane can take off quite well without them. But for short runways or when operating in lower air pressure conditions (during hot weather or at high altitudes), you can use flaps to increase wing lift. For our flight we'll use 10 degrees of flap, although as much as 20 degrees is acceptable. Just know that the more your flaps are extended, the greater the penalty in drag. It's also true that, as the flaps are extended, an aircraft's stall speed is lowered slightly. So if an aircraft's specification list happens to list stall speeds for both clean (flaps and landing gear retracted) and dirty (flaps and gear extended) you'll know what it means.

Now release the brakes (press Ctrl + . [period]) and then smoothly advance the throttle to full. In a real Cessna you would also adjust the fuel mixture to full rich and perhaps even set the propeller pitch angle, but the default settings in Flight Simulator take care of these items for you. The plane will start moving, quickly building up speed as it tracks down the runway. Don't move the controls at all since the plane can veer quite easily on its takeoff run, depositing you rather unceremoniously in the airfield coffee shop, or worse, trying out the Cessna's capabilities as a sub in Lake Michigan. (Give a yell if you find the *Edmund Fitzgerald*.)

Keep an eye on the ASI, and when it's reading around 60 knots, pull back on the stick slightly to lift the nose, although the plane may rise by itself before reaching 60 knots, since we are using flaps. This is known as rotation and on airliners (especially those operating from short runways) is

Keep your wings level as you climb.

With those big wings, the Skylane lifts easily and quickly.

usually followed by a sigh of relief from passengers the world over. At this point, or maybe just a bit before, we come to our first great debate in flying—the proper takeoff technique.

The traditional way to take off is to let the plane rotate up as soon as the lift of the wings will allow it. In aircraft with high lift wings such as STOL craft (Short TakeOff and Landing) or planes with flaps extended, it's all a pilot can do to keep the plane from lifting off, but our plane needs a bit of help with its rotation. With the traditional takeoff the plane rotates, lifts off, climbs a bit, and then levels off, to allow speed to build up again. This is because, as the plane rotates on takeoff), the wings' higher angle of attack (the angle at which the wing, moving forward, meets the air) cause extra drag which slows the plane down, even as it is generating more lift.

The other technique is to keep the plane on the runway longer by pushing the stick forward, which deflects the elevator down. This lets the plane build up more speed on the ground, and consequently more than enough lift is generated. The plane finally takes off with more upward momentum, obviating the need for the respite provided by the leveling-off phase of the traditional technique. The second technique requires a bit more finesse with the controls because you don't want to overcompensate with the elevator. It also requires perhaps a little more daring, particularly if you're operating from a very short runway.

For now we'll go with the traditional technique, letting the plane gradually climb for a couple of hundred feet, leveling off for a moment or two, and then resuming the climb, still at a very shallow angle. It's best to climb no faster

than about 200-300 feet per minute on this first flight to eliminate any chance of stalling the aircraft. You'll probably notice that the plane takes off this way almost by itself, climbing a bit, leveling to gain speed, and then resuming the climb. This is one result of that excellent balance between engine and airframe mentioned earlier; the plane will literally fly itself under normal conditions.

You're Not in Reno, You Know

A good climb speed is around 80 knots, and you should try to stay in the neighborhood of this figure. Remember that the Cessna's stall speed is 54 knots, and you definitely don't want to flirt with the stall speed, most especially during takeoff. Any time the speed drops below 70 knots during the climb phase, lower the nose a few degrees to build up speed again. You're not in a race to gets to 1500 feet. So take it easy and keep that airspeed up.

We'll cover stalling more completely in Appendix B, but for this flight you should know that stalling has nothing to do directly with the engine (although performance of the engine can be a factor in a stall). Instead, stalling is caused by problems with the wing and the flow of air over it. A wing generates lift because the air flowing over its upper surface (which is curved) must travel faster than the air flowing below the wing.

The faster that air moves, the lower is its pressure. So the air moving below the wing has higher pressure and thus lifts the plane. If, however, the wing meets the air at too high an angle of attack, the airflow above the wing is disrupted and lift is lost. This is called stalling, and it causes the nose of the plane to drop quickly. A plane can also stall if its airspeed drops below the minimum necessary—its stall speed—for the wing to provide lift. If you're not both attentive and quick, the plane can go into a spin (a total loss of aerodynamic integrity) from which it may not be able to recover. And even if there's no spin, you may be in serious trouble. An airplane is not very high during takeoff, so any sudden loss of altitude—even a hundred feet—can be deadly. But back to the flight...

Once you're up to around 1500 feet (the tower won't penalize you for 10 or 20 feet, but try not to vary your altitude any more than that), throttle the engine back to around 2200 rpm, retract the flaps completely, and we'll take a minute to trim the plane out for level flight. Actually, the plane should be fairly in trim already, set to an ever-so-slight positive angle of attack. This may not be acceptable, however, for a couple of reasons. First, with this setting it's almost impossible to maintain the traffic pattern altitude of 1527 feet unless you play

The default setting
for elevator trim
is for a slight
nose-up attitude.

You can also change views with the keyboard.

around with the engine settings, something we want to avoid on this first flight. Second, the differences in joysticks or flight yokes may result in changes in trim as well. With some sticks you can adjust this out, but with others you may not have this option. So let's make our trim changes from the cockpit.

In the lower right corner, next to the landing gear and flap indicators, is a small vertical scale with a cursor. That's the elevator trim gauge, and as we look at it now, you'll see that the cursor reads slightly above the midpoint. That means that small tabs on the trailing edge of the elevator are deflected upward slightly to raise the nose a bit, resulting in a positive angle of attack. To adjust the trim, you use the keys K+7 (to move the trim indicator down) and K+1 (to move it up). For this flight we'll want the indicator to read close to the midpoint so that the plane neither climbs nor descends without direct input from you. Move the indicator in small increments until the plane is flying level and at a speed of around 80 to 90 knots.

Basic Turns

Once we're flying straight and level, we'll prepare to make our first turn. If you were flying a real plane, you'd want to look completely around the plane to check for nearby air traffic before making any maneuver. Let's do the same thing now, just to develop a good habit. In any Skylane, you're going to have some blind spots, mostly due to the wing placement, but you can still get a fairly informative view. In the Flight Simulator Cessna, you even have a bonus view. It helps if you're using a joystick such as the Microsoft Sidewinder or the CH Flightstick Pro which have a "viewing hat" option that lets you change your view quickly. Otherwise you'll need to use the keyboard, although this isn't necessarily a bad thing. Using the keyboard (press the Shift key plus the numeric keypad key corresponding to the direction of your choice), you can also select views in 45-degree increments instead of the 90-degree increments of the joystick view hat. Then there's that bonus view—directly below the plane—that real Skylane pilots don't have unless they enjoy sticking their heads out the window and into a 90-knot slipstream.

After ascertaining that the immediate airspace is clear, you can begin your turn. In most cases you'll be making what are known as standard turns, which involve a wing bank angle of about 30 degrees. There are a couple of reasons for staying around this angle of bank. The plane's nose will have a tendency to drop in any turn, and the more inclined the bank the greater that tendency is. Steep banks also affect the way your controls react, since, as you bank, your horizontal stabilizer gradually approaches the vertical, and thus the elevator begins to act more like a rudder and less like, well, an elevator. The rudder's moving towards the horizontal at the same time, so a very steep bank, aside from being rather disconcerting to you and your passengers, can make your controls go all wonky, too.

A standard turn means that, in the case of a light plane, your rate of turn is three degrees per second. Holding a turn at this angle means you make a complete 360-degree turn in two minutes. Larger aircraft, such as airliners, use a standard turn rate half that amount, or 1.5 degrees per second.

This first turn is done with Auto-coordination on so that the ailerons and the rudder work in unison. This means your turns will be according to proper technique, but keep an eye on the turn indicator anyway, to get a feel for how to read it correctly. Later we'll try a turn without Auto-coordination, and you'll

The four views available using a joystick's view hat, starting with the front view.

You can see an airship to the right.

need to watch this gauge more closely to make sure you're not either slipping or skidding in the turn.

All the turns on this flight, including this one, will be 90-degree turns. You can either keep your eye on the Magnetic Compass or the Heading Indicator because one's data mirrors the other. Try to get a feel for the turn rate at this angle of bank so you can judge accurately when to finish the turn. It will probably take a few turns before you can stop the turn exactly, without going past the intended heading. With the Skylane it's usually best to begin pulling the stick back to neutral about 15 degrees before your intended heading. This first turn goes from 180 degrees to 90 degrees (heading due west), so you should start easing

the stick back around 115 degrees. This varies from plane to plane (the Extra 300S, for example, is much more responsive—you can almost turn it on the proverbial dime) and also varies depending on the angle of bank and the airspeed. But then, that's one of the true and never-ending joys of Flight Simulator—learning the characteristics of each plane in a variety of situations.

Well, we're finally on a heading of 90 degrees, so check your altitude and speed and adjust accordingly before we move on to our next maneuver. You should know that most airports and airfields have a standard traffic pattern or patterns, and normally the pattern at Meigs is all left turns. We'll be making a couple of right turns

This is your view to the left...

...and this is the perspective out the back of the plane.

A standard turn is performed here (with a 30° banking).

on this flight, but since we'll be considered "out of the pattern" for those maneuvers, we won't be violating airfield protocol. And we'll finish up with a standard approach to Meigs that will be part of the standard pattern.

Okay, we're ready to make another left turn, this one onto a heading of 360, for our lengthy downwind leg. We nominally took off into the wind (even though the day is calm), and so our first leg was upwind. We're now flying crosswind, in preparation to turn downwind. As before, take a quick look all around for other traffic, and then begin the turn. Again, sense the turn rate of your plane and finish up the turn so that you nail 360 degrees dead on.

Stalls

Now that we're on a rather long downwind leg, it's time to try a few things to get a feel for just how the 182 handles. First of all, we'll try a stall. With the plane in level flight, pull the stick back all the way. The nose will rise, and the plane will begin to climb. But airspeed will begin to drop. As you continue to pull the stick back, the wing's angle of attack increases to the point where the air flowing over the top of the wing breaks up into turbulence. Once this happens, the wing loses all lift, airspeed falls off to almost nothing, and the nose drops quickly, sending the plane into a dive. With the Cessna, most stalls are pretty harmless affairs if you have enough altitude. During this particular

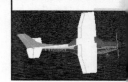

stall, you'll notice that the nose dropped straight down while the wings stayed more or less level. You then went into a moderately steep dive in which the plane picked up speed quickly and the nose began to rise. At the point where the plane is once more level, a little forward pressure on the stick prevents the nose from rising too high again and precipitating another stall. Pretty painless, huh?

Stalls, though, are not always this benign. Depending on the weather conditions and the plane you're in, a stall can be much more serious. With the Cessna the stall was rather gentle, but often it can be more violent, with the plane falling off to one side or the other. In that case you need to coordinate the rudder and ailerons quickly in order to

This figure shows how the gradual recovery from a stall...

...leads you back to straight-and-level flight again.

If you try to climb too steeply...

...you can trigger a stall, causing you to descend dramatically.

prevent going into a spin. Later on, in Chapter Seven, we'll actually put the airplane into intentional spins in some of the maneuvers, but for now be glad that the Cessna Corporation designed such a forgiving aircraft as the Skylane.

That was fun, wasn't it—sort of like a roller coaster ride? Let's hope you didn't need to reach for an airsickness bag (and if you did, boy, do we have some interesting times ahead in Chapter Seven). Since the plane stalled so benignly, you should still be on the same heading, 360 degrees. If not, adjust accordingly, and we'll go on to our next experiment.

Maybe You Slipped When You Should Have Skidded?

For the next maneuvers we must deactivate Auto-coordination so

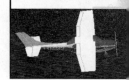

that we have independent use of the rudder and ailerons. Access the Aircraft heading on the menu bar and scroll down to the Realism and Reliability selection. Once the menu pops up, you'll see that the Auto-coordination button is lit. Click on this to deactivate Auto-coordination, and then close the menu to return to flying.

Switching Auto-coordination off.

The controls you're using will determine how hairy this next segment is. If you have a joystick or yoke with separate rudder controls or if you're fortunate enough to have dedicated rudder pedals, such as CH Pro Pedals, then this should be easy. If, however, you must control the rudder from the keyboard, you'll need a bit more dexterity. In any event, we're just going to try a couple of turns to gauge the effectiveness of the rudder and the ailerons.

First, let's try a rudder-only right turn. You can watch the control surface position indicators located between the altimeter and the attitude indicator to see whether the selected control is working. The ailerons are the top gauge, the elevator is in the middle, while the bottom gauge shows the position of the rudder. When using only the rudder you should be careful not to overcontrol, as most planes, the Skylane included, are fairly sensitive to rudder inputs. Too much rudder and you can put yourself into a nasty little spin very quickly.

As you turn, notice that even without the ailerons, the plane still banks in the turn. Also notice that where before the turn indicator showed a nice smooth turn, now the lower ball is probably sliding right and left, as the plane moves sideways. If the ball moves toward the inside of the turn (that is, in a right turn the ball moves to the right), then the plane is slipping. A slip means the rate of

The plane slipping in a rudder-only turn.

A skid, resulting from a rudder-only turn.

the turn is too low for the angle of the wings' bank. To correct for this condition, you can either use the ailerons to decrease the bank or use the rudder to increase the rate of turning. In this flight, let's nudge the rudder a bit more to bring the ball back to center.

If the ball moves in the opposite direction of the turn, the plane is skidding because the rate of turning is too high for the current angle of bank. Correcting this requires, quite naturally, control input opposite to those for a slip: that is, either less rudder or more aileron. Again, we'll correct with the rudder, easing up a bit until we've completed a 90-degree turn, to a heading of 90 degrees. Make sure to center the rudder after completing the turn if the controller you're using doesn't do that automatically.

If you watch either a slip or a skid from behind the plane, it's obvious that the plane is not pointed in the direction in which it's actually traveling. As you might imagine, this isn't the most efficient way to fly, but in certain circumstances it can be an essential technique. The most common instance where slips or skids are used is in landing during a crosswind. You may

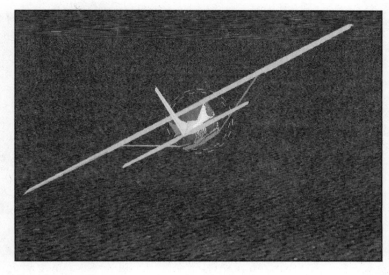

An aileron-only turn.

have noticed in films or on television that airliners are sometimes shown landing with their noses pointed noticeably away from their direction of travel. This is called crabbing and is used to compensate for the tendency of a crosswind to push the plane away from its flight path. Using the rudder to cause the plane to either slip or slide is one of the real arts of basic flying. The crabbing technique isn't used all that much, but when you do need it, you really need it.

You might also notice, when you're using only the rudder, that the plane tends to lose altitude a bit. This brings up another situation when you want to allow the plane to slip sideways. There will be times during a landing approach when you'll want to increase your rate of descent without increasing your airspeed. It takes a fine touch, however, to do this without taking the plane away from its intended line of flight.

Did You Know Aileron Is French for, "Oh, Look—I Can See My House!"

Okay, let's get back on our heading of 360 degrees by making a 90-degree left turn, but this time we'll do it using only the ailerons. As soon as you begin the turn, you'll notice that it feels almost identical to an auto-coordinated turn, except that the turning rate is lower, more on the order of 1.5 to 2 degrees per second. There's also a tendency during aileron-only turns for the plane to yaw or turn its nose opposite to the direction of the turn. This occurs because banking the wings of a plane changes the angle of attack for each wing, which in turn creates more drag. The higher wing has slightly more drag, and its this extra drag that pulls the nose of the plane away from the turn. To compensate for this yaw, the rudder must be used.

Letting It All Hang Out

Back on the downwind leg, a heading of 360 degrees, let's try one more experiment before heading back to the airfield. To get a feel for how flaps affect aircraft performance in the air, try extending them 10 degrees. Before doing so, check your airspeed—extending the flaps above a certain speed can cause damage to any plane. In the case of the Skylane, never extend flaps when your airspeed is above 140 knots. (This same figure applies to landing gear extension, as well.) Your airspeed should be around 80-90 knots, so there should be no problem. Now drop the flaps, but be prepared to ease the stick forward a bit because extending the flaps will cause the nose to pitch up slightly. Dropping them another 10 degrees changes the

Lowering the flaps changes the shape of the wing airfoil, providing greater lift.

pitch again, but this time there's also a slight reduction in speed. Although you can't properly call flaps air brakes, pilots do use them to slow down, especially on landing approach.

Approach and Landing

Now that we've finished playing with the flap settings, retract them fully again and make another left turn, onto a heading of 270 degrees. This will be our final crosswind leg and will take us up to our final turn and approach. Keep checking the view out your left window, and when the plane seems to be fairly even with Meigs Field, start making your final turn upwind to a heading of 180 degrees. Given the variations in our flight path, you'll probably have to correct your course a bit as we get closer to the field, but for now hold it steady on 180.

As you near the field, but before you can see any real detail, start making preparations for landing. If you haven't already, drop your flaps 10 degrees and throttle the engine back until the tachometer reads around 2000 rpm. You can adjust this a bit to keep your airspeed from falling below 75 knots.

With the field more clearly visible now, but before you can actually see the stripes of the runway, run through the landing checklist (found in the Flight Simulator manual). Lower your gear and set the plane up for your final approach. Start a slow descent until the altimeter reads around 1600 feet (which, at Meigs Field, means you're about 1000 feet above the runway). Lower the flaps another 10 degrees (they should now be at 20 degrees) and continue to adjust the plane. Try to keep the nose level with the horizon. If the plane won't hold that attitude by itself, adjust the elevator trim until it does. If you can't get the trim exactly right, just remember it's better to have the trim a little too positive (that is, set so that the nose has a slight tendency to rise when flying the plane "hands-off") than the opposite.

The stripes of the runway should be visible now. Check your landing gear again, and then drop the flaps to 30 degrees. This should slow the plane down noticeably, as well as pitch the nose up slightly. A slight nose-up attitude is just what you want.

Although it sounds contradictory, to make a good landing, you must try to keep the plane from touching down. The theory is that, as you reduce power and drop the flaps, your aircraft will eventually come down of its own accord.

Beginning your approach.

When you can see the white runway lines, extend the flaps to 30 degrees.

Keeping the thought in your head that you must prevent this (even though you can't) results in a light, smooth landing.

Keep your eye on the airfield, and as you sense the plane crossing the outer marker of the runway, cut the throttle down to idle and apply very slight back pressure to the stick to bring the nose up a bit more. Ideally the attitude you want right at touchdown is nose up about 10 to 12 degrees. This nose-up attitude is called flaring and is essential to a proper landing because it creates more drag and slows the plane down until it settles on the main landing gear. It also prevents you from bending or breaking the odd nose gear or propeller. In older planes, such as the Piper Cub, where there's only a main

gear and a small tail wheel (these planes are affectionately called tail-draggers), flaring is even more critical.

If you haven't come in too fast or at too steep an angle, the plane should settle down easily for its landing roll. Don't apply the brakes too soon, or you could nose the plane over. As soon as the speed drops to around 40 knots, you can lightly apply the brakes until you reach a manageable taxiing speed. (You can nudge the throttle up a bit to get rolling again, should you inadvertently stop completely.) Keep the plane rolling until you reach one of the runway access lanes, take a right turn onto the apron, and taxi until you find your parking spot on the flight line. Then cut the magneto switch by clicking in the lower-right corner with

Don't try to fly the plane onto the ground—it will come down without your help.

Flaring on landing lets the main gear touch down first...

...followed by the nose gear.

your mouse to kill the engine, and you're home.

Now that you've had a little taste of flying, you'll almost certainly want to learn about the proper ways to handle an airplane and the rules that all pilots adhere to. For that you should return to Chapter Two, where the next session of Flight Simulator Flight School is just about to begin...

Chapter Five

Instrument Flying

By now you've had your first flight and a taste of what all pilots face in ground school. Although there's been a lot of data on aircraft and flight procedures to assimilate, getting into a plane and flying has been relatively easy. There's a bit of the "seat of the pants" feel to flight, even though all your flying has been done in front of a CRT. The actual act of flying is, indeed, relatively simple, at least compared to what we have lined up for you in this chapter.

Radio Navigation

Up to this point, most of your flying has been fairly informal. Certainly, you've learned to pay heed to the "rules of the road" of flying, but you've yet to go beyond flying a few simple traffic patterns. As you learned in Chapter Four, you can fly from point A to point B with only the basic flight instruments, but for more involved flights your navigational experience must encompass considerably more than flying simple headings and rough calculations for distance flown. Really to get to where you want to go, you'll have to take that next

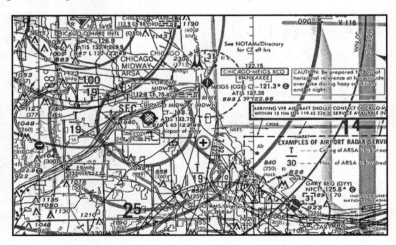

A Typical Navigation Chart with VOR Information.

step into the near-mystical area of radio navigation. It's either that or a stop at the local quickie mart to ask for directions. And guys (you know who you are), do we really want to resort to that?

That's One Big Flashlight

In the days following World War I, as commercial aviation made its first tiny and uncertain steps, a major stumbling block was navigating by means other than dead reckoning or celestial navigation. In the daylight, if you were well-versed in the landmarks along your route or if you possessed a fairly accurate map of what roads there were, you could usually find your destination without too many white-knuckle moments. But let the conditions darken or cloud up or otherwise become visually challenging, and Rand McNally's best couldn't help you. An experienced pilot, familiar with his plane and the effects of wind on it, might navigate by noting heading and distance flown (figured as airspeed multiplied by time, with allowance for wind drift), a technique once known as dead reckoning, but which now goes by the more benign phrase, deduced reckoning. Celestial navigation, on the other hand, meant using star positions to establish headings, much as sailors do.

A rather novel solution, albeit a short-lived one, appeared in the mid-1920s with establishment of a series of powerful, vertically aimed spotlights. These light beacons, placed every 25 miles or so along well-traveled air routes, literally lit the way for commercial pilots. Of course, these lights were only effective as long as the visibility was acceptable, but when extreme visual range dropped below a mile or two, you were just as lost as you'd be without these mega-flashlights.

A Dim Bulb's Better Than No Bulb at All

It didn't take long for someone to figure out that the nascent technology of radio might provide an answer. However, it did take a few years before anyone could effectively harness radio waves' ability to travel a relatively long distance, penetrating both the darkness and most weather. The first successful adaptation of radio to navigation was the Non-Directional Beacon, or NDB, which first appeared in 1932.

The NDB is actually nothing more than an unmanned AM (Amplitude Modulation, where the strength of the signal is modulated, or controlled, as

opposed to FM or Frequency Modulation) radio station that sends out a continuous signal, or carrier, instead of music or talk shows. If you look at the dial of any AM radio, you'll see that the tuner starts at 530 kilohertz. NDBs use frequencies below regular AM radio, in the 200-kilohertz to 400-kilohertz range, though some come close to the lower range of commercial AM radio.

Even though it's a relatively old technology, there are several advantages to the NDB. It remains in use even today. First of all, it's cheap. The transmitter itself is relatively inexpensive, given the price of more sophisticated (and more expensive) VOR (Very high frequency Omni-directional Range) equipment. Maintenance

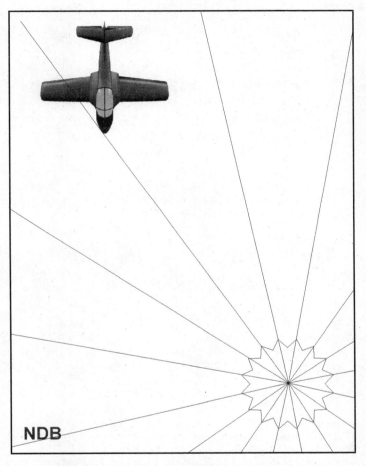

An NDB's single frequency signal radiates 360 degrees from the transmitter.

costs are low as well, since there is little to go wrong with the beacon, meaning even airfields with rather modest means can have a transmitter.

Like ordinary AM radio stations, NDBs have quite a long range under the right conditions. If you've ever fiddled with the dials of an AM radio late at night, you've probably found stations coming in clearly even from a thousand miles away or more. Some of the big stations during radio's heyday, such as

WLS in Chicago or WOR in New York, blanketed the country with their broadcasts. The reach of AM radio diminishes considerably during the daylight hours, however.

NDB technology is very mature, and little can go wrong with the transmitters. Several generations of pilots have learned to fly with NDBs, so there's little that can go wrong from the pilot's end either. A further and final advantage is, simply, that it's everywhere. So many NDB transmitters dot the map that it's difficult to let go of the technology, even though we now have superior alternative technologies.

On the minus side, NDB is extremely limited in the kind of information it can provide a pilot. With the air lanes becoming more crowded each day, there are some situations where the inherent inexactness of NDB technology has proven not just inconvenient but deadly. Also, the range varies considerably from day to night and during thunderstorms as well.

What sort of information does an NDB provide? As you might have guessed from the "non-directional" part of the name, there's some ambiguity involved. The name is a bit misleading. "Omni-directional" might be more accurate. An NDB transmitter broadcasts its signal (on a single frequency) in all directions. VOR transmitters do this as well, but with a critical difference, as we'll soon see. The transmission radiates in all directions, to be received by any airplane equipped with an ADF, or Automatic Direction Finder, which has been tuned

Adjusting and Using the ADF in the Cessna 182 RG

The ADFs in both the Cessna 182 and the Learjet 35A do double duty with the two VOR Indicators. In the Cessna, these indicators are located in the center of the instrument panel, one above the other, just to the right of the Altimeter and Vertical Speed Indicator. You can set the frequency of the ADF receiver either on the instrument panel (just to the right of the VOR Indicators, and labeled ADF) by using the mouse or the keyboard. To use the mouse, just click the cursor to the right of the digits to increase the frequency or to the left to decrease it. If you look closely, you'll see that the cursor becomes a hand when it passes over the ADF display and that a + or - sign appears on the hand, depending on whether the cursor is to the right or left of the display. Using the keyboard is actually a bit simpler and quicker—just press A, which highlights the first digit of the frequency readout. The + key increases the frequency, while the - key (you guessed it) decreases the value. When you reach the desired number, hit A again, which takes you to the next digit. A third hit of the A takes you to the final digit.

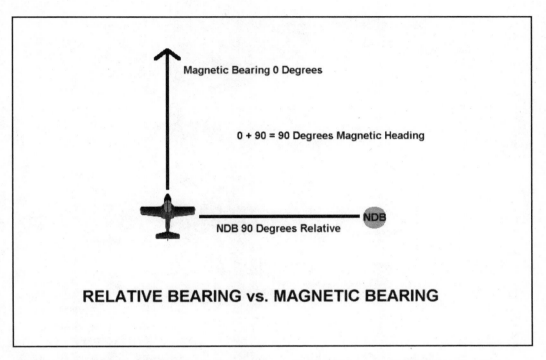

Magnetic Bearing 0 Degrees

0 + 90 = 90 Degrees Magnetic Heading

NDB 90 Degrees Relative

RELATIVE BEARING vs. MAGNETIC BEARING

The Magnetic Bearing is calculated from the Magnetic Heading and a Relative Bearing figure.

to the frequency of a particular NDB. An ADF functions like any AM radio, except that the transmissions it receives are not converted into sound but are read by the ADF, which relays the data to a needle on the indicator dial. The needle then points in the direction of the NDB. ADFs can, in fact, indicate the direction of commercial AM radio stations, too.

Using Radio Navigation Resources

Okay, so now you know the location of an NDB. But just what do you do with that information? Obviously knowing the general direction of an NDB isn't going to help you much unless you want to fly straight for the beacon. For actual navigation you must take the data supplied by the ADF and compare it to your true magnetic heading. There's a simple formula to do this that soon becomes as ingrained in a pilot's mind as the multiplication tables or the Pythagorean Theorem. The formula is MB = RB + MH, where MB is the

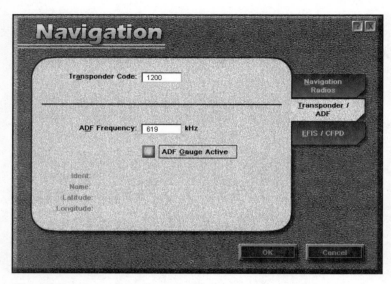

The ADF radio can be adjusted with the mouse, the keyboard, or in the Navigation menu.

Magnetic Bearing, RB is the Relative Bearing (that's the information you get from the ADF), and MH is the Magnetic Heading, which you get from your aircraft's compass (after compensating for wind drift, as discussed in Chapter Four).

Let's assume you've tuned your ADF to the specific frequency of a station you know to be nearby (you did look at the Airport/Facilities listing in the Pilot's Help, didn't you?), and you see the ADF needle swing around to the right to read 90 degrees. This means the transmitter is 90 degrees, relative to the nose of your plane. By the way, most ADFs don't indicate relative bearings in increments less than 45 degrees, so you'll have to do a bit of eyeballing to get close to the right value.

If all this seems a bit much, the frequency can also be set in the Navigation menu by clicking on the Aircraft menu heading, then clicking on Navigation, and then on the Transponder/ADF tab. Then all you have to do is type in the exact frequency.

Where do you get these NDB frequencies? All this information, along with other important data (including the VOR frequencies we'll use later on) can be found in the Airport/Facilities Directory under Help. Access this, and you're presented with a world map. From here you can click on a specific area, which takes you to another map where you can refine your search. Eventually, you'll find listings for not only airports but also for various navigation beacons as well.

Now check your magnetic heading, which we'll say is 270 degrees. If you add these two values per the formula above, you'll come up with 360 degrees, the magnetic bearing to the NDB. This would put you due south of the NDB station. So you're somewhere south of the beacon, with *somewhere* being the operative word here. And now you've stumbled on the biggest shortcoming of NDBs—they tell you where you are, but only roughly where. For more accurate information, we'll have to go on to the next level.

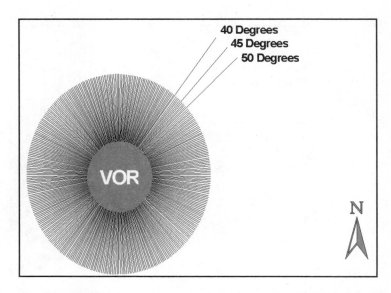

| Back | Print | Map | | | | |

North Carolina

☐ Airports
☐ VORs
☐ NDBs

NDBs

Location/Name	Ident	Freq	Lat	Long	Elev
Ahoskie	ASJ	415	N36°17'	W77°10'	218
Airli (LOM)	IL	281	N34°11'	W77°51'	
Alwood	AQE	230	N35°42'	W77°22'	
Anson Co	AFP	283	N35°01'	W80°04'	302
Ashee (LOM/NDB)	JU	410	N36°26'	W81°19'	3123
Broad River	BRA	379	N35°16'	W82°28'	
Burlington	BUY	329	N36°02'	W79°28'	605
Camp	CPC	227	N34°16'	W78°42'	90
Carolina Beach	CLB	216	N34°06'	W77°57'	
Cherry Point Mc	NKT	245	N34°50'	W76°48'	
Chocowinity	RNW	388	N35°30'	W77°06'	40
City Lake	CQJ	266	N35°42'	W79°51'	750
Clinton	CTZ	412	N34°58'	W78°21'	
Davie	DVZ	354	N35°54'	W80°27'	810
Dixon	DIW	198	N34°34'	W77°27'	54
Doone (LOM)	GR	367	N34°54'	W78°56'	170
Dorchester Co	DYB	365	N33°03'	W80°16'	100
Edenton	EDE	265	N36°01'	W76°33'	
Elizabethtown	TGO	398	N34°31'	W78°30'	115

An NDB listing provides frequency information for all the stations near your flight path.

The VOR System Ahead

It was obvious, almost from the start, that NDBs weren't the final answer to the complexities of aircraft navigation. There was still too much ambiguity to the data, and it didn't

40 Degrees
45 Degrees
50 Degrees

VOR

N

A VOR station, oriented to magnetic north, produces 360 radials, each representing one degree.

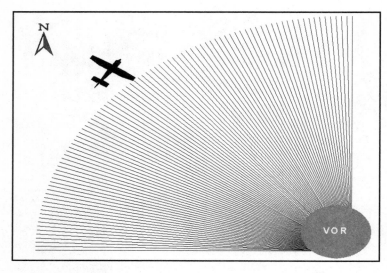

Flying abreast of a VOR station, the indicator numbers change as you pass each radial.

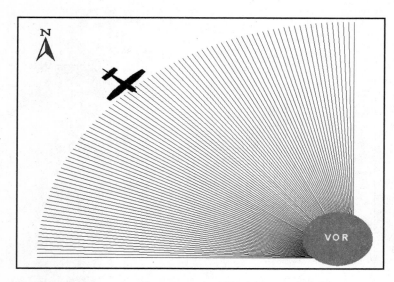

Keep the indicator needle centered to fly along a selected radial toward the VOR station.

take a gifted prognosticator to see that the burgeoning world of aviation would need something better—and soon.

In the late 1940s the United States instituted the VHF Omni-directional Range, or VOR, system. It was immediately recognized to be such a great improvement over NDBs and the myriad other schemes that had been tried in the thirties and forties. By the mid-1950s, VOR had become the de facto international standard. It remains the primary system of radio navigation today, even as technologies such as the satellite-based GPS (Global Positioning System) threaten finally to end its reign over the airways. VOR has become such a standard that the lanes between primary VOR stations have become known as "airways."

VOR and the earlier NDB do have one thing in common—they broadcast their signal in all directions. That's just about where the resemblance ends, however. Whereas the NDB station sends out one signal, on the AM radio band, in all directions, the VOR station transmits two signals. One signal is constant in all directions, while the second cycles, like a lighthouse or a spinning quasar. Both of the VOR's two signals are modulated in VHF (Very High Frequency), a part of the FM (Frequency Modulation) band that is also used by broadcast television channels 2–13, as well as by commercial FM radio. Indeed, just as NDBs broadcast in the area just below the commercial AM radio band, VOR stations transmit their signals in the 108–117.95-MHz range, which is directly above the commercial FM radio band.

As the two VOR signals go in and out of phase, they combine to broadcast 360 lines, or radials. Each of these radials has a unique signature, and it's that signature that is read and interpreted by an aircraft's VOR receivers. As an airplane passes a VOR station, the VOR indicators display each radial (in degrees). If that plane is either headed toward or away from a VOR station along one of the radials, the indicators will let the pilot know this.

The biggest drawback to VOR is its relatively short range. This is not a result of broadcast power but of the nature of VHF waves. Like television and FM radio signals, VOR transmissions

Adjusting the NAV Radios

Right next to those big round VOR Indicators are the little boxes that make them both work. Among the many radios your plane has are two NAV (navigation) radios, labeled NAV1 and NAV2. And as *with the ADF, you can adjust the NAV radios by three different methods. Mouse clicks on the digits to the right will increase the radio frequency, clicks on the left-hand digits will decrease it.*

The NAV radios correspond to the respective VOR indicators. To use the keyboard approach, first press N to select NAV1, and then use the + key to increase the number to the left of the decimal point or the - key to decrease it. Pressing NN moves you over to the right of the decimal point, where you use the same keys to change the numbers. To select NAV2, press the N and 2 together, and then change the numbers on the left to the desired value before pressing NN to adjust the numbers right of the decimal.

Finally, you can access the Navigation Radios tab in the Aircraft/Navigation menu, which is located under the Aircraft heading on the menu bar. Type the correct frequencies, close the menu, and your radios are set to receive. And as with the ADF, you can find VOR frequencies for stations along your course in the Airport/Facilities Directory in the Help menu.

Using the VOR Indicators

You really get your money's worth with the VOR Indicators. No dedicated functions here—multiplicity is the name of the game. You've already been using one of your VOR indicators as your ADF, after all. There are two main parts to the VOR indicator: the OBS, or Omni-Bearing Selector, which allows you to input VOR radial data, and the OBI (Omni-Bearing Indicator). The latter itself consists of a CDI, or Course Deviation Indicator, a vertical needle that, on the Cessna 182, moves from side to side (although on some VOR indicators it pivots at the top), and an Ambiguity Indicator, which actually reduces ambiguity because it displays whether you're heading toward (TO) a VOR station or away from (FROM) it. When the Ambiguity Indicator reads OFF, it means you're simply not receiving a particular station's signal. With some OBIs there's also a horizontal needle that indicates the glide slope when you're using your VOR for landing approaches.

The three parts of a VOR indicator are the OBS, the OBI, and the Ambiguity Indicator.

Told you these babies did a lot of things. Really, though, it's not as complicated as it sounds. The OBS simply lets you select a specific radial so that you can "follow the needle" and fly to that radial, while the OBI tells you either the radial you're already on or the radial you've selected with the OBS, as well as whether you're moving toward or away from the VOR station. And with that amount of information you can do a lot of precise navigating.

To change radial data with the OBS, the drill is the same as with the other radio navigation gauges. The mouse will let you increase (click to the right) or decrease the values (click to the left) for each indicator. Pressing V and 1 on the keyboard simultaneously accesses VOR1, after which you can increase or decrease values using the + or - keys. V plus 1 accesses VOR2. And, of course, you can type in the values in the OBS course box on the Navigation Radios tab in the Navigation menu.

are pretty much "line of site" phenomena which can be easily blocked by obstacles such as buildings or, more commonly, mountains. This blocking can be overcome to an extent by climbing to a higher altitude, but there's a limit to the signal's range, no matter how high you climb. Over uneven terrain, and at altitudes below 18,000 feet, a VOR transmitter's range can be as little as 35 nautical miles. Flatten out the terrain, and the range can extend to around 130 nautical miles. Above 18,000 feet, the blocking effects of ground obstacles no longer come into play (unless someone has foolishly located a transmitter at the foot of a mountain and you're on the side opposite the transmitter), but maximum range still tops out at about 130 nautical miles.

VOR is a more versatile navigation aid, compared to NDBs. First of all, you immediately have a much more exact positioning of your aircraft, since the radials read by the VOR indicators correspond to your magnetic compass and heading indicator. That is, 360 degrees

means north, 90 degrees is east, 180 is south, and 270 is west. So if you're flying toward a VOR station on the 225-degree radial, you know your position is due southwest of that station.

Finding out where you are relative to a VOR station simply means adjusting the radial values with the OBS until the CDI is centered and the Ambiguity Indicator reads FROM. For example, you twiddle

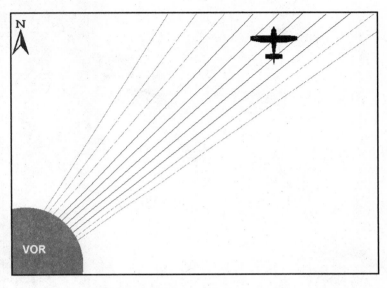

The most basic use of VOR is to find your position relative to a specific station.

with the OBS until the vertical needle centers, which means you're tuned exactly to one of the VOR station's 360 radials. In this case, the OBI identifies it as the 90-degree radial. Match that up with a FROM indication, and it says you're somewhere due east of the station.

To reverse the process in order to fly to a specific station, again adjust the radial values with the OBS until the CDI needle is centered, but the Ambiguity Indicator shows a TO reading. The value you read in the OBI is the course directly to the VOR station.

Fine, you know where you are in relation to a VOR station...sort of. You don't, however, know how far away from that station you are. Unlike NDBs, VOR can give you that information as well, with a little help from one of its cousins. Perhaps you've noticed that you have not one but two VOR receivers and indicators. Now a suspicious mind might surmise that this is just the sad and costly result of a fast-talking used-plane salesman and an extremely low level of sales resistance on the part of the original buyer. Or maybe you're one

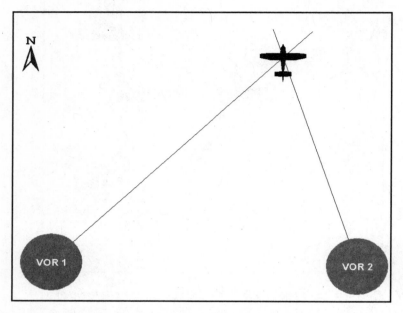

The point where the radials of two VOR stations intersect is your position.

of those overly cautious "belt-and-suspenders" types who figured a little redundancy couldn't hurt. After all, this little Cessna has two magnetos and two fuel tanks, hasn't it?

Wrong on both counts. (Okay, as a slight twinge of paranoia passes, we'll grudgingly award a half point to the redundancy group.) You need two VOR receivers to figure out exactly how far you are from a station. There is another way to do this, which we'll cover in a moment, but for now, let's take a crack at pinpointing our plane's position with those dueling indicators.

This is actually one of the simpler things you can do with your VOR receivers. First, consult your Airport/Facilities listing or a handy navigation chart and find two VORs in your immediate vicinity. This takes a little guesswork on your part, but if you're so lost that you don't have even the slightest inkling where you are, well, "Reset Flight" is right there in the File menu. Once you have two prime VOR candidates, set each of your VOR receivers to one of the frequencies. (See the sidebar above for instructions on setting the receivers.) Now center the OBI needles on each VOR indicator, making sure that both of them read FROM. Then you can read the radial information from the top of both needles. From there it's a quick look back at the chart to see where those two radials intersect. Find that point, and you've found yourself.

With VOR so ubiquitous, it stands to reason that airports have become primary locations of the transmitters for the VOR network. And since that's the

case, it's also true that air travel between these nodes has been greatly simplified because pilots can just fly the radials, or airways, between airports. The problem is, how do you find a particular radial. In a sense, this is like asking how to get to the on-ramp for one of the many aerial superhighways.

To intercept a radial, you first need to know the frequency settings for the two nodes, or VOR stations, of a specific airway, as well as the course between the two stations. For the sake of this example we'll keep it a nice round number—90 degrees. (Radials read as from a VOR, so this means a heading of 90 degrees from the first VOR to the second.) Tune one of your NAV radios to the first VOR station, the station you're flying away from. Then set the OBI to read 90 degrees, and FROM. Your initial course depends on which way the needle falls. If it moves to the left, for example, your course should be to the left of 90 degrees. A generally accepted intercept course would be about 30 degrees, so in this case your intercept heading will be 60 degrees.

As you hold that course, keep a close eye on the CDI needle. It will eventually begin to slowly move toward the center of the indicator. As it nears center, start your turn (to the right) so that your heading reads 90 as the

ILS

We'll be using ILS, or the Instrument Landing System, in Chapter Six, but because its technology is linked with that of the other radio-navigational instruments, a quick overview is in order. In the Cessna the VOR indicators serve as ILS indicators, once you begin a landing approach.

An ILS system consists of two main transmitters—the localizer and the glide slope— along with several short-range transmitters, called markers, that tell you when your plane is a specific distance from the airfield. The localizer transmitter operates in the same VHF band as VOR and is usually located at the far end of the runway. While a VOR signal radiates 360 degrees, a localizer signal is much narrower—only five degrees in width—and highly directional—so much so, in fact, that the signal, or beam, cannot be picked up at all by any aircraft flying more than 35 degrees off the approach heading. Like all radio signals, even highly directional ones, there is some signal spreading. This spreading is taken into account when a localizer is adjusted for a particular runway so that the beam's width at the threshold of that runway will be 700 feet. The spreading continues so that, at a runway's outer marker (approximately five nautical miles, depending on the runway), the width of the beam has grown to nearly 3000 feet. Still not all that big a target to aim at, and with the beam narrowing as you approach the runway, staying "on the beam" becomes increasingly difficult. You stay on the beam by using the CDI, or vertical needle, on the VOR indicator to establish your position in relation to the localizer.

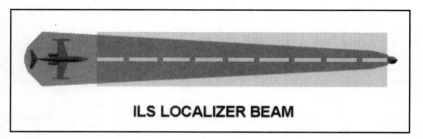

ILS LOCALIZER BEAM

A Typical Localizer Layout.

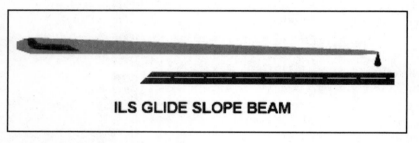

ILS GLIDE SLOPE BEAM

The Glide Slope and Marker Layout.

needle finally centers. Unless you're flying in dead calm, you'll probably need to correct for wind drift to keep the needle centered.

At some point along the radial you must tune in the frequency of your destination's VOR since it will eventually become stronger, just as the signal of the VOR you're flying away from becomes weaker. Remember that we mentioned how radials are described as radiating from a VOR? That means that, once you tune to the station you're heading toward, the radial you find yourself on is not 90 degrees, but its reciprocal (180 degrees opposite), in other words, 270 degrees. But to maintain your course, set the OBS to 90 degrees.

The glide slope transmitter, situated off to one side of the runway and usually relatively close to the runway threshold, shares the UHF band with DME. Its signal is even narrower than the localizer's—only about 1.5 degrees—so its spreading is less. At a mile the beam has only spread to a vertical width of about 140 feet, so it's much more difficult to stay on the glide slope than it is to stay within the beam of the localizer. The glide slope information is relayed to a horizontal needle on the VOR indicator—the needle shows the position of the slope, so, for example, if on approach the needle drops below center, you'll need to increase your altitude to get back on the

slope. Together, the localizer and the glide slope transmitters use radio waves to create an ever-narrowing tunnel down which a plane flies to a successful landing.

The final part of ILS is the marker system, a series of short-range transmitters whose signal can only be received when a plane is very close. Each marker has a signature signal, broadcast in Morse code. On approach we can hear this signal, as well as see it because the signals also activate different lights on the instrument panel. The outer marker is situated at the point where a plane would normally pick up the ILS system, usually around four to seven nautical miles, depending on the runway. The signal for the outer marker is three dashes in Morse code, with an accompanying blue light on the instrument panel. The middle marker, located 3500 feet from the runway threshold, sends out a dot-dash-dot-dash signal and illuminates an amber light. And though not always present, there is often an inner marker at the point in the glide slope (usually 200 feet) designated as the Decision Height (the height where you must decide whether you can land the plane). This marker sends out a four-dot signal with a white light.

Taken together, these components comprise the ILS. Designed during World War II, it operates 50 years later, essentially unchanged, at airports the world over. And in Chapter Six we'll see just how important ILS is when trying to daintily set down 65 tons of prime 737.

Distance Measuring Equipment

The third part of the radio navigation triumvirate is also the newest technology of the three: DME, or Distance Measuring Equipment. Operating in the Ultra High Frequency band (yep, that's UHF, the same band used by television channels 14 and above), DME is a close cousin to radar. A transmitter on your aircraft sends out a signal that is intercepted by a selected ground station. Unlike radar, where the original radio pulse is simply reflected back to the aircraft, a DME station sends out a pulse of its own, triggered when it receives your airplane's signal. The elapsed time between when the original signal is sent and the DME station signal is received by your aircraft is used to calculate the distance between aircraft and station, with the value displayed on the DME indicator, in nautical miles. DME stations are almost always a part of a VOR

station (these stations are called VOR-DMEs, or VORTACs), so you don't have to select a DME. You get the DME data along with VOR information.

The distance between your plane and the VORTAC transmitter is measured as distance along the ground, which reveals the one flaw in the DME system. Imagine the DME system as a right triangle, with the airplane at one vertex, the DME station at another, and the right angle formed by a vertical line drawn from the plane intersecting a horizontal line from the station. Radio waves travel at the speed of light, so in the relatively small area described by this triangle, the time difference between a radio wave hitting a plane at, say, 20,000 feet and the same wave reaching a point on the ground directly below the plane is negligible. But, and this is a really big but, the actual difference in distance from the plane to the station—the hypotenuse of the triangle—as opposed to the point on the ground to the station, can be considerable. In this case, the DME might tell you that you're 20 nautical miles from the station, when in reality, because of your altitude, you're only 17 nm. This is called the slant range, and all pilots take this measurement with one or more grains of salt, depending on their experience. And for a little icing on the cake, this distance distortion effect increases as you approach the DME station. Just a little more fun for all.

There's one more navigation technology to consider before we leave this chapter. Although you'll find it on only one of the planes we'll fly in Flight Simulator, the RMI (Radio Magnetic Indicator) is an

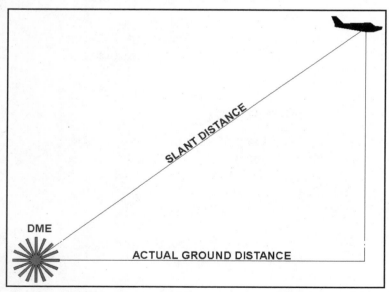

The slant range (the line from your plane to the DME) is always greater than the actual range.

important instrument on most airliners. The RMI really is a jack-of-all-trades, combining the functions of an ADF, a VOR Indicator, and a Heading Indicator. The instrument itself usually features two needles—one for ADF and the other for VOR (with the head of the needle always pointing to a VOR station so that a separate Ambiguity Indicator is not needed). Combining the functions simplifies headings since you don't have to worry about relative bearings.

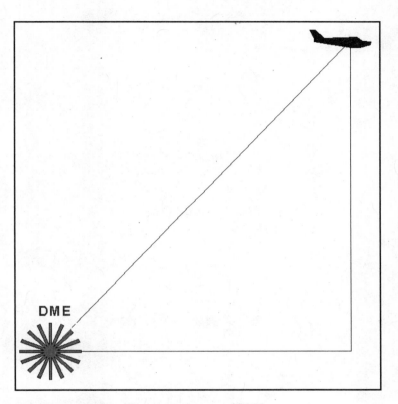

DME

Very high altitudes affect the accuracy of DME.

We'll look more closely at the RMI, and a lot more goodies as well, in the next chapter, when we take the big 737-400 for a spin. And maybe we'll discover a few more inside tips on piloting an airliner. Just don't expect us to reveal any of the dark secrets of airline food. The world's simply not ready for that horror yet.

Chapter Six

Commercial Pilot

There are few occupations with a more immediate effect on people's lives than that of airline pilot. A pilot's decisions and actions could end the lives of as many as 400 people. With that in mind, it's certainly no surprise that the training and certification procedures for airline pilots rank among the most stringent and closely monitored.

In Microsoft Flight Simulator for Windows 95 we don't experience the true feeling of having responsibility for so many people, but we can experience the techniques and procedures a pilot must master to be worthy of that charge. In this chapter we'll take an overview of what goes into making an airline pilot, as well as look into the planning of a typical flight (even if there is no such thing), the aircraft preparations, the flight itself, and a bit about how airliners manage to find their way around.

Basic Knowledge for the Airline Pilot

It goes without saying that airline pilots don't start out as airline pilots. You don't use multiengine aircraft for flight training any more than you'd learn to drive on an 18-wheeler. Airline pilots begin the way all pilots do, with basic flight training, usually in a small Cessna or Piper (if they happen to be American). As we've seen in Chapter Two, even the steps required to become a private pilot are quite difficult, and not everyone can make it. It is not enough to have good coordination and a talent for handling an airplane in flight. There must be a certain mental discipline as well, and an attention to detail that an outsider might

A pilot's eye view of the office.

view as bordering on paranoia. But these are essential characteristics for any pilot, and expecially for airline pilots.

While there may seem to be many systems and gauges to attend to in any aircraft, the truth is that the complexity of today's modern airliner would overwhelm someone whose only experience had been piloting a Cessna 182. Of course, the basic functions to be monitored —engine performance, aircraft status, communication equipment, navigational concerns —are the same. But the way they're monitored and acted upon is much more complex. To compound the difficulty, most modern airliners have much smaller flight crews than planes of 40 years ago. In the spacious cabin of an old Douglas DC-6, there would usually be four, or even five, crew members. The pilot, copilot, navigator, flight engineer and, sometimes on longer flights, a relief pilot, all had specific responsibilities. By contrast, modern flight crews usually have only three members, and sometimes only two. Today's airline pilot must be a combination of aviator, navigator, and flight engineer.

Planning the Flight

A flight actually begins well before an aircraft pulls away from the terminal gate. (On longer flights, it really seems this way to the passengers.) Usually the aircraft's pilots confer with flight operations personnel over the configuration for the aircraft—that is, how loaded the plane will be, what the actual course is, and other items. Then it's on to the meteorological center for the latest reports, not only on the weather at takeoff but also on conditions along the route, as well as at the destination. Naturally, on a longer flight, weather evaluations for a destination 3000 miles and seven hours distant are tenuous at best, but then, that information will be constantly updated during the flight. Given the inprecision of weather forecasting, it's at least possible to have some idea of the weather seven hours hence. These days, satellite imaging has made forecasting reasonably accurate, especially in the case of large weather formations.

A thorough understanding of weather and how it affects an airplane is important to any pilot. Much of this information is acquired in ground school and through experience, but when dealing with the upper atmosphere, an area most light plane pilots see only from the window of an airliner's passenger compartment, a pilot's knowledge must go deeper. For a discussion of weather factors and flying, you should consult Flight Simulator's extensive help files under Weather. These mini-lessons provide not only a basic background on how weather systems form and change, but also on how these systems affect aviation.

Armed with weather data, pilots can then make very educated estimates on how much fuel will be needed for the flight. Contrary to popular belief, airliners almost never take off with a full load of fuel, particularly on shorter flights. Full tanks mean that much more weight the plane will have to lift off the ground. In comparison with earlier jets, modern high by-pass turbofan engines are much more economical, as well as quieter. The old Boeing 707, pioneer that it was, was a real gas guzzler (well, kerosene, really) and noisy as well, which is why you don't see

A meteorological chart.

many of them flying any more. Many of those you do see have been re-engined with newer, fuel-efficient powerplants. A complete flight plan can now be created, signed off on, and filed with flight operations. Finally, before going out to the plane, the pilots make sure that all the radio navigation aids along the route are functioning properly. If there's a problem here, they can nominate alternate beacons.

In most cases, an airline pilot already knows the route he'll be taking like the back of his hand. These days there are very few instances where an airliner, either regular or charter, will take a flight path not already frequented by many other aircraft. With Air Traffic Control's need to know where all large aircraft are at all times, it's essential that airliners fly predetermined flight paths. These routes are not set in stone —they are updated daily to reflect variations in weather patterns, air traffic density, and other factors.

```
WA CASCDS WWD
CSTLN...SCT015 BKN040. TOPS 100. WDLY SCT -SHRA. AFT 09Z OCNL
   BKN015. OTLK...VFR.
RMNDR...SCT025 BKN050. TOPS 120. WDLY SCT -SHRA NR MTNS. 09Z
   BKN025 BKN050. TOPS 120. SCT -SHRA. OTLK...MVFR CIG BECMG VFR
   18Z.
.
WA E OF CASCDS
SCT-BKN060 BKN100. TOPS FL250. WDLY SCT -SHRA. NERN MTNS ISOL
-TSRA TIL 05Z. CB TOPS FL280. OTLK...VFR.
```

Typical weather report.

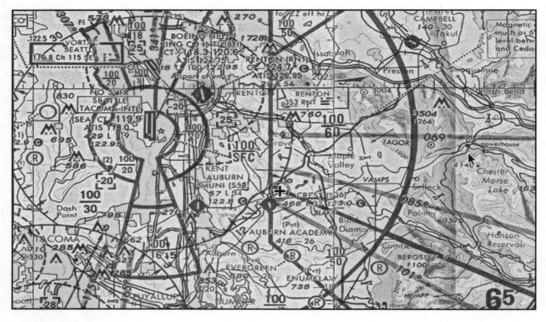

Chart of the Seattle area.

This is especially true of long-distance flights where pilots might want to take advantage of the jet stream (a high-level "river" of air flowing west to east, sometimes at near-supersonic speeds). Much of the variation in flight paths comes not from actual course changes, but in altitude adjustments.

Preflight Checks

The plane has been undergoing inspection since before it pulled up to the terminal gate, as the ground crew readies it for flight. The fuel figures are given to the ground crew for final fueling, and the pilot makes his checkup. There's really not much that you can see externally on a plane, although the odd loose rivet or fluid leak can pop up during an inspection. One of the last things the pilots do before boarding the plane is to ascertain that the plane has been balanced—that both fueling and cargo loading have been carried out with a critical eye toward balancing the craft, fore, aft and laterally. To be sure, it would take a gross violation of cargo-loading procedure radically to relocate a

plane's center of gravity, but sometimes even minute changes can result in altered flight characteristics.

Once inside the cockpit and situated, we can take a look at the 737's instrument panel and consider the difference between this panel and the others you've seen in Flight Simulator. Obviously it's more complex than a light plane's instrument grouping, although the panel is much cleaner than those of earlier airliners because electronics and miniaturization have allowed many instruments to perform multiple functions. The two

The HSI and the RMI.

biggest changes between this panel and, say, a Cessna's, are the HSI (Horizontal Situation Indicator) and the RMI (Radio Magnetic Indicator). The HSI is one of those multifunction instruments we were discussing. It combines a heading indicator with sections for VOR (yellow arrow) and ILS (red arrow). The indicator shows an overhead view of the

The Boeing 737-400, featured in Aircraft Handbook in Pilot's Help. A complete set of pilot checklists is available there, too.

aircraft, with the magnetic heading displayed at the top of the circle. The RMI indicates bearing relative to a VOR (green arrow) and to an NDB (yellow arrow). We'll cover the function of both gauges more fully once we're in the air. Another addition to the panel is the spoiler switch, situated to the right of the thrust levers (the name for the throttle levers in jet aircraft). If you've ever

It's Boeing This, and Boeing That...

A time traveler from the 1950s would certainly be shocked at the preponderance of Boeing aircraft on the commercial-aviation scene. Almost every airliner seemed to be a Douglas DC-4 or DC-6, and the few that weren't made by Douglas were usually graceful Lockheed Constellations. And ever so occasionally, you'd hear in the news of a revolutionary new jet aircraft named the Comet by the English company de Havilland. But Boeing? They made bombers for the Air Force, didn't they?

Yes, they certainly made bombers—the B-17 and the B-29 were stalwarts of the Second World War. It was the fact that Boeing did make bombers that is partly the reason for Boeing's dominance in commercial aviation today. In the closing year of World War II, the Army Air Force decided it needed to take the next step in bomber design and asked all the major aircraft companies to submit designs for an aircraft powered by the still-new jet turbine engine.

The other companies submitting designs went a very conservative route, for the most part grafting jet engines onto what could just as easily been piston-engined planes. Boeing, however, with the advantage of aerodynamic information gathered from German designers, made a bold leap with the B-47, a swept-wing, six-jet aircraft that looks modern even by today's standards.

All the while Great Britain, seeing how Douglas aircraft were flooding the market, came up with the de Havilland Comet, a radical design for the late forties, with four de Havilland Ghost jets buried in the wing roots. The plan was to leapfrog the U.S. companies in the race for the future of airline travel—and it almost worked. Tragedy, in the form of several Comet crashes in the early fifties, indefinitely grounded the plane. Metal fatigue was discovered to be the culprit, and the Comet eventually flew again (a Nevil Shute novel of the time—and eventually a similarly titled movie—called No Highway *chronicled a fictional airliner known as the Reindeer that was suspiciously similar to the Comet). But the damage to the Comet's reputation was already done.*

In the intervening years, both Douglas and Boeing (benefiting from its design experience with the B-47 and the later, larger B-52) came out with designs that significantly improved on the Comet. The Douglas DC-8 is now generally considered the better of the two aircraft, but Boeing managed to come out on top with some last-minute modifications to what would eventually become the 707.

Of course, today the big names are not just Boeing and Douglas, but Boeing, Douglas and the European aircraft consortium Airbus. Douglas still makes short- and medium-range aircraft such as the MD-80, while Airbus has the 300, 310, and 320 models. Lockheed, which was for many years something of a player, blew everything on its ill-fated L-1011 Tristar jumbo jet, the failure of which nearly ruined the company. And Boeing...well, the next time you hear an airliner pass overhead, look up. You shouldn't be surprised if it's a Boeing 707 (yep, there are still a bunch of them flying nearly 40 years after their maiden flights), 727, 737, 747, 757, 767, 777...well, you get the picture.

watched the wing of an airliner a few minutes before landing, you'll get the disconcerting feeling that the whole structure is coming apart. A modern airliner's wing is a patchwork of aerodynamic devices, some used to enhance lift, others to degrade it, and a few to perform both functions. The spoilers on the 737 are used to disrupt lift in landing approach situations and simply to slow down the plane by creating extra drag. We'll let you know when to pull this lever...whatever you do, don't try using it during takeoff.

By the way, if you don't see the controls for the various radios, don't fret. Like the Learjet 35A, the 737 is meant to be flown by two people, and so it has a wide instrument panel in order to enclose all the instruments needed. Putting all those instruments on the screen at once while maintaining the correct aspect ratio for panel to windscreen would make the panel too small to be easily read. So Microsoft has put the engine and radio controls on a toggle. Any time you want to change the panel, just hit the Tab key.

A Typical Flight Aboard the 737-400

Our flight today is not an actual, passenger-carrying flight (the FAA would almost certainly frown on a novice taking charge of 150 or so passengers), but rather a ferry flight. We'll be taking off from legendary Boeing Field (a.k.a. King County International Airport) in Seattle, Washington, delivering this shiny new 737-400 to San Francisco International Airport. It's not a terribly long flight—and navigation considerations along the way will be minimal—but it will give us the chance to practice getting a 60-ton airplane from point A to point B. And we'll have the opportunity to practice one of the more arcane arts of flying, the ILS landing approach.

Now that you've got some idea of what does what on the 737's instrument panel (don't worry, we'll help you out if you forget), why don't we get settled, get the engines started and warmed up, and get ready for takeoff.

It's basically a truism to say that the takeoff is the most dangerous and, for the pilot, the busiest part of any flight. This is especially the case with an airliner. There is so much that can go wrong, and although it usually doesn't, allowances must be made. Pilots undergo a great deal of on-the-job training, but it's easy to forget that they also spend many hours "flying" on the ground. Flight trainers have come a long, long way since the rudimentary Link Trainers. These days, there's a dedicated flight simulator for every major type of aircraft so that a pilot's practice sessions aren't the generic affairs they once were. With computers and elaborate servo systems to control the attitude of the simulator

module, a modern 737 pilot can experience the complete range of aviation situations, all the while sitting in a cockpit that looks and reacts just as the one on a real 737.

By the time you've earned the right to sit in the left-hand seat of a major airline's plane, you will have undergone thousands of hours of flying, in both smaller aircraft and computerized simulators. When the time comes to make that split-second decision, there can be no hesitation, no confusion—seeing it all before in the flight simulators prepares a pilot for the worst that can happen.

Okay, we'll run up the engines, back away from the parking apron, and move onto the taxiway leading to the end of Runway 31 at Boeing Field. It's a busy day here (business must be good for Boeing), so we can take the time to review our takeoff procedure as we await our turn to take off. First of all, we need to discuss V speeds and how they relate to the 737. V speeds represent the points during a takeoff when decisions must be made and, more importantly, followed through. The first V speed, V1, is the speed at which the decision must be made to continue with the takeoff. Thatis, the speed beyond which the takeoff cannot be aborted. With a fully-loaded 737-400 at sea level, this speed is around 150 kts. Given a normal takeoff roll, you should still have enough room to bring the plane to a stop on the runway should you abort the takeoff while below this speed.

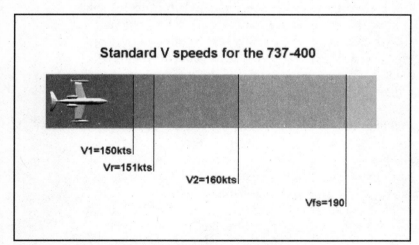

Standard V speeds for the 737-400

V1=150kts
Vr=151kts
V2=160kts
Vfs=190

The speed chart.

Vr is the next speed of note. The "r" stands for rotation, the point along the takeoff roll when the nose of the plane is lifted in anticipation of takeoff. In most cases, Vr and V1 are close to the same speed; you should rotate at just over 150 kts. Finally, V2 is actual takeoff

speed, noted as the point along the airspeed continuum where the plane can become airborne even if an engine fails. Early large jet airliners were almost always four-engine affairs, mainly because turbine engines just weren't as powerful as today's models. Newer, more powerful engines have allowed designers to drop the requisite number to two, which makes a plane both lighter and more streamlined. No surprise, then, that way back in the late sixties, the 747 was the last plane Boeing designed with more than two engines. The power of these newer engines is such that, once a plane has accelerated to V2 speed (about 160 kts in the 737), it can continue on—albeit at a very low altitude—to make an emergency landing. Post-takeoff speeds (such as when the landing gear is retracted) are expressed as V2 plus a number, V2+15, for example. The various V speeds, as well as other critical points along the takeoff roll, are usually read off by the copilot and ascertained by the pilot.

With takeoff only a few minutes away, we complete our final checks (all aircraft checklists can be found in Pilot's Help) and prepare the aircraft for departure. As we taxi onto the end of the runway, extend the flaps to the five-degree setting. (By the way, as we refer to the various controls, we'll simply direct a certain action as it would be peformed with a real plane. For a rundown on the keyboard, joystick, or mouse inputs for each action, please refer to Chapter One.)

There are eight flap settings on the 737, starting with one-, two- and five-degree settings, and then in five-degree increments up to a fully extended 40 degrees. These settings are indicated by the round dial in the upper right-hand corner, just above the landing gear lever. This wide range of adjustment is a result of the necessity to configure the wing for many different flight situations. While you're at it, adjust the elevator trim to neutral for takeoff. (It will be readjusted later.)

Jet-turbine engines operate a many times the rpms of reciprocating engines, but it's still possible to over-rev them. Taking that into consideration, it's a wise pilot who keeps an eagle eye on the engine-monitoring instruments, and on the N1 gauge in particular. It's located atop the main engine instrument column. and monitors the rotation speed of the engines' main turbines. Under normal circumstances, it should never indicate an engine speed above 96 percent, even during takeoff.

If you're ready to start the takeoff roll, ease the thrust levers up smoothly and rather slowly. These engines, with their large-diameter turbines, don't respond very quickly to changes in thrust settings. Even more than the much

smaller turbines in the Learjet, the 737's turbofans have a noticeable lag time, so you'll need to plan ahead whenever you're adjusting them.

As the N1 reading moves to 60 percent, you can release the brakes. The aircraft will start rolling slowly—so slowly, in fact, that you almost think there may be something wrong with the engines. Some pilots, in a effort to maximize the available runway length, time their turn onto the runway so the plane keeps rolling right into the takeoff run. The Flight Simulator 737 is pretty much a hands-off machine as far as tracking down the runway goes. For that matter, the real plane is much the same way, although the dynamics of flight do have some adverse effects.

For example, as the plane begins its takeoff run (and until it reaches a speed of around 140 kts), its direction is easily controlled by the steerable nose gear, which, in turn, is controlled by the rudder pedals. After the plane lifts off,

Rotation at Vr.

the rudder takes over to correct any minor yawing motion. But there's a gray area in the takeoff—where the plane is just beginning to lift, but isn't yet completely airborne—where the issue of control gets a little confusing. If the wind is blowing at an acute angle (not directly along the plane's flight path, but just to one side or the other), the plane can sometimes act like a weathervane in a high breeze or a sailboat in a strong current and point its nose into the wind. A great deal of care must be taken at this point since the nose gear has little or no authority by this time, but rudder inputs may lead to over-control.

As we said, at any speed past 150 kts you can pull back on the yoke to lift the nose to about a 15-degree angle. This change in wing incidence increases lift to the point where the plane should lift off within a couple of seconds. Almost as soon as you feel the plane completely lift from the runway, retract the landing gear and drop the power until the N1 gauge reads 91 percent. Increase the climb angle to somewhere between 15 and 20 degrees and keep the airspeed below 250 kts until you reach about 10,000 feet. The reason for this speed limitation is rather interesting: it minimizes the damage should a bird hit the windscreen. Because there aren't many birds that can make it up to 10,000 feet—or more to the point, want to—you should be safe from there on up.

The climbout after takeoff is a particularly tricky balancing act. On the one hand, you must prevent the aircraft from stalling from a too-high climb angle. Stalls this close to the ground are always disastrous. On the other hand, there are the ever-more-strict noise abatement regulations that strictly limit an airport's noise output. And let's face it, an airplane, whether jet- or propeller-driven, is never more noisy than at takeoff. The engine is at full revs, of course, and in a prop plane, the propeller pitch is usually set to a higher angle for more thrust (and more noise). So what's a pilot to do? Well, a climb-out angle that's as steep as possible without flirting with a stall helps get the plane well above the houses and businesses below as quickly as possible. And the slight throttling back helps as well, even though turbofan engines at 90 percent are still shouting at the top of their frenetically spinning lungs.

The higher you go, the thinner the air gets. And despite their many differences, jets and piston engines do have one thing in common—they need to breath the air. The combustion chambers in both depend on oxygen, so as the air gets thinner volatile combustion is reduced. For a given throttle setting, engine output drops as a plane climbs higher. To counteract this, keep an eye on airspeed and adjust the thrust levers to keep it

A noisy climb out over a peaceful city.

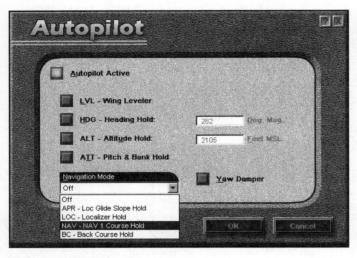

Setting up the Autopilot.

constant. Once you've passed the 10,000-foot mark, your airspeed should be about 270-280 kts. And by the way, once a plane reaches a height of 20,000 feet or so, the IAS (Indicated Airspeed) shifts from being expressed in knots to Mach numbers. After 20,000, the plane should be tooling along at around .75 Mach, or 75 percent of the speed of sound. (The sound barrier increases as altitude increases.)

As we climb out of Seattle we'll make a gentle left turn to bring us to a heading of 179 degrees. It will take us several minutes to climb out to about 20,000 feet, where we would be instructed by ATC to continue our climb to Flight Level 310, which is the level we specified on our flight plan. Once we get to that level, we can set the autopilot to hold both heading and altitude. Our first VOR station will be the Battle Ground, Washington station (BTG), with a frequency of 116.60. Go ahead and set NAV1 to this frequency, and we'll reset the autopilot to home in on the station. Remember, even though the radial we're flying toward is the 359-degree radial, we must set the OBS to the reciprocal of that radial, or 179 degrees.

The flight itself is pretty uneventful, which is always good when you're trying out a new plane for the first time. Fortunately, Boeing knows how to build them right, which is one reason why the 737 is the all-time sales leader for jet airliners. But enough of this reverie—there's more navigation to perform. The following are the remaining VORs and their frequencies:

Eugene, Oregon (EUG)	112.90
Fort Jones, California (FJS)	109.60
Redding, California (RDD)	108.40
San Francisco, California (SFO)	115.80

As we approach San Francisco, the cockpit suddenly becomes a much busier place. About 100 miles out from our destination, we will begin to make a slow, steady descent. In the real world we would contact ATC at this point to request permission to reduce our altitude. It's important to call in whenever you're making radical changes of altitude, but it's essential for such a busy airway as the one we're flying. While we can't experience quite this level of

Advanced Navigation

While we're pretty much limited to VFR and basic IFR flying with Flight Simulator, there are more advanced forms of navigation for aircraft. Some are proven technologies already in use, while one in particular—GPS—has only recently come on-line. But it promises the sort of pinpoint accuracy in navigation that pilots have only dreamt of.

LORAN (LOng RAnge Navigation) has been used for quite some time for aircraft on long flights, especially over oceans. Used by ships as well as aircraft, the LORAN system consists of several master transmitters and additional slaves placed about 200 miles apart. The master transmitters send out signals which are relayed by the slaves and picked up by anyone with the proper receiver. As the signals from three consecutive transmitters are received and compared, a position can be fixed with a fair degree of accuracy, depending on the distance from the transmitters.

Another multiple-signal positioning technique is the Omega system. Extremely powerful transmitters are positioned around the world, all sending out three precisely timed signals to ships as well as aircraft. An on-board computer in an airplane then compares the signals against an internal clock synchronized to the Omega transmitters, and a position is established, usually to an accuracy of no more than a couple of miles.

Another technique, inertial navigation, is an outgrowth of the gyroscopic instruments most planes already carry. Actually, pilots perform inertial navigation every day, using the information gained from their gyroscopic instruments to make better-informed flight decisions. Advanced inertial navigation goes a step further, using extremely sensitive gyroscopes to sense the slightest change in movement along all three axes of flight. Cruise missiles (such as those used in Desert Storm) use a form of inertial navigation to guide themselves to a target. It works like this: information about a course is entered into a computer connected to the gyroscopic measuring devices. The computer constantly compares its course information against the data it receives from the inertial instruments, and then makes the appropriate corrections. The obvious advantage of inertial navigation for airplanes is that weather conditions or visibility problems don't affect its operation.

A further improvement, the laser gyroscope, eliminates the one major problem of inertial systems, the mechanical gyro. With no moving parts, the laser gyro isn't affected by friction or gyroscopic precession. The name "gyro" is something of a misnomer for these laser devices—there is nothing rotating, as you might infer from

(continued on page 122)

Microsoft
Flight Simulator
for Windows 95

(continued from page 121)

the name. Rather, by precisely measuring the changing length of a laser beam as it is affected by movement along the axes of flight, a computer can compare directional changes against a pre-determined course and, as with the mechanical gyro system, make the appropriate corrections.

Satellite navigation, usually called GPS (Global Positioning System) uses a network of 24 satellites circling the earth at 11,000 miles, sending out signals to special receivers. This system, developed by the U.S. military, is called the NavStar system. Each receiver contains a computer which can interpret the signals of a minimum of three satellites, and then fix the user's position. Every satellite's signal transmission is set to a very precise interval, so the GPS receiver on the ground knows exactly when to expect it. Measuring the difference between expected and actual reception supplies an important value in the positioning equation.

The GPS got its first real test in 1990 during the Gulf War, and soon after it was made available to the public, albeit in a rather limited form. The 24 satellites send out two signals—the CA (Coarse Acquisition) signal, which is what you receive when you operate one of the many commercial portable GPS receivers available, and the PPS (Precise Positioning System), which is available only to certified users (i.e., the military).

For reasons known only to the U.S. military, the CA signal contains a deliberate error in its transmission, which makes the signal most of us can receive accurate only to about 100 meters (although in practice the error is closer to 50 meters). PPS signals, on the other hand, are accurate to within a couple of feet. GPS receivers have become so inexpensive and commonplace (you can even buy models that hook up to PCs and work with mapping programs) that it's only a matter of time before the NavStar system—or its successor—completely replaces the complex, confusing, and often archaic aeronautical navigation system still in use. When you can buy a $200 GPS receiver for your Cessna and—the government finally willing—you have accuracy of less than your sleeve measurement, who would want to fool around with VORs and NDBs?

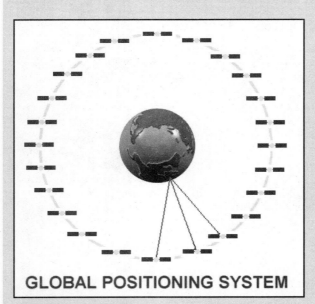

GLOBAL POSITIONING SYSTEM

The NavStar GPS

The 737 descending.

realism with Flight Simulator, we can at least go through the motions of descending to the various flight levels and leveling off for a moment before losing more altitude. Be sure to disengage the autopilot before beginning the descent.

While it may not seem like much of a glider, the 737 can fly a long way without power, which is just the way it's going to fly for the next few moments. Pull the thrust levers down to idle and we'll coast for a bit. Note that the 737, usually a very docile and stable plane, may become a little more sensitive flying in this mode. Don't over control the plane; make nice, gentle corrections. And when descending, don't try to do it all at once. You've got a hundred miles or so to work with, so there's no big hurry. Certainly, no more than two degrees downward is warranted at this point.

As we drop below 10,000 feet, there are a couple of items to note. First of all, remember that the speed limit below this altitude is set at 250 kts. And second, be sure to reset your altimeter. By this time we should be able to pick up the ATIS transmission out of San Francisco, and it includes the correct setting for the altimeter. Power at this point in the approach should be around 70 percent, although it may vary by a few percentage points either way as you keep airspeed right around 250 kts.

Instrument Landing System (ILS)

We're going to try something new on this flight: a true ILS approach and landing. The ILS system has become so foolproof—and autopilots so sophisticated—that many new planes (the 737 included) can, in theory at least, land themselves. We won't quite put that to the test, but we will rely solely upon information from the ILS system to land the plane. If you recall from

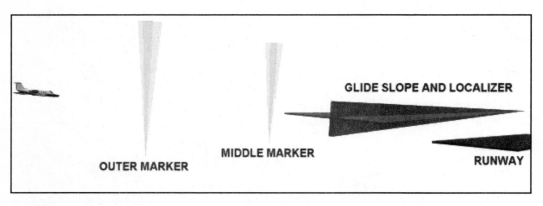

The complete ILS system.

Chapter Five, the ILS system is made up of three separate systems. The two main systems are the Localizer and the Glide Slope. The third, ancillary, system is the Markers.

Now that we're close to the San Francisco Airport, it's time to give ILS a try. The golden rule when attempting an ILS approach is always to fly toward the needles. The needles represent the position of the glide slope and the

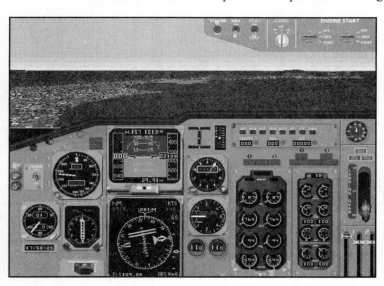

Acquiring ILS.

localizer in relation to the plane. Think of the ILS system as two flat spreading cones, one oriented vertically, the other horizontally. They combine to produce a radio signal shaped sort of like a cross. The intersection of that cross is the correct approach path. The horizontal needle on the ILS Indicator (part of the HSI on the 737) represents the glide slope, while the vertical needle represents the localizer. Before you can acquire the ILS, you must turn onto your final approach. Set your power to about 60 percent and use the spoilers sparingly (if they're needed at all) to bring the airspeed down to about 210 kts. Don't let the airspeed drop below this, or you'll run the risk of stalling when you make your turn onto final approach. You should also extend the flaps to the five-degree setting

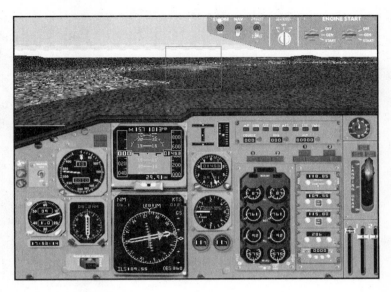

Holding the glide slope and localizer.

in anticipation of the turn. Lowering the flaps will both slow you down and bring the nose up a degree or two. It also slightly reduces the chance that the aircraft might stall in the turn. Just before you make the final turn, drop the flaps to 15 degrees.

As you turn onto the final approach, you will immediately acquire the ILS transmitters. You'll know this by the change in the positions of the needles, and probably by the beeping of the Outer Marker indicator as well (which will flash a blue light). If the vertical, or localizer, needle is to the right of the center, that means you're to the left of the localizer beam, so steer the plane to the right until the needle centers up. Or say the horizontal, or glide slope, needle is above the center of the gauge. You're too low and must climb a bit until that needle centers.

Between the localizer and the glide-scope indicators, it's usually more difficult to stay on the glide slope. The localizer remains constant, and unless you actually steer the plane away from it or let the plane drift to one side or the other, you can stay nailed on the localizer. The glide-slope transmitter, however, sends its beam out at a slight angle—about three degrees up. This inclination means you literally fly down the glide slope, constantly reducing altitude to stay within the relatively narrow beam. Drop your flaps to 25 degrees and adjust

Flight Simulator
for Windows 95

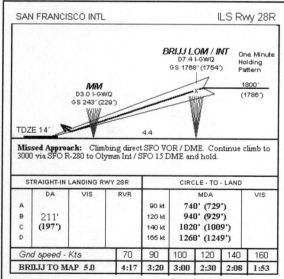

Approach Diagrams for San Francisco International.

power so that you're in the neighborhood of between 140-150 kts. Again, use the spoilers if you're coming in too fast. By the way, you can lower the gear now...things might get a little hectic soon and we wouldn't want to forget an essential point like that.

Note the ILS approach chart we've included here (courtesy of Final Approach, a good program by Georges Lorsche—see the appendix for more details) shows a decision height for San Francisco International Airport. The decision height is similar in concept to the V speeds used during takeoff—decision height denotes a specific point in the landing approach where the decision must be made to continue with the landing or choose the missed-approach option and try another go-round. The chart also describes the procedure for a missed approach for this particular airport.

With both needles—or in the case of the 737's HSI, the yellow arrows—centered, your approach is right on the money, and you can attend to the business of actually setting the thing down. At about 3500 feet from the runway threshold, you'll acquire the middle-marker signal along with its yellow or amber light. If you are right on the ILS beam, this marker will tell you that you're 200 feet above runway level.

With the speed at around 140 kts, extend the flaps to 30 degrees and just let the plane fly itself in. If you must make adjustments to stay within the glide slope, make them very delicately.

Just before you cross the threshold of the runway at an altitude of about 50 feet, cut the power back to idle and let the plane ease itself down. Because of the flap setting, the plane will already be flying nose high, so resist the temptation to tug the yoke back a bit to raise the nose further. It doesn't need it. The instant you hear the main landing gear touch the runway, deploy the spoilers and apply full reverse thrust (you'll probably have to use the keyboard—the K3 key— to do this, since the throttles on most joysticks will bottom out at idle). Watch the rollout speed, and when it drops below 60 kts, move the thrust levers back to idle and apply the brakes. Don't hold the brakes on too long. You want to so keep the plane rolling enough to drive it to the gate. And just like that, Microsoft

Over the threshold.

Touchdown.

Airlines has a new 737-400 to add to its stable. And you have your first instrument landing under your belt. Life is good.

Chapter Seven

Dancing with Clouds

For many aviation enthusiasts, nothing captures the essence of flight quite so completely as aerobatics. Wringing out an agile plane, pushing it to the limit, flying on a razor's edge boundary between "perfect-10" aerial gymnastics and total disaster—that gets right to the heart of flying. Amid the myriad regulations, rules, and procedures that are part of modern aviation, the aerobatic pilot stands as a true link to flying's romantic past.

Flight Simulator's Extra 300S, arguably the best aerobatic aircraft in the world today, lets you experience the peculiar combination of analytical precision and pure adrenaline rush that is aerobatics. In this chapter we'll try to give you a few pointers on mastering the maneuvers that are the staple of modern aerobatics.

A Short History of Aerobatics

It would be stretching things to say that pilots have been doing aerobatics since the dawn of the Aviation Age. Those early pilots might indeed have longed to cavort through the air like birds, but the first aircraft simply weren't up to it. In fact, it was all most planes could do to get into the air in the first place, given their anemic engines. And once off the ground, staying aloft demanded all of an aircraft's meager flight resources. Finally, even if there had been enough power, the construction of those early craft would never have withstood even the moderate stresses of a simple loop.

The case could be made that practically any of the first generation aircraft were aerobatic—albeit unintentionally so—because of their quirky flying characteristics. The first truly aerobatic aircraft would not appear until nearly a decade after the Wrights flew those first 120 feet at Kitty Hawk, and by that time there were plenty of pilots skillful enough (or crazy enough) to put these new planes through previously unimaginable contortions.

The Blériot monoplane.

In the first decade of aviation, almost anything anyone might try was a "first:" first flight, first turn, first crossing of a river. In 1908 poor, unfortunate Thomas Selfridge even made history as the first fatality (with the pilot of his ill-fated flight, Orville Wright, nearly becoming the second). But there were some pilots who seemed to specialize in being the first. English Channel-spanner Louis Blériot quite naturally comes to mind, but an employee of his, young Adolphe Pégoud, had a few claims to fame of his own. Not satisfied with being the first pilot to parachute from an airborne plane, he managed to do something in 1913 that changed aviation forever—the first loop. There's something of a controversy on this point, some maintain that the first loop was actually performed by Petr Nesterov, one of the early pioneers of aerobatics. (The Nesterov Cup, awarded to the winning team at each World Championship, was named after him.)

Regardless of who actually looped that first loop, from that moment there was no stopping Adolphe, Petr, or their peers. Not even a war, as it happens; indeed, a world-wide conflagration was just the kick in the pants that aviation, and in our case, aerobatics, needed.

Building on their successes just prior to the war, a new generation of innovative designers such as Fokker and Nieuport brought forth planes that not only flew well in a straight line but could also turn, climb, and dive quite well, all without threatening to disintegrate in midair.

Many of the maneuvers flown by today's aerobatic champions had their origins in The Great War—the turn for which Max Immelmann is renowned, for instance, has now outlived its creator by 80 years. There's just something

about the feel of hot lead whizzing past your head that inspires aerobatics sense, although the thought processes involved in creating a maneuver as bizarre as the twisting, tumbling Lomcovak surely must be more the result of alcohol in the bloodstream, rather than adrenaline.

It was between the World Wars that the traditions of organized aerobatics began. By the early 30s, there was no shortage of great pilots or great airplanes. In fact, the aerobatics scene of the decade preceding World War II was something of a golden age, with pilots idolized in much the same way that Formula 1 auto-racing drivers are today. There was a great deal of national pride involved—especially in Europe—as the major countries supplied their aerobatic champions with state-of-the-art aircraft. In the U.S., air-racing was king, with heroes like Jimmy Doolittle and Roscoe Turner. But Europeans loved their own aerobatics. Men such as Gerhard Fieseler and Michel Detroyat were esteemed for their exploits.

Legendary Aircraft: Bücker Jungmeister

At first glance the Jungmeister hardly appears the aerobatic legend it is. Wire-braced and a bit dumpy looking by modern standards, the little biplane was nonetheless the choice of several champions.

The Bücker Jungmeister.

Deceptively agile, the Jungmeister first flew in 1933 as a single-seat variation of Swedish designer Anders Andersson's popular Jungmann two-seat trainer. It was manufactured by the Bücker Company in Germany and continued to be flown with great effectiveness even after World War II, as newer, more powerful aerobatic craft were in ascendancy.

The meister *in the name—German for* master— *is apt. Although well past its prime by the time the modern World Aerobatics Championship began in 1960, the Jungmeister nevertheless holds an honored position in international aerobatics.*

Look at the Aresti Cup, the top award in Championship Aerobatics, and you'll see the Bücker Jungmeister. It sits atop that trophy because it was the favored plane of Count Jose Luis Aresti, one of the fathers of modern aerobatics. If there's one plane that epitomizes aerobatics, it would almost certainly be the evergreen Jungmeister.

The first World Cup of aerobatics was held in Paris, in 1934, with others held throughout the decade, until war once again brought a harsh reality to aerobatic flying. After the war and until 1960, aerobatic competitions were relatively low key—at least compared to what they had been before the war. The Lockheed Trophy competitions were the best known, but given the more informal nature of these events, the more intensely professional flyers were looking for a greater challenge.

Perhaps because aerobatic flying was for so long the domain of the European pilots, Americans have not had the sort of success in World Cup competition one might expect. To date, and including the World Cup of 1996, there have been only four World Cup champions from the U.S.—Mary Gaffney, Betty Stewart (who has won twice), Charlie Hillard, and the inimitable Leo Loudenslager. His plane, the Laser, is noteworthy as the inspiration for two fine aerobatic designs, the Super Star and your very own Extra 300S. Loudenslager himself is noteworthy as one of the true originals of aerobatics.

But enough history! It's time to put all those years of aerobatic experiment to good use.

Patty Wagstaff flies the Extra 300, as shown in the Flight Simulator Help section on Aerobatics.

Getting to Know the Extra 300S

When Walter Extra showed up with his new Extra 300 at the 1988 World Championships, spectators were treated to something special. Extra flew a full program of figures with ease...while carrying a passenger. It was absolutely shocking, but this

auspicious debut was no fluke, as the many renowned aerobatic pilots who have flown the 300 since then will tell you. With the introduction of the 300S ("S" for single seat), the aerobatics plane many feel flirts with perfection was born.

You're sitting in its cockpit, under the panoramic canopy, wondering just how you got yourself into this. It's one thing to be Patty Wagstaff, who flies her 300S as if it were a part of her, and quite another to be a rookie with most of his hours behind the yoke of a nice, sedate Cessna Skylane.

Before we go any further, we'll need to effect a change of scenery. Access the World menu heading, scroll to Go to Airport, and select the Avra Valley airport in Arizona. We're heading there for a couple of reasons. First, it's pretty barren out there, so you won't have to worry about a lot of tall buildings. More important is the area just south of the airfield where an official aerobatic box is set up.

The Aerobatic Box

As in several other sports, the so-called "level playing field" exists in aerobatics as well. When aerobatic pilots fly their programs in competition, they do so within a construct called the aerobatic box. It takes a bit of imagination because the box doesn't really exist—it's defined by a set of white markers on the ground. The markers describe a box with both a length and width of 3300 feet. The top of the box is at 3500 feet above the ground, while

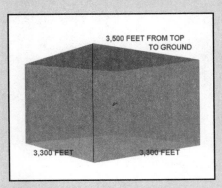

The Aerobatic Box.

the bottom boundary depends on the skill level of the pilot. The Sportsman classification, the lowest rung on the competition-aerobatics ladder, specifies a lower limit to the box of 1500 feet above the ground. As the pilot classification goes higher, the bottom of the aerobatic box drops. Intermediate pilots may maneuver as close as 1200 feet to the ground, while advanced pilots can venture down to 800 feet. Unlimited pilots such as Patty Wagstaff are allowed all the way down to 300 feet, the length of a football field. Given the skill of these pilots, that may not seem all that close, but just think of this—a car going at only 60 miles per hour covers 88 feet every second. The 300S can perform maneuvers at three times that speed and can eat up 300 feet in the blink of an eye.

The Extra 300S, a classic tail-dragger.

All maneuvers must be performed within this box, with points deducted for flying outside it, much the way gymnasts are penalized for stepping outside the boundaries during their floor exercises.

What may be most disconcerting at first is the angle at which you're sitting. After some contortions to insert yourself into the seat (you don't sit in this airplane, you wear it!), you discover that you're seated at a rather odd angle compared to the nice, level seating in the Cessna 182. Moreover, while the view's great to the sides, above, and behind, you can't really see much over the nose. Well, this is where you missed joy (and pain) by not doing your flight training in a Piper Cub, Aeronca, or Taylorcraft. Those old tail-draggers were a horror to land—at least for a novice—but they really taught a pilot the importance of attitude (the plane's, not the pilot's).

After you get over the odd angle at which you're sitting, the next thing that strikes you is how close everything is—wingtips, tail, propeller, and so on. This is a very cozy aircraft, and with good reason. Remember back in Chapter Two when we discussed the makings of a great aerobatics plane? One of the most important factors was to have as much of the airplane as possible as close to the center of gravity as possible. This makes a lot of sense if you try a little experiment: Sit in a swivel chair and spin yourself around. (This comes very natural to most people anyway, especially while seated in one's office around 2:30 in the afternoon, any day of the work week.) Okay, are you spinning? Good. Now extend your arms straight out on each side and notice how you quickly slow down. Pull them back in, and the rate of deceleration decreases.

Aircraft have the same problem, which is why you don't see any aerobatic aircraft with long wings. Indeed, for many years pilots felt the best kind of plane for aerobatics was the biplane, since you could have shorter wings, yet have plenty of wing surface for lift. But the biplane configuration exacts other tolls in performance, most notably extra aerodynamic drag and the added weight of two sets of wings. So the monoplane became the design of choice, but with wings as short as possible to decrease roll resistance—the tendency for a plane to resist rolling (rotating) along its longitudinal (front to back) axis.

Now that you've made yourself comfortable in the cockpit, take a look at the instrument panel. While not as complex as the 737, it is a considerable leap upward from the Cessna 182. The majority of the instruments and controls should be familiar to you, even if their positioning is not. The extra

The Legendary Aircraft: YAK-18

Ask anyone to name a make of Russian or Soviet aircraft, and the answer will almost invariably be the MiG. But Russia has had many outstanding aircraft designers through the years, and none more prolific, influential, or versatile than Alexander Yakovlev.

The YAK-18P.

Unlike many of his peers (such as Mikoyan, who mainly designed fighter craft) or Tupolev (who specialized in large planes), Yakovlev could design simply anything. He came to prominence early in World War II with a series of fighters and cemented his reputation in the post-war years with his versatile jet fighters and bombers. But the aerobatics world will remember him for his YAK trainers, beginning in 1946 with the YAK-18. In appearance a bit like a scaled-down North American AT-6, the YAK-18 was much more agile, even in its basic-trainer guise.

The YAK-18P was a single-seat version of the basic plane, much lighter and with more horsepower (originally 260 hp, quite a lot for the fifties and early sixties). Even though considerably larger than its competitors, it was still an extremely maneuverable plane that inspired confidence in its pilots with its robust structure and edge in sheer horsepower. Its only weakness—its rather ineffective rudder—derived from its trainer heritage where extreme control surface movements are a liability. A souped-up 300 hp version, the YAK-18PM, took the Soviet aerobatic team to a clean sweep of the first three positions in the 1966 World Championships.

G-Meter.

instruments in the 300S are devoted almost entirely to helping you perform aerobatic figures. The one you'll be most concerned with is the G-meter, which you'll find on the lower left-hand side of the instrument panel. The G-meter aids the pilot on a couple of counts. First, it tells you when the g-force, the force of gravity, is approaching either the pilot's or the aircraft's limit—pretty important in a real airplane, but of a more academic nature in Flight Simulator. However, it's also used to set up some maneuvers where the pilot uses the g-force to provide momentum.

One thing that's missing from the instrument panel is the flap indicator. That's because of what's missing from the Extra's wings—flaps! For the type of flying it does, flaps simply aren't needed. With all the power the 300S has relative to its weight, it will literally leap into the air at full throttle, but the lack of flaps does make for interesting landings, as we'll see at the end of our flight.

Okay, if you're ready, let's get this bird up where it belongs. If you've been flying the Cessna, or perhaps even the Learjet, you should be prepared to revise your flying technique a bit. The Extra is a much more responsive plane, as befits a cloud dancer. When you apply a control input—any input—there's no lag time, no "slop" in the controls. So always keep in mind that you should approach flying this aircraft with a smooth touch. There will be maneuvers, to be sure, when you'll need to jerk the plane into a certain attitude. But for the most part, be as light-handed with the controls as possible, while still being firm and decisive. If that sounds like contradictory advice, rest assured that, once in the air, it will make perfect sense.

By the way, if you haven't already, go into the Realism menu under the Aircraft heading and deselect Auto-coordination. Some of the following maneuvers are impossible to perform with the rudder and ailerons linked. You might as well get used to using the controls separately now, although having either rudder pedals or a joystick with rudder control (such as the Microsoft Sidewinder) is almost essential for successful aerobatics.

Many aerobatic maneuvers require that you look to the side, and sometimes to the rear, as you perform them. While you don't absolutely need a joystick with a view hat switch, life will be so much simpler if you do. Having to take your hands off the controls to switch views with the keyboard simply won't cut it when events start coming fast and furious.

The engine's turning over, so let's obtain clearance from ATC, release the brakes, and smoothly (there's that word again—remember it) advance the

throttle. Here's your first big challenge, namely taking off without bending the prop—or worse. All the other planes in Flight Simulator (excepting the Sopwith Camel) have tricycle landing gears supporting the aircraft on the ground in a level attitude. The nose cannot drop because the nose gear prevents it. Not so with tail-draggers like the Extra. If you advance the throttle too quickly, the little plane will nose over faster than you can say "gemütlichkeit."

The tail lifts.

Advance the throttle enough to get the plane going, and then gradually move the lever to about three-quarters throttle and wait for the speed to build up and the tail to lift. Keep your hands (and feet) off the controls, and the plane should track straight down the runway. We're assuming a clear day with little wind for this first flight, but later on, if you choose to fly with a crosswind, you may need to steer a bit into the wind to keep the plane straight. Once the tail is off the ground, you'll finally be able to see where you're going, and you can apply full throttle. The plane should lift quickly.

Aerobatic box markers.

You'll notice right away how rapidly the little Extra climbs at full power. You'd almost believe it would climb straight up, and you wouldn't be far wrong. Unlike earlier aerobatic planes, the newest generation—planes like the Extra, the Mudry Cap 231, and the YAK 55—have the power-to-weight

ratios of fighter planes. With that sort of power, we climb up to 2000 feet in no time.

Although we won't be flying in competition for a while, let's head over to the aerobatic box area so we can fly in nonrestricted airspace. Take a heading of 180 degrees immediately after takeoff. You'll be flying toward what appears to be a valley, where you'll soon see the nine white markers that define the aerobatic box. We won't concern ourselves with the box for now. Continue to climb, leveling off at about 4000 feet.

Legendary Aircraft: Pitts Special

It's a rare airplane that's so influential as to be considered a landmark in aviation. The Wright Flyer qualifies, of course, as do the Boeing B-17, the North American F-86, and the Hawker-Siddeley Harrier. In aerobatics the Pitts Special is definitely a contender for landmark status. In the late sixties, while companies in Europe like Zlin and Mudry were opting to perfect the monoplane for aerobatics, the U.S. took a perceived step backwards when Curtis Pitts designed the S1-S, known as the Pitts Special. But it wasn't a real step backward because the tiny biplane proceeded to take the aerobatics world by storm.

With 180 hp it had a lot of power for its weight and, with double the number of ailerons, possessed a nimbleness unmatched by its monoplane peers. It didn't hurt that the Pitts Special was so small that competition errors were barely noticeable, while the same missteps stuck out like sore thumbs with larger planes. Its knife-edge performance was even helped by the unique design of its fuselage, which presented a fairly efficient airfoil when the plane was at 90 degrees of bank.

In 1972 the late Charlie Hillard became America's first World Aerobatics Champion flying the Pitts, and he continued to fly it—along with Gene Soucy and Tom Poberezney—for 25 years as a member of aerobatics' premiere exhibition team, the Eagles. The Pitts Special is the only biplane to win the modern World Championship, a status it's likely to keep for the foreseeable future.

Loops

It isn't long before we reach the aerobatic box markers. See them? Good. Now forget about them except as a reference point for returning to the aerobatic practice area. Now that we're at a suitable altitude, let's consider the maneuvers we'll be performing. If you've ever seen an aerobatic champion perform, you'll see a number of complex, often stomach-twisting figures, but at the heart of each maneuver are a few basic figures.

Asked to name the first aerobatic maneuver that comes to mind, most people

will unhesitatingly say, "The loop." Most sport pilots will give the same answer, mainly because, of all the maneuvers, the loop is the easiest to perform. That's a bit misleading however because, while the loop is easy to perform, it can be quite difficult to perform *well*. And if you plan on progressing to more difficult maneuvers, you'd better make sure you can do a nice clean loop.

Probably the trickiest part of the loop is making sure that your exit is at the same altitude as your entrance. You usually won't have to worry about exiting the loop higher than your entrance, but a pilot's first few loops almost always end at a lower altitude, making the whole maneuver look less like a loop than a comma.

Loop diagram.

As with many maneuvers, you'll need to find a reference point on the ground to line up a loop. Most pilots use a straight road, and so will we. Fortunately for us, there's one just below, so adjust your heading so that the nose of the Extra is lined up with the road. Before we start the maneuver, take a quick look at a diagram of a loop.

We want our airspeed to be around 140 kts, so adjust the throttle accordingly. The Extra's throttle response is just as immediate as that of the other controls, so don't overdo it. In nonaerobatic planes a pilot often has to enter a loop from a dive to gain enough momentum to complete the maneuver. The Extra has more than enough power to loop from level flight, but don't let that fool you into thinking there's unlimited power to pull you out of any situation.

This initial climb, the loop entrance, is where you get your first experience with the G-meter, so keep an eye on it as you begin the loop. Pull back on the stick until the G-meter reads between three and four Gs. The nose will rise quickly, so be ready to ease back on the stick a bit once the plane goes past the vertical. A quick glance to the side is advisable here, since it's often difficult to tell where the nose is after you've lost the horizon as a reference point. As you

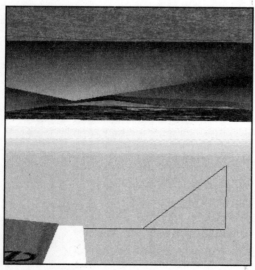 

The Loop. The wing tip guides (visible above) are equilateral triangles segmented to show 45, 90 and 180-degree angles. The guides provide an accurate guage of your plane's position relative to the horizon. For a detailed explanation on using these visual guides, see page 142.

look to the side, you'll see the wingtip describe a small circle on the horizon. If the circle flattens out or elongates, you'll need to adjust the pressure on the stick slightly. A circle flattened on top means there's too much back pressure on the stick (so ease up a bit more), while an elongated circle signals the need for more back pressure.

At the inverted part of the loop, you must ease up on the stick anyway, or you may stall out. Don't ease up more than a second or two before pulling the stick back again for the downward part of the loop. In a proper loop, the aircraft must remain in a vertical plane throughout the maneuver. So keep checking your reference point and adjust the plane's path with the rudders if necessary. The wings must stay level, as well, although that's not usually a problem unless there's a strong crosswind. As you can see even with a simple loop, independent control of the rudder and ailerons is nearly a requirement.

Because you're in a dive, airspeed may increase considerably. The Extra's structure is stressed to permit maneuvers at speeds up to around 160 kts, so if you discover airspeed creeping up toward that figure, retard the throttle a bit. Look to the side again—is the wingtip still forming a true circle?

The exit of the loop should be identical to the entrance. That is, the g-force on exit should also be between three and four Gs. Too much speed out of the loop will cause you to experience higher g-force in order to pull the plane back to level at the same altitude as the entrance.

There, that wasn't so hard, was it? Well, maybe it was. For anyone who thought a loop was just a matter of pulling back on the stick and letting the plane (and the physics of flight) do all the work, the preceding sequence must be a real eye-opener. But the truth is that flying a loop is like playing the guitar—easy to do, but difficult to do well. It's an aerobatic skill well worth perfecting, however, because experience gained flying the loop will serve the pilot well in learning other maneuvers. Any aerobatic figure you perform will require three things: constant use of visual reference points during the maneuver, awareness of the aircraft in all three axes of flight, and sensitive management of the plane's inertia.

Once you've practiced the loop several times (making sure to stay within the aerobatic area near the aerobatic box markers), it's time to move on to some variations. And don't forget to climb back to 4000 feet before trying the next figure.

Square Loop diagram.

Square Loop

While some aerobatic maneuvers have rather exotic names that provide little or no indication about what they actually are, the square loop (and the eight-sided loop that follows) are exactly what they sound like. They're loops where the turn radii have been altered to square off the figure. To perform a square loop from level flight, you need a plane with a high power-to-weight ratio like the Extra, since you have a more pronounced vertical climb, at least for the first leg of the figure.

Once again, adjust your airspeed to about 140 kts, sight on the road as a ground reference, and pull back on the stick as you did with the regular loop, pegging the G-meter at between three and four Gs. But this time, rather than waiting to ease back on the stick until the plane noses over from the vertical, push the stick forward to center just before the plane attains a vertical attitude and let it climb straight up for three or four seconds. You'll need to look to the side to check that your attitude is 90 degrees to the horizon. Fortunately, the Extra has visual guides attached to each wingtip that let you easily judge the plane's attitude relative to the horizon, with segments displaying level flight, a 45-degree angle, and a 90-degree angle. The vertical component of the guide will be level with the horizon when the plane is flying at 90 degrees, or perpendicular to the ground, while the diagonal component is level when the plane's attitude is 45 degrees.

After the short climb, resume back pressure on the stick until just before the plane is completely inverted, and then quickly center the stick. Again, check your visual reference to the side to make sure the plane is flying level, as well as your reference point on the ground to keep the aircraft flying within the same vertical plane.

If you were flying a nonaerobatic plane, this maneuver would be much more difficult. It all has to do with the shape of the wing's cross section, or the airfoil. As we've seen, a usual airfoil is curved at the top and nearly flat at the

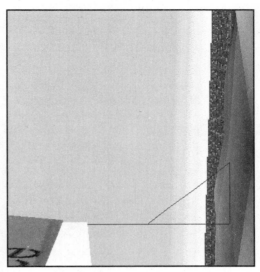

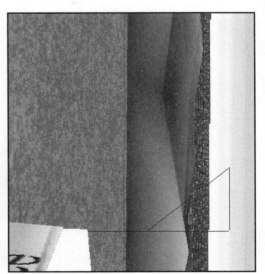

The Square Loop.

bottom. This is the optimum design for normal flight and works quite well in 99 percent of flying situations. But invert that airfoil in flight, and suddenly it's a nightmare. Enter the symmetrical airfoil, featured on the Extra, other aerobatic planes, and most fighter planes since World War II. As the name implies, this airfoil has the same curve for the top and the bottom, and so behaves the same whether level or inverted.

The inverted component of the square loop should last a bit longer than the first vertical since you've lost some speed from your initial climb. A few of these square loops will give you enough experience to know how long to hold inverted flight. Pull back again on the stick to bring the nose down into the third leg of the loop, and then center it again just as the plane approaches vertical again. (Check those visual references!) A three- or four-second pause in this attitude will bring you to the final corner of the loop, and another backward pull on the stick will—if everything went according to plan—bring you back to level flight at an altitude close to where you began.

Eight-sided Loop diagram.

Eight-Sided Loop

Think of a stop sign, and you've pictured the eight-sided loop. Another variation on the standard loop, this figure has eight components, each connected by a 45-degree angle. Needless to say, it requires even finer control of the aircraft's attitude. Once again, here's where the wingtip visual guides come in handy. While it's fairly easy to judge when a plane's at 90 degrees vertical without a guide, nailing 45-degree angles is much harder without some reference aid.

Speed is the same—140 kts—going into the figure, but because your pull up into the first leg of the loop is only 45 degrees, the G-meter reading will be lower, on the order of about 2.5 to 3 Gs. Constantly check your reference points and remember that, because of the figure's complexity, maintaining your airspeed will be critical. By the time you reach the third leg of the figure (the semi-inverted 45-degree

The Eight-Sided Loop.

segment), airspeed will have dropped off considerably unless you apply more power. Just be ready to back off on the throttle quickly once you reach the fourth segment—fully inverted flight—so that you don't have too much speed going into the downward sections of the figure.

Rolls

Now that we've gotten the basic loop and its variations down pat, let's try something on a different "plane" (spatially speaking, that is).

Aileron Roll diagram.

Aileron Roll

The aileron roll is an easy maneuver for most pilots if it's set up correctly before execution. In the roll, the plane rotates along its longitudinal axis. Seen from the front, a correctly performed roll has the nose of the plane moving in a very small circle. In a perfect world the nose wouldn't move at all, but we all know how imperfect a world this is, and the many physical forces acting simultaneously on a plane in flight rule out true perfection. Even the super fast computers that control a "fly-by-wire" fighter plane such as the F-16 Falcon don't compensate quickly enough to allow the plane to rotate perfectly along its axis.

To begin an aileron roll, we'll once again adjust our speed to around 140 kts and find the road for our reference. Now comes an essential part of the roll—pulling the nose up slightly. Because there will be a tendency for the nose to drop during the maneuver, we must begin the roll with the nose up at an angle of between 20 and 30 degrees (depending on the plane). Because the Extra can easily perform very tight rolls, we'll use the lower figure of 20 degrees.

Gently pull back on the stick until the nose angle is 20 degrees (you can monitor this with a look to one side), and then center the elevator. This will be a roll to the left, so quickly—but smoothly—push the stick over to the left and hold it there. You will not touch either the elevator or rudder controls in this maneuver. The Extra, as we've mentioned before, handles like a hummingbird

and can rotate a complete 360 degrees in less than a second, so you won't have to hold the stick over very long. In fact, until you get the feel of the Extra's roll rate, you'll probably over-roll by 30 or 40 degrees. Timing is critical in centering the stick a split-second before the wings reach horizontal. Just keep practicing until you can stop the roll with the wings dead level. By the way, if the roll is executed correctly, the nose angle at the finish of the figure should be the reciprocal of the starting angle. That is, if you began the maneuver with the nose at a positive 20-degree pitch angle, you should finish with the nose at 20 degrees negative pitch.

Slow Roll

The basic aileron roll is not a competition figure, but a variation of it—the slow roll—is. The slow roll demands more

The Aileron Roll.

attention to the other controls—rudder and elevator—because it's, well...it's slower. Depending on whether the slow roll is continuous, two-point, four-point, or eight-point, the plane must fly for short periods at various angles of bank, each applying a unique set of aerodynamic forces to the aircraft.

You enter a slow roll at the same speed and attitude as the regular aileron roll—140 kts and 20 degrees nose up. The roll rate is slower, however, because you don't push the stick over nearly as far. Just remember: the slower the roll, the more you'll need to adjust the plane's attitude with the other controls. Attention to all the controls is even more critical with the hesitation or point rolls. In these figures, the plane actually hesitates at various points in the roll. In

The Slow Roll.

a two-point roll, the pilot momentarily stops the roll after rotating 180 degrees, and the plane is inverted. As you've learned from the square loop, flying a plane, even a specialized aircraft like the Extra, demands more from the pilot when inverted. Once you're inverted, you'll need to find the road again to make sure you're still lined up. (Use the rudder to make slight adjustments.) Also, make sure that your nose has not dropped below the horizon before resuming the side pressure on the stick and finishing the roll. And it's also essential with all these figures to keep an eye on your attitude indicator since the actual horizon is not always visible.

The four-point roll has stops every 90 degrees and puts your plane into a unique new position, the knife edge. This occurs when the plane has rotated the first 90 degrees and is held momentarily with the wings perpendicular to the ground. The knife edge seems impossible

since the wings couldn't possibly generate lift in that position. And they don't— it's the *fuselage* that now serves as the airfoil, and the shape of the fuselage determines how well a plane will fly the knife edge. Usually aircraft that have more rounded profiles are better, becoming a lifting body much like the predecessors of NASA's Space Shuttles.

The fuselage becomes a wing.

At this attitude the roles of the rudder and elevator are reversed—if you need to adjust the nose level, you must use the rudder. In a roll to the left, this would mean that right rudder would raise the nose while left rudder would lower it. Corrections for deviation right or left of your reference road are made with the elevator. (Up elevator moves the nose left; down elevator moves the nose right.) The plane returns to this knife-edge attitude once more in the maneuver but banked the other way, so the reversed controls are themselves reversed. (Right rudder = nose down, left rudder = nose up; up elevator = nose right, down elevator = nose left.) Is it any wonder that strong spatial reasoning and a quick mind are prerequisites of a good aerobatics pilot?

An eight-point roll adds four more hesitation points placed every 45 degrees. It also adds a little more ambiguity because at 45-degree angles of bank, the rudder and elevator are just beginning to swap roles. The rudder still yaws the nose, but at that angle of bank it also acts a bit like an elevator as well. Same with the elevator, so you'll need to try these maneuvers several times to get an idea of what the controls are doing at various bank angles. The best way to do this is to isolate the controls, trying all permutations on one before testing the other.

The Four-Point Roll.

Barrel Roll

The barrel roll had its genesis in air combat back in the World War I as a maneuver that evades an attacker while at the same time turns the tables. Perhaps the best way to describe the barrel roll is as a sideways loop. Viewed from the side, the plane does seem to describe the shape of the loop, with the aircraft pointed 90 degrees away from the plane of the loop. The plane does a standard aileron roll, rotating about its longitudinal axis, but at the same time the pilot is using the elevator movements associated with a simple loop. The inverted section of the roll should coincide with the inverted section of the loop so that the plane, rather than reversing course as in a loop, continues to fly along the same heading.

Begin by sighting on the reference road and adjust the throttle so that your speed is around 140-150 kts. Begin the maneuver by rolling quickly to one side; in our example, we'll roll to the right. (Your initial roll determines the direction of the barrel's rotation.) As you begin the roll, pull gently back on the stick and maintain this roll and climb

Barrel Roll diagram.

Legendary Aircraft: CAP 20

Cooperatives des Ateliers Aéronautiques de la Region Parisienne opened its doors in 1953 under the ownership of Auguste Mudry, but it wasn't until 1966 that the company (which became Avions Mudry in 1968) first rolled out the CP.100. With a few modifications, this aircraft was to begin production in 1970 as the CAP-10 two-seat trainer. The French Air Force loved the little plane, and it was only a short time before the plane's aerobatic potential was recognized and a single-seat version produced. The CAP-20, also introduced in 1970, was a revelation to aerobatic pilots and a dominant aircraft of the 1970s.

By 1980 the CAP-20's design was getting a little long in the tooth, and it was no longer competitive with newer designs. The CAP-21 appeared as something of an interim model, replaced in 1985 by the powerful (300 hp) CAP-230. This quickly evolved into the CAP-231, an aircraft still being flown in competition today.

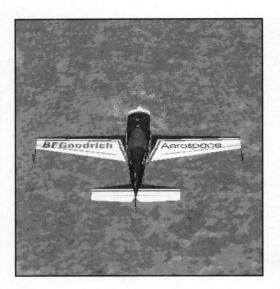

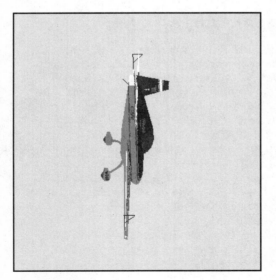

The Barrel Roll.

attitude through the maneuver. The back pressure on the stick keeps the elevator in the up position, while the constant roll makes the plane climb and dive during the maneuver. That is, as you roll over to the inverted position, "up elevator" becomes "down elevator."

We've all seen so many films of military pilots performing barrel rolls that we naturally assume it's an easy maneuver. Once again, like many other figures, the barrel roll is fairly easy to perform, but very difficult to perfect. In an ideal barrel roll, there is no difference in altitude between the starting and ending positions, but unless you make subtle stick adjustments throughout the maneuver, you will invariably end up at a lower altitude than where you started. The way to avoid this altitude loss is to keep the nose pointed slightly toward the inside of the barrel. Sighting on a reference point on the horizon will help you keep the nose where it belongs.

Turns

Turns are, as you might expect, also a basic part of the aerobatics vocabulary. They not only function as figures in themselves, but they also provide smooth and artistic transitions from figure to figure.

Competition Turn

The basic competition turn is usually steeply banked—none of this gentle 30-degree stuff. In competition we're talking about banks from 60 to 90 degrees. First let's try a basic turn of 90 degrees, with 60 degrees of bank. Airspeed remains the same—140 kts—so let's begin the turn. The two most important factors in a competition turn are maintaining a constant bank angle and a constant altitude. When you bank, the plane will naturally want to turn, so correct as needed with the elevator and rudder. Remember, however, that as you approach the 60-degree bank, the controls do reverse roles to an extent, so remain sensitive to that.

Competition Turn diagram.

When your bank angle is 60 degrees, commence the turn using the rudder. A proper turn will register from 3.5 to 4 Gs. Just prior to reaching your new heading, first center the rudder to end the turn, and then bring the stick back to center to level the wings.

The Competition Turn.

Rolling Turn diagram.

Rolling Turn

A variation on the competition turn, the rolling turn is one of the most difficult maneuvers to perform well because the pilot must think and control the plane in all three flight axes simultaneously. Ideally the aircraft will roll 360 degrees for every 90 degrees of turn so in a complete 360-degree turn, there will be four rolls. The rolls are always to the inside of the turn and must have a consistent roll rate. The turn must stay within the horizontal plane as well. (Use the horizon for reference.)

With the rolling turn airspeed is dependent on the radius of the turn. Generally, keep the speed around 120-140 kts. Don't forget that, aside from the complexity of maneuvering in all axes, you must pay close attention to keeping

The Rolling Turn.

your airspeed constant. This should be no problem with the Extra, but what might be a problem is the Extra's excellent roll rate. This may cause you to roll too fast, so don't peg the stick all the way over.

The biggest obstacles to overcome are the constantly changing roles of the rudder and elevator. As we've mentioned before, as a plane banks, the rudder and elevator begin to swap places. At a 90-degree bank, they've completely changed positions and, therefore, their respective influences on the aircraft's attitude. Flying a plane in a rolling turn is akin to patting your head and rubbing your stomach while riding a unicycle. Try this maneuver only when you've perfected the others covered here—or when you feel the need for a good dose of humility.

Spins

It's sometimes difficult to think of a spin as an aerobatic maneuver, since a spin usually means a plane has lost all aerodynamic integrity. It looks it, too, as the aircraft tumbles wildly through the air. An out-of-control spin is the result of an uncorrected stall and can have serious—even fatal—consequences should it

Spin diagram.

Flight Simulator
for Windows 95

happen near the ground. The aerobatic spin also starts with a stall, but intentionally Even though the aircraft appears to be tumbling totally out of control, it isn't.

In an aerobatic competition, a spin lasts only for a predetermined number of rotations and must end with the plane's resuming a predetermined course. As you'll see, the spin's easy to invoke and, although it looks frightening, isn't quite as difficult to recover from as you might think.

As we said, spins begin with stalls, so the first thing we'll do is induce a stall. After lining up with the reference road once again, throttle back the engine until you're doing about 90 kts. (If you haven't turned off Auto-coordination, you'll need to do so for this maneuver.) With the great g-forces an airplane experiences during a spin, you really don't want to be going all that fast when you enter the spin. Too, it's easier to induce a stall at lower speeds. Okay, pull back on the stick smoothly but quickly to bring the nose up to around 40 degrees (this angle varies somewhat with different aircraft) while fully cutting the throttle. As the plane approaches the stall, you'll experience a little sinking, accompanied by the stall-warning alarm. Continue pulling the stick back while pushing the rudder pedal for the direction you want the spin to take. We'll go left for this spin, so stick back and full left rudder. Be prepared—the nose will drop very quickly.

As you're headed downward in the spin, maintain the control positions (difficult not to try and correct, isn't it?) and watch the ground for your reference point so that you can count the number of spins. Spin only three times (since you didn't bring along an airsickness bag). As you begin the third spin, apply full right (reverse) rudder and center the stick. Once the spin stops, quickly center the rudder as well. But don't try to pull the plane back up to level too quickly or you'll stall again. Just advance the throttle and let the airspeed build as gradually ease back up to level flight. Still on the same

The Spin.

heading as before? No? Well, don't feel bad. Just getting out of the spin cleanly the first time should be cause enough for celebration. As you get more of a feel of the Extra's spin behavior, you'll be able to better judge when to reverse rudder to stop the spin.

Advanced and Combination Figures

Hammerhead diagram.

Hammerhead

The Hammerhead is sometimes called a zero-airspeed turn or the Hammerhead stall, even though it's not quite either a turn or a stall. The plane's never completely dead in the air, (the control surfaces would have no effect whatsoever if it were), and the plane never actually stalls. But after climbing straight up, the plane is almost stopped in the air and appears to pivot around one wingtip. It takes very precise timing and plenty of speed—as well as some tricky coordination of rudder, ailerons and elevator—to produce a high-scoring Hammerhead.

As we said, speed is essential for entry into the Hammerhead, so crank up the throttle until indicated airspeed reads 175-180 kts. Find the reference road, then quickly (don't jerk it) pull back on the stick as if you're entering a loop. With the higher speed this pull-up should read around six Gs. As you're climbing, be sure to look to the side, using your wingtip guide to maintain a 90-degree climb with the stick centered. Even with the power the Extra has, you'll begin to lose airspeed. The plane will also have a tendency to wander from the vertical, so you may have to make slight adjustments with the rudder and elevator to maintain a perpendicular attitude.

Watch your airspeed indicator and begin your pivot as the plane approaches zero airspeed. If you wait until the plane stops completely, you'll almost certainly do a tail slide, which is a maneuver for another time. On the other

The Hammerhead.

hand, if you make the pivot before airspeed has dropped to almost nothing, you'll perform a sloppy Hammerhead. It has to appear as if one wing is nailed to a cloud while the rest of the plane pivots around that point. To pivot, apply full left rudder while you compensate with just a bit of right aileron and down elevator. This is necessary to keep the plane from rolling over into a spin. Remember, be gentle. Not much control input is needed here.

As the aircraft completes its 180-degree pivot, ease the throttle back quickly to about half power and apply opposite rudder to stop the pivot. A perfectly done Hammerhead should have a pivot no wider than one wingspan, which in the case of the Extra, is about 25 feet. Quickly center the controls and the plane should recover by itself, perhaps helped a bit by a slight pullback on the stick until you regain level flight.

Cuban 8

When viewed from the ground, the Cuban 8 resembles a figure eight lying on its side. Technically, it consists of two partial or three-quarter loops tied together in the middle with half-rolls, although it could also be said to consist of two modified Immelmann turns (see below). The two components of the figure must be identical in size, and the aircraft must remain on the horizontal plane for the entire figure.

Start as you would with a regular loop, lining up the plane with the reference road and pegging the airspeed at around 140 kts. Begin the loop by pulling back firmly on the stick to climb at approximately four Gs. As you're climbing, you'll also be advancing the throttle. You should be at full power by

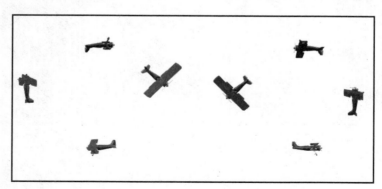

Cuban 8 diagram.

the time the plane reaches vertical. As with the loop, an occasional visual check to the side will tell you when you're vertical, and if your loop is the right shape. (Remember, the

The Cuban 8.

wingtip should be describing a circle on the horizon). Make any slight adjustments with the ailerons to keep the wings level as you nose over to inverted, and monitor airspeed to keep it relatively constant. As you nose over, you will pick up speed, and it's important for your entry into the second loop that you don't gain too much momentum.

Maintain back pressure on the stick until the nose drops to a 45-degree angle (check the wingtip guides for this), and then push the stick forward to keep the plane flying at the

A Typical Aerobatic Program

Competition-aerobatic programs are not comprised of isolated figures, they're choreographed performances, with each maneuver tied to the preceding and succeeding maneuvers by transition figures that are judged as well. Below is a listing of figures in a typical aerobatic program, followed by the program shown in Aresti Notation as the pilot would plan it out.

Aresti Notation was developed as an aerobatic shorthand by Spanish count Jose Luis Aresti, a driving force behind the birth of the modern World Championship. There had been many forms of aerobatic notation over the years, so when Aresti developed his system, he drew upon much of what had gone before. Although there was some resistance to adopting Aresti's system, it nonetheless prevailed. When it first became the accepted notation standard in 1964, there were around 3000 figures noted in the Aresti Dictionary. Today there are some 15,000.

A Typical Program.

Hammerhead, 1 and 1/4 Snap Up, 1/4 and Full Roll Down

Humpty Bump, 1 and 1/2 Rolls Up, 4-point Roll Down

2 of 4 Up—3/4 Loop

Tailslide—Inverted Out

2 of 4 on 45-degree Upline—1 and 1/2 Snaps Down

Vertical 2 Point Up

2 of 4 Down

Humpty Bump—3/4 Snap Up, 1/2 Roll Down

Hammerhead Roll Up, 3/4 Roll Down

Roll Up on 45 Degrees Inverted

Down Loop—1/2 Inside, 1/2 Roll, 1/2 Outside

1 and 1/2 Snap Split-S—2 Point

Half Loop—Plus Snap

Rolling Circle - 4 Alternating—Inside/Outside

45- degree angle. Push the stick full over in the direction you want to roll and hold it until the plane has rolled 180 degrees. Once the roll is finished, begin a gradual pull back on the stick to level the plane momentarily before repeating the process for the other half of the Cuban 8.

Split-S

You can immediately see the tactical value in the Split-S from a fighter pilot's standpoint. This combination of a half-roll with a half-loop is an effective evasive maneuver because the aircraft not only reverses direction quickly, but it also gets a boost of speed from the diving produced by the half-loop. The plane trades altitude for speed—and usually a lot of altitude—so make sure you climb back to 4000 feet before trying the maneuver.

Let's get right to it. Bring the airspeed down to between 90-100 kts and sight on the reference road. Keep your hand close to the throttle because you'll want to throttle

Split-S diagram.

The Split-S.

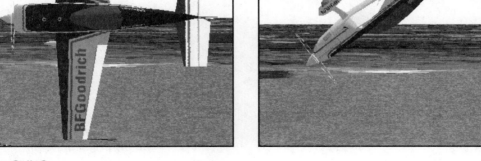

The Split-S.

Legendary Aircraft: Zlin 50

One of the older aircraft firms in Eastern Europe, starting business in 1934, the Czechoslovakian firm Zlinska Letecka spent World War II making (involuntarily, no doubt) copies of Bücker's Bestmann low-wing monoplane trainer for the Luftwaffe. As Czechoslovakia rebuilt after the war the company continued to build the trainer, until 1946, when they debuted their replacement, the Z-22. It's direct descendant, the Z-26, provided the foundation for Zlin's first great aerobatics plane, the 226 Akrobat. The Akrobat in all its varieties reigned supreme in the aerobatics renaissance of the 50s and 60s—the first World Champion of the modern era, Ladislav Bezek, flew a 226 to victory in 1960, and his family to freedom in the West in 1971—but by the early 70s the Zlins had been left behind by Goliath—the Russian YAKs—and David—the American Pitts Special.

With the greater demands of modern aerobatics on aircraft structure, Zlin came out with the Zlin 50 in 1975 and immediately rose to the top of the aerobatic world once again. Sharing the stage with the French CAP-20, the Zlin 50 nevertheless captured the imagination of pilots the world over with its combination of power, strength and agility. Zlin was so on-target with the 50 that the plane still competes in World Championships over 20 years after its introduction.

back completely as you begin the first part of the figure, the half-roll. Okay, roll the plane to the left as you would in a simple aileron roll and pull back the throttle smoothly. Stop the roll once the plane is inverted by centering the stick, quickly checking the view over the nose to make sure you are indeed inverted and level.

The finish of the half-roll and the beginning of the half-loop (really the second half of a normal loop) should be seamless. That is, start your loop just as the wings level off. Begin the loop by pulling the stick back (yes, back—remember, you're upside down). Because we literally dove into the half-loop from level flight, the plane will be carrying more airspeed into the loop than in a normal loop. Keeping constant back pressure ensures that the plane won't build up too much speed in the dive, plus it helps the loop retain its shape as the plane inevitably gains speed. Center the controls as the plane exits the loop and bring the nose back to a level attitude.

Immelmann

Because the pilot trades speed for altitude, the Immelmann Turn can be considered the opposite of the Split-S. Otherwise, it's much like the Split-S, a half-loop (the first half of the loop, this time) with a half-roll. It was borne out of necessity during wartime so flyers could make sudden and hard-to-follow evasive maneuvers. It became more of an offensive maneuver as practiced by its supposed originator, the German ace Max Immelmann. If you can believe that he really did come up with the maneuver, you might also believe that he should have practiced it a bit more, as he managed to last only about a year in combat before being shot down (no doubt by a crafty pilot also using an Immelmann Turn).

The biggest difference in flying technique between the Immelmann and Split-S turns is airspeed. While you might have been close to stall speed for the Split-S, with the Immelmann you'll want plenty of airspeed— in the vicinity of 160-170 kts. Imagine you're starting a loop. Smoothly pull the stick all the way back (you did check the reference road, didn't you?). As with the loop, the G-meter should register 4 to 4.5 Gs. Simultaneously with the climb, advance the throttle so that the engine is at full power as it reaches a vertical attitude. (Check those wing tip guides!)

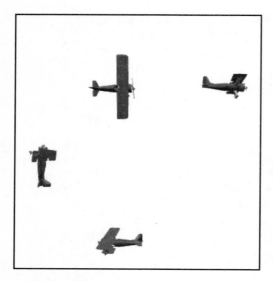

Immelmann diagram.

The Immelmann Turn.

The plane will continue to nose over into inverted flight. As it approaches level and inverted, apply side pressure to the stick to begin the roll. When you can see the horizon to the rear of the plane, you know it's time to start the roll. Keep the back pressure on until the plane does level out, and then center the stick completely when the wings level out.

Chandelle

The Chandelle is not actually part of the championship figures, but with a name like that, who can resist trying it? At least the name's more attractive than its description, which is "a maximum performance climbing 180-degree turn." Which means that the Chandelle is a quick and graceful way to change both direction and altitude.

For our Chandelle let's adjust the throttle until airspeed is around 170 to 180 kts, pick up our reference road, and then put the plane into a bank of about 35 -45 degrees to the left. Pull the stick back smoothly, slowly increasing the pitch angle on the nose to about 35 degrees. Hold the bank steady

Chandelle diagram.

through the first half of the turn, and then smoothly begin to level the wings as the second half of the turn progresses. The plane will be losing speed during the climb, and this—combined with slight left rudder—should keep the turn radius constant, even as the bank angle decreases. Just remember: despite the speed you take into the Chandelle, it is a gentle maneuver, a graceful climbing turn.

Care must be taken to keep the plane from stalling. By the time you reach the midway point of the turn, the plane will be perilously close to stalling. This is prevented by decreasing the bank in the second half of the turn, but speed will still be critical, so be alert for any signs of stalling during the climb. Just as the turn is completed, bring the nose down to recover to level flight

After the racing pulses and sweaty palms of aerobatics, let's drop the excitement level a bit and enjoy the pleasure of flying cross country. In the next chapter, we'll take the Schweizer 2-32 in search of thermals, wring the Learjet out in a cross-country cruise, and take the Sopwith Camel up into the skies over France to relive a typical mission over the trenches of World War I.

The Chandelle.

Chapter Eight

FLIGHTS OF FANCY

In this chapter, we'll fly up the east coast to scenic Martha's Vineyard—in our personal Learjet, of course—and then hop over to San Francisco for a day of picturesque sail planing. From there we're off to visit France, exploring the countryside in our Sopwith Camel.

East Coast Flight in a Learjet 35A

As aircraft types go, the business category is a relatively new one, and the business jet class is even younger. Although a few businesses owned their own aircraft prior to World War II, they were few and far between. Prices for suitable aircraft were beyond the means of most companies. The postwar glut of aircraft changed this to some extent, as thousands of cheap surplus military aircraft flooded the market. Most of them were military conversions of civilian aircraft designed prior to the war, planes like the Beech 18 and the Cessna T-50 (which, in its military guise as the UC-78, was more often called the Useless 78). These aircraft met the criteria for business-aircraft classification, but only just.

Something bigger and faster was needed, and a few imaginative designers immediately began drawing up plans to convert the plethora of deactivated medium bombers to business-plane status. Aircraft such as the North American B-25 and the Douglas B-26 were gutted of all military hardware and rebuilt. This worked better with some models than with others, but the sad fact remained that these planes were designed to carry bombs, not businessmen. No amount of plush upholstery and soundproofing would ever disguise that fact.

The first designer to recognize that a true business plane would require starting from scratch was Ted Smith. His company, Aero Design and Engineering, would produce in 1948 the first of a new breed of aircraft —the Aero Commander. Mid size, twin-engine and high-wing, Aero Commander

This is the Learjet 35A, from Flight Simulator's Aircraft Handbook in the Pilot's Help, which also includes a number of flight checklists.

begat many imitators and took a large part of the market for the next decade, until Lockheed brought out the prototype business jet in 1957, the Jetstar. Grumman and North American flew their own minijets the following year, with European firms like Dassault not far behind. And so the stage was set for a true American original, Bill Lear, to make business jets commonplace when he brought out the original Model 23 Learjet. (It was two words back then.) He must have known he'd made it when the Byrds released the song, "Eight Miles High," supposedly inspired by Roger McGuinn's flight in a Learjet.

And so we come to our own Learjet 35A, parked on the flight line and waiting for us. It certainly looks like a fighter, as indeed was its earliest ancestor, the failed Swiss P-16. Since the first Model 23, all Learjets have shown a strong family resemblance, with the high-mounted T-tail, wings set far back on the fuselage, and, more often than not, wingtip fuel tanks. Later Learjet designs may sport winglets (small up-tilted wingtip extensions) but are otherwise true to the original Lear design philosophy.

After a preflight check we'll climb into the 35A and situate ourselves. This is not a big plane, as is obvious once we climb (almost crawl) through the door. It seats six passengers and a crew of two, but doesn't hold much more. The Learjets weren't designed to be bulk carriers.

Slipping into the cockpit, you're immediately struck by the difference between this cockpit and those of the other aircraft in Flight Simulator. The 737's cockpit is every bit as sophisticated—and then some—but it feels about

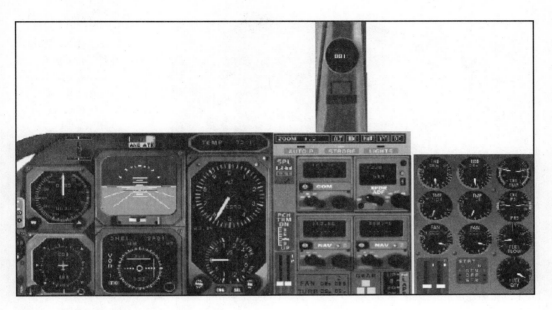

The Learjet 35A Instrument Panel.

twice the size of the Learjet's. The other cockpits are cozier, but nowhere near as complex. Let's check out the panel and controls right away to get an idea of the actual differences and what you need to be aware of.

The basic instruments are quite recognizable, even though their placement might be odd. You might notice that there are no provisions for monitoring engine operation. Well, the 35A was meant to be flown by a pilot and a co pilot, and so engine function monitoring is shared. Should you need to check the engines, just hit the Tab key to toggle between the radio and engine instrument panels. Also, the VOR indicator is now only one instrument and combines the functions of VOR with indicators for ILS.

With the new panel fresh in your mind, we'll take a look at our itinerary for this shakedown flight. Normally before we'd even think about settling down behind the flight yoke, we would work out a detailed flight plan, consulting the MET (the METeorological center) for the latest weather reports for our flight path. We'd also file a detailed flight plan, specifying our general course and whatever way points we plan to use. We'll take all these, as well as the preflight inspections, as givens and proceed with our flight. For a more detailed

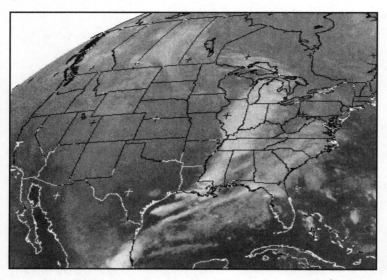

A meteorological report.

explanation of what goes into a flight plan, as well as basics of flying under IFR (Instrument Flight Rules), see Chapters Four and Six.

We'll be taking off from the Raleigh-Durham International Airport, just to the northwest of Raleigh, North Carolina. You'll find your way there by selecting Go to Airport in the World menu, and then scrolling until you

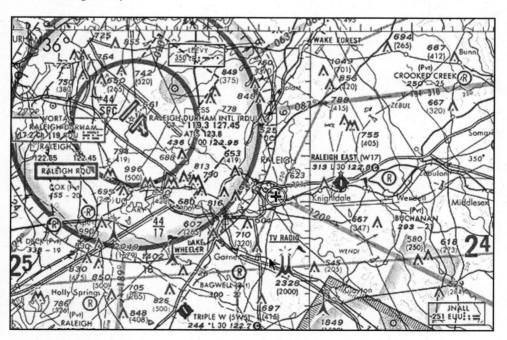

Chart showing the Raleigh-Durham area.

find North America. The airport listings there are in alphabetical order. After takeoff we'll be climbing to a cruising altitude of around 34,000 feet, on a northeast heading up the Atlantic coast, to a well-deserved vacation on Martha's Vineyard. After all, we've got a Learjet, so we must be able to afford this. Got your toothbrush with you? Then let's go.

There's one thing to keep in mind when flying the Learjet—or any turbojet aircraft for that matter. Turbine engines run differently from the reciprocating engines found in planes like the Cessna 182 RG or the Extra 300S. The term "spool up" (rev up) is an apt term for turbines, since these engines react more slowly to throttle changes, needing to build gradually, or spool up, rpms. You'll notice this right away as you advance the 35A's throttles. The response is much slower, something you can hear in the gradual frequency increase of the engine's whine and also see on the engine power monitors. And while standard procedure with the prop planes is to release the brakes and then advance the throttle, with turbojet engines it's advisable to keep the brakes applied while the engine builds up thrust. Using this technique means you're a lot less likely to run out of runway before rotation.

If you have ATIS (Automatic Terminal Information Service) switched on, you can get automatic reports on weather conditions and other useful information as you taxi out to the end of the runway. The data will be displayed in a crawl across the top of the screen. While you're at it, turn on the aircraft's transponder so that ATC can track us. Were we flying on VFR, we'd simply set the transponder to 1200, but since we'll fly the entire trip by IFR, we'll enter the "squawk" code in the transponder as we receive it from ATC. (To reach these settings, select Communication under the Aircraft pull-down menu.)

Once we obtain clearance, set the flaps for eight degrees (20 degrees if the runway is particularly short—less than 6000 feet—or if the outside air temperature is above 35 degrees Celsius). Then spool up those turbojets, pop the brakes and let's get this puppy airborne.

In Chapter Six we went over the system of V speeds used by airline and small jet pilots. These are points during the takeoff and climb out where certain decisions must be made. Aircraft engines are, on the whole, some of the most dependable and sturdy machines ever made, but nothing is perfect. Pilots must take this into account when the plane is most vulnerable and sensitive—during takeoff. Decision points and V speeds are not nearly as important in aircraft like the Cessna Skylane, but for jet-powered aircraft, the time available to make critical decisions decreases as the speed increases. If you have chosen a low

Rotation and Liftoff.

reliability setting in the Realism & Reliability menu, then you might want to jump back to Chapter Six and review the entire V speed litany. But for our flight we're mostly concerned with Vr, or rotation speed. For most flights a Vr of 143 knots is about right, although you should bump the speed up a few kts if the weather is very hot.

As speed reaches 143 kts, gently pull the yoke back to raise the nose 10 degrees. The plane should lift almost immediately after rotation, but don't expect it to leap into the air. It is a jet, but it's not an F-16. The 35A is heavy for its size, and although 7000 lbs of thrust will eventually get this bird moving at a high percentage of Mach (the speed of sound—around 760 miles per hour at sea level), it's not instantaneous.

To keep the FAA off our backs, the first thing we need to do after we're in the air and the gear and flaps are retracted, is to throttle back the engines until fuel flow drops to about 1000 lbs. per hour. This should give us a fairly decent rate of climb to cruising altitude, with the nose at a positive 15-degree angle. The aircraft will slowly build speed up to about a .7 Mach number, but below 10,000 feet we'll need to limit airspeed to 250 kts as a safety precaution. If you notice that airspeed begins to drop slowly at a constant throttle setting, don't worry. The engines will lose some thrust as they climb into thinner air. Be ready to apply more throttle as needed to keep airspeed a constant .7 Mach. By the way, the airspeed indicator will change from reading in knots to showing fractions of Mach as you accelerate beyond about 350 kts.

As we decided earlier, we'll cruise at around 34,000 feet, or Flight Level 340 (FL340, which is how altitude is expressed above 18,000-feet), an

economical cruise altitude for the 35A. As you climb past the 18,000 foot level, be sure to reset your altimeter to the 29.92 inches of mercury. Once we get to around 100 miles of our destination, Martha's Vineyard, we'll reset the altimeter once again, according to information received from ATIS at the Martha's Vineyard Airport. Failure to

The climb to FL340.

reset the altimeter could spell big trouble because your altimeter may tell you you're higher than you really are.

The elaborate network of radio navigation beacons on the eastern seaboard offers us a number of options for our flight path. There are, however, airways (or standardized VOR headings) which most pilots use, partly as a matter of convenience, and partly because it's so much easier for ATC to track the many aircraft that are in the air at any one time. Since we were able to take off to the northeast, it's only a slight adjustment to fly onto the 020-degree radial of the VOR at Raleigh-Durham. This is a common airway, and is often the flight path taken by airliners heading for Washington, D.C. We'll eventually fly onto the VOR at Washington's Dulles Airport, where we'll make a course change for New York's JFK Airport. We'll probably lose the VOR from Raleigh around from 50 nm to 60 nm out, but if we hold the course, we'll eventually intercept the 220 radial from Washington Dulles.

You can go ahead and set VOR 2 to the Dulles frequency, 111.0. If you have any questions about how to intercept a radial, refer to the VOR section in Chapter Five. Just remember that once you intercept the radial and turn to fly onto it, you should have the OBS set for the reciprocal of the 220 radial, or 020. The Ambiguity Indicator should read TO as you fly along the radial, and you'll be able to watch the DME count down the distance. You'll know when

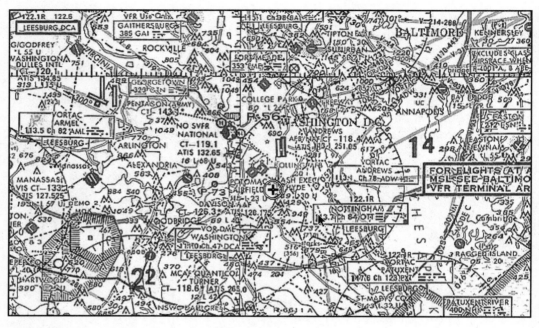

Chart showing the Washington, D.C. area.

you've actually passed the VOR station (the DME does become more inaccurate the closer you are to the station) when the Ambiguity Indicator changes to FROM. If you have a question about our location en route to intercepting the radial, we can tune into the VOR at Richmond, Virginia, (114.0).

It always seems that airliners and business jets spend so much fuel getting to the 30,000 + heights that economy must fly out the door. True, pushing a nine-ton bullet to altitudes of six miles or more does gobble up the kerosene, but the energy savings once a plane gets to cruising altitude more than make up for it. You must remember, it takes a lot of energy to push a plane through the dense air at near sea level, even an aircraft as sleek as the Learjet.

The weather must be on our side. About 130 nm out from Raleigh we're able to tune into the VOR at Washington National, and now we're "riding the beam" into D.C. Don't forget that, on these longer trips, you can set the aircraft's autopilot to maintain either the heading or, as in our case, the VOR radial. With a Mach 0.7 speed it doesn't take long to turn the TO on the VOR

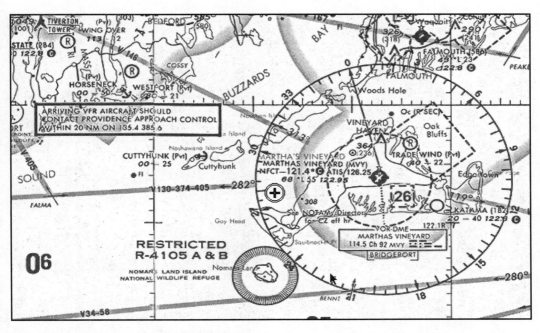

This chart shows the Martha's Vineyard area.

indicator to a FROM. Fortunately, we'll stay at our present cruising altitude, so high we can just barely make out the Potomac tidal basin. Good thing, since we don't have time to sightsee—we need to make a course change and get on the 41-degree VOR radial leaving National in order to intercept the 221 VOR at JFK in New York. Then it's the 70-degree radial from JFK until we intercept the 255 radial into Martha's Vineyard. (But remember those reciprocals!)

As we approach Martha's Vineyard, we'll contact ATC to get info on resetting our altimeter although being at sea level, we can anticipate the setting. At our altitude we'll need to start our descent about 100 nautical miles out. Keep in mind, you don't "horse" the 35A down to a lower altitude. At these altitudes the plane is performing a delicate balancing act, and any coarse control inputs are likely to have you descending a lot faster than either you or your passengers would enjoy. (The wrenching sound as the wings are torn off is particularly upsetting to the faint of heart.) Use very small control movements, lowering the nose only a degree or so after you've throttled the engines back, so that your descent rate is 2800 to 3000 feet per minute. At times during the

Cruising the beautiful sandy shores of Martha's Vineyard.

descent you may experience some control flutter as you pass into increasingly denser air. And above all, don't let your airspeed exceed 350 kts. (The Overspeed warning message will let you know if you do.) Below 10,000 feet, it's back to the 250 kts maximum airspeed limitation.

Before we actually land, let's take a little trip around the island to see what a nice job Microsoft has done in fixing up the place. Just be careful to keep the speed down to below 200 kts—don't want to rattle the windows of the rich and famous, now do we?

Landing the 35A is a real eye-opener, especially if you're used to the nice, slow approaches afforded you in the Cessna 182. For a private aircraft, the Lear comes

in awfully fast. Even with maximum flap settings (40 degrees) you're still looking at a touchdown speed in excess of 130 kts. Engine power should be set to approximately 50 percent as you lower the flaps in anticipation of turning onto your final approach.

Intercepting the glide slope.

As we acquire the ILS localizer and glide slope, you should be throttled back to about 40 percent power. Lower the flaps to 20 degrees. Your airspeed at this point should be around 135-140 kts. You may lower the landing gear as you center on the ILS localizer. At the point when you intercept the glide slope beam, you can lower your flaps fully to 40 degrees, and increase power to around 75 percent. With the flaps at 40 degrees, the nose is raised to the right landing attitude.

Final approach.

Touchdown.

Unlike other aircraft, you won't flare the 35A just prior to landing—the attitude you carry over the runway threshold is the attitude the plane will be in when the wheels touch. Another difference with the Lear is that, instead of using the elevator to adjust your position on the glide path, you make slight adjustments with the throttle.

Cut the throttles completely as you cross the runway threshold. At this point you should be no more than 60 feet above the runway. Just hold the attitude and let the plane settle by itself. Rest assured, this is no glider —those stubby, thin wings are just the ticket for cutting through the atmosphere at 30,000 feet. But down here just above the ground, with near zero engine thrust, they have about as much lift as a couple of bricks.

At the point of touchdown, activate the spoilers and apply full reverse thrust (by moving the throttle levers into the red area at the bottom). Advance the throttle back to zero as soon as the plane slows to below 60 kts. Brakes can be applied below 50 kts, but very gently. Retract both the flaps and the spoilers, and taxi off the runway as soon as possible to avoid what appears to be a B-52 coming in right behind you.

Now we'll head west for a different flying experience.

Soaring Techniques with the Schweizer 2-32

Even with their sleek and graceful looks, sailplanes still manage to confound some people. It's hard enough to accept the fact that powered aircraft can remain aloft, much more so that a motorless plane can not only fly, but can fly for hours at a time, too.

Our Schweizer 2-32 represents the lower end of the sailplane spectrum. In production since 1965, its overall design, as well as its basic construction, belong to the old school. Newer, high-performance craft boast state-of-the-art aerodynamics and the latest in composite construction techniques, but very few can offer the Schweizer's combination of performance and good flying manners. A sailplane pilot may end up in one of the flashy competition models, but odds are that, at least in the U.S., he or she started soaring in a Schweizer.

Let's look at the Schweizer for a moment. Externally, it appears fairly conservative for a sailplane. Most modern sailplanes have a high-mounted horizontal stabilizer, sometimes called a T-tail (a few even have a V-shaped tail assembly, similar to a Beech Bonanza light plane), but the Schweizer's is located in the usual position, simplifying the elevator linkage while making for a much stronger tail structure.

The cockpit is covered by the usual bubble canopy, and inside there are seats for two people. Lift the canopy, and we'll climb inside. It's a pretty snug fit, though not nearly as cozy as some of the competition single-seat models.

The Schweizer 2-32, as shown in the Pilot's Help. Get a complete rundown of the Schweizer's performance specifications there, too.

Layout of the instrument panel.

Right away, the instrument panel with an austerity that makes the Sopwith Camel's ancient panel look elaborate catches your eye. There's certainly not a lot to worry about here. You've got an altimeter, vertical speed indicator, airspeed indicator, and magnetic compass, along with a switch for the wing spoilers (more on them later). That's it. Actually, the Flight Simulator version of the Schweizer has no variometer, so it's even a bit more basic than the real thing. A variometer might be thought of as an ultrasensitive vertical speed indicator, able to sense quickly minute changes in the sailplane's altitude. A pilot uses the variometer to seek out thermals—rising columns of air—and stay within those thermals once they're found. Of course, the pilot has to know where to look for thermals in the first place, something we'll cover in a moment. By the way, if you haven't already, check out the airspeed indicator—it reads in miles per hour, not knots.

Since we're already in the plane, let's buckle up the safety harness and get going. Now normally we'd already be on the tarmac of the runway and waiting for our tow plane. A towplane can be just about any powered propeller-driven craft in the light to medium range, that has at least 150 hp. The most common towplanes are Cessna's—172s, 182s, and 210s although these days cropdusting

The view forward.

The view right.

aircraft such as the Piper Pawnee serve as well. We could wait for the towplane, but it would be a long wait, since that feature hasn't been included in Flight Simulator yet. To get into the air, we can go one of two routes—using the Slew control to take us up to the altitude we desire or choosing one of the flights from the Flights Challenges menu. We'll try the latter for this flight, selecting the Sailplane (Difficult) challenge, which puts us at an altitude of about 2000 feet above the hills outside San Francisco.

This area is idea for soaring, with terrain that will allow us to practice the two main types of soaring—ridge and thermal. Once we arrive at our release

The view left.

Looping the Schweizer 2-32.

point (where we'd disconnect from the towplane cable, were we being towed), hit the P key to pause the simulation for a moment. Since we'll begin to drop almost immediately, it's a good idea to take a look around first to see where we might want to go. Pilots usually do this as they're being towed to the release point, but since we're being taken there instantly, we'll use the simulation's facilities to help us out.

To the right of the plane you'll see green hills, while just ahead lies San Francisco. On the left there's nothing much but flat land and water, so you'll want to make your way to the right as soon as you resume the simulation. You've got a little time, so try out the controls to get a feel of the Schweizer's responsiveness. You'll discover that it's a fairly nimble craft, with a roll rate that will really surprise you, given the long wing span. Many people think that sailplanes aren't very maneuverable, which is far from the truth. Actually, sailplanes can perform just about any aerobatic maneuver a powered plane can. It just takes a bit more planning.

Sailplanes are also thought to be slow, again a total misconception. Certainly, a good part of any soaring session is flown in the neighborhood of 60-70 kts, but most sailplanes, including the venerable Schweizer 2-32, can dive at speeds in excess of 150 mph. Some sailplanes do this on a regular basis, but the Schweizer, owing to stress limits, should always be kept below 150 mph. That switch in the lower left-hand corner operates the wing spoilers, which act as air brakes and should be used to slow the plane before it passes its maximum allowable speed. The spoilers are also useful, as we'll see, in sailplane landings.

Press P to resume flying. Once the simulation continues, you'll feel the plane drop. A slight back pressure on the stick will bring the nose back up, but this brings up a basic tenet of soaring. All sailplanes, no matter how long they may stay up, are always losing altitude. Sounds like a contradiction, doesn't it? Not really. It's true that a sailplane, despite the high-lift wings and

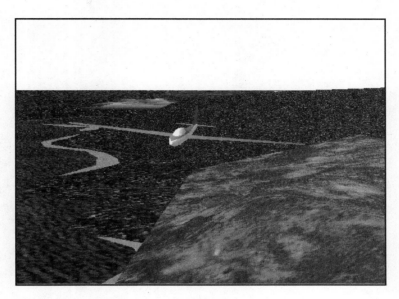

A sailplane using the ridge soaring technique.

low drag, is always coming in second in the battle with gravity. But this is not as bad as you might think. Gravity is actually the sailplane pilot's friend, pulling the airplane down so that air will flow around the wings to provide lift. Indeed, many modern sailplanes carry extra weight, or ballast, usually in the form of water, to make them soar more efficiently.

But if a sailplane is always dropping, how can it stay aloft so long, and even gain altitude? It's because, while the sailplane is dropping, the air around it, called relative wind, that is rising. Rising air is created in several ways, but the most common sources are updrafts caused by winds being deflected upward by hills or mountains and thermals, which are warm air columns rising from sun-heated areas on the ground.

Since we're literally heading for the hills, we'll try our hand at ridge soaring first. This is the easiest of the two types of soaring, requiring only a defined ridge—hills or mountains—and a prevailing wind blowing against either side of the ridge. This can be likened to surfing in the air, with the wind rising from the ridge acting as a wave would in the ocean, supporting the surfer. You can stay aloft as long as the wind blows, and since the wind blows almost all the time around San Francisco, ridge soaring is nearly always possible.

A thermal forming.

(The Wright Brothers knew about ridge soaring and made all their early gliding experiments along the dune ridges of Kitty Hawk, North Carolina. Jockey's Ridge has become famous as the launching point not only for the Wrights' many gliders but also for ground zero on December 17, 1903, and the first flight of the Wright Flyer.)

Once you reach the first ridge, you'll immediately notice that the plane climbs much more quickly above the side of the ridge facing the sea. While it's not always true that the wind comes from the sea, it usually does. We can experiment with this. Build up some altitude by flying along the seaside ridge until you're back up to about 2500 feet. Now position the plane on a line following the crest of the ridge. Fly slightly toward the ocean side and watch both the nose of the plane and the Vertical Speed Indicator. There should be a noticeable rise in both.

With that in mind, move the plane over until it's just to the land side of the ridge crest. As you move more inland, you should notice a drop in the climb rate, or even a slight descent, depending on conditions. Take the plane back over to the ocean side of the ridge so we can gain some altitude before going off in search of thermals. The best way to do this is to fly along the ridge as far as it will take you, and then turn around and head the other way, staying with the updraft.

Now that we've got a little distance between us and the ground, let's try out the second, and more challenging, type of soaring—thermal soaring. As we said before, thermals are columns of warm air that rise, hopefully lifting your plane

along with them. To search out thermals, you first need to know what creates them in the first place and what, if any, clues to their location they offer to the experienced sailplane pilot.

When the sun hits the ground, or objects on the ground, it warms them to varying degrees. Something white is hardly warmed at all, reflecting most of the sun's energy away. That's how snow can survive the bright winter sunlight (especially the snow-covering driveways and sidewalks). The darker an object is, the more it converts the sunlight into heat. So to find thermals, all we have to do is look for dark areas on the ground, right? Well, yes and no.

Dark objects do often warm the air above them, but not always. A dark patch of ground may absorb the sunlight, but if it's wet ground, the moisture will conspire to cool it, and we have thermal stalemate. Or dark ground could be exposed to wind, which would also cool it, preventing thermals from forming. Forests are another type of area, usually dark in color, that don't generate thermals because the trees themselves absorb the heat and circulate it back to the shady ground below.

What we're looking for, then, are open areas of dark ground, such as a plowed field, or maybe even a cultivated field, depending on the plants growing in it. Large sandy areas are good candidates for thermals, too. And before you think, "Wait a minute—sand is a very light color. How does that create thermals?" consider this. The multifaceted design of a grain of sand would reflect light in many directions, enough so when multiplied by billions of grains, heating would take place.

Checking the ground for the above signs is one way to find a thermal, but there's another effective method—if there's enough moisture in the air. Look for cumulus clouds: the white, puffy, benign-looking type. Spot one of these, and you can be sure it was created by moist air rising from a thermal. (The moisture reaches a certain altitude then it condenses, forming the cloud). The big problem here is finding a *forming* cloud, rather than a mature cloud, or worse, one that's dissipating. This takes a little practice and a good deal of patience, as you scan the sky in search of the first wisps that signal the formation of a cumulus cloud. Once you see that, head straight for it.

After you've reached the general neighborhood where a cumulus cloud is forming, you still have to find the thermal. If there's any wind at all, you probably won't find the thermal directly below the cloud, but somewhere to its the downwind side. The technique for finding a thermal is to begin circling in the most likely area, as you keep an eye on both your wingtips and the VSI.

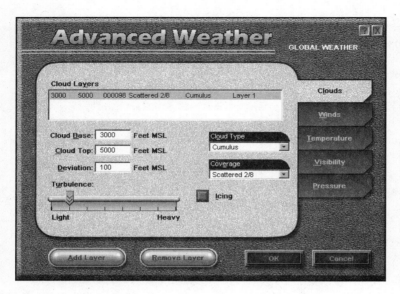

Generating clouds with the Weather menu.

You'll usually sense a thermal first with one of the wingtips, and once you do, steer toward that wingtip. As you enter the thermal, the VSI should indicate that you're going up. Keep circling, first to map out the boundaries of the thermal and then to stay within the thermal as it takes you up. Since a sailplane loses altitude more quickly the faster it goes, you might want to keep your speed down as low as possible by judicious use of the wing spoilers. Just remember that stall speed is 48 mph, so stay at least 5 mph above that speed. A stall isn't the worst thing that can happen in the Schweizer—it's actually quite docile in its stalling characteristics. It's just that a stall will almost certainly take you out of that thermal you've worked so hard to find.

There is a third type of soaring, not usually practiced by the average soaring pilot, that depends on a phenomenon of air passing over irregular surfaces. It's called the lee wave, or sometimes the mountain wave. In this case the air acts like water, supporting a sailplane along a series of waves. Some of these waves can be very powerful and can send a sailplane up 40,000 feet or higher. This is obviously a lot higher than we'll want to venture with the basic Schweizer, but in mountainous areas the lee wave is a powerful source of soaring propulsion. The major drawback to this type of soaring is that the lee wave is very directional. As long as you're soaring along with it, everything's fine. But fly into a lee wave at an angle perpendicular to its course, and it's like trying to swim through an ocean riptide.

With the default settings on our Challenge flight it's a fairly cloudless day, so we may want to create a couple of cloud layers for soaring purposes. You can do this by going to the World Weather menu. From there, click on the Add Layer button, select Cumulus from the Cloud Type scrolling menu, then Scatter 2/8 from the Coverage menu. For Cloud Base, type in *3000 feet MSL*, and for Cloud Top, enter *5000 feet MSL*. You might also want to check your General Preferences settings (under Options) to make sure you have the Weather Generation button selected. These settings should give you enough cloud generation to provide for some nice thermal soaring, using the techniques outlined above.

Nimitz Field as seen from the Bay Bridge.

At the Runway Threshold. Next up, a major change of scenery and aircraft...

Although we didn't have to take off, you might want to try your hand at landing a sailplane, if only to see whether that tiny little semiretracted wheel about two feet below your posterior can really do the job. First you'll need to find the Bay Bridge, which shouldn't be too hard to spot if you have enough altitude from your thermal riding. Head for the bridge (skew the plane there if you don't think you can stretch your glide that far), and by the time you get there, you should be able to see the airport just beyond.

Normally you won't see sailplanes landing at Nimitz Field, but we're special, aren't we? So pick any runway you'd like and line up for your approach. Remember: this is like the Space Shuttle—you must nail the landing first time because there are no go-arounds. The best way to insure that you stay out of the bay is to maintain as much altitude as you can right up to the airport, and then use a dive and your spoilers to bring you down quickly. Just be prepared—when you open the spoilers, as the effect on your speed is immediate and very noticeable.

Landing speed is around 55 mph. The plane will want to float above the runway, as those long wings really make use of the ground effect, so once you're positioned correctly on the runway centerline (about 20 feet or so above the ground), open the spoilers and pull back ever so slightly on the stick. With this plane you don't really want to flare the landing fully. You just want the nose up enough to make sure the landing wheel touches down first. The wings should stay level until just before the Schweizer stops rolling, unless you've tried a sharp turn onto one of the taxi strips in an effort to get to the airport cafeteria before they stop selling the sirloin special.

A Fighter Pilot's Life with the Sopwith Camel

The morning is crisp and clear, with just a hint of the sun on the horizon to the east. This must have been what it felt like those many years ago, in the early spring of 1918, in that corner of northern France where so much blood was spilled. By that time, the Allied forces could finally see the end of four miserable years of war. But as the earthbound fighting slowly ground down to the stalemate that would eventually end the "war to end all wars," the skies above that embattled part of Europe were still filled with the howls of Clerget, Hispano-Suiza, and Oberusel engines. The air warriors were still at it, still braving the new territory where their exploits would become part of the lore of aviation, as well as the basis for all air combat.

In that spring of 1918, the Sopwith Camel was still in its ascendancy, though its fighting career would not last beyond the end of the war. Indeed, had the fighting gone on only a few weeks more, the nimble but treacherous Camel would have disappeared completely from the battlefield. New and better aircraft, like Sopwith's own Snipe, were waiting in the wings.

The Sopwith Camel, waiting on the tarmac at Reims.

And now we (digitally) stand on the tarmac of the airfield at Reims, France, soaking in as much of the atmosphere as possible before taking the tiny fighter up once more to revisit some of the areas drenched in blood and aviation history. (Under Options, select Go To Airport, and then Scenery Area: Europe. Then select Reims, France.) We'll also put the Camel

First light of dawn.

Liftoff.

through its paces to find out just why, despite its shortcomings, it was so phenomenally successful as a fighter plane.

A left foot on the trailing edge panel of the wing and a swing of the right leg over the cockpit coaming and you're in the Camel's cozy cockpit. Right away, you can see where the aircraft got its unofficial name—the fairing, or hump, if you will, over the twin .30-caliber Vickers machine guns completely encloses the rear breeches of the guns, and so completely blocks your forward vision. Of course, that the aircraft sits at such an extreme angle doesn't help visibility either, but these were the days before tricycle landing gears. You can almost console yourself with the fact that the visibility in the Fokker Dr.I Triplane was even worse.

The motor's already running, so let's take a minute to check over the cockpit and its painfully sparse instrumentation. Beyond knowing how fast you're going, how fast the little nine-cylinder Clerget rotary engine is turning, how high you are, how the fuel and oil are doing, and in which direction you're headed, there isn't much else in the way of flight data. But back then flying was still more intuition and feel than technical expertise. Most pilots learned more from listening to their planes and feeling how they handled than from those often wildly inaccurate instruments. Some even claimed they could judge the engine's condition from the smell and the temperature of the castor oil as it was flung back on them from the spinning cylinders of the rotary engine.

Ready? Then tighten your scarf, button your flight jacket, lower your goggles, and let's go. As a concession to modernity, Flight Simulator's Sopwith has brakes, but the real thing was kept immobile by wheel chocks until flight time. Another concession here is the throttle; the Camel had a very rudimentary a throttle. Engine speed was governed for the most part by turning the engine off and on. That's why in old WWI films, some planes often sound as though they had the hiccups when landing. The pilot is blipping the engine to slow down. Flaps, spoilers, and airbrakes were still several years away, so a plane often had to be flown down to a landing, and even ancient planes like the Sopwith were pretty fast when the engine was running at full song. Some pilots were more fortunate—they had planes with in-line engines, such as the British S.E. 5 or the French SPAD.

If you've already flown the Extra 300S, another tail-dragger design, you know the care required when you're taking off in a plane with no nose gear. Since the Sopwith Camel has considerably less horsepower than the Extra, there's less possibility of nosing the plane over onto the ground, but it could still happen. Advance the throttle smoothly, and the plane should track straight down the runway. Let's hope so, at least because with the obstructing nose and the tail-down attitude of the Camel, you must take it on faith that you won't end up in the drink.

Even with the lift provided by two sets of wings, the Camel may need some urging to lift off, depending on conditions. Just a bit of back pressure on the stick should do the trick, once your ground speed reaches the 55-knot range. In any event, the Sopwith isn't going to leap into the air. And as you climb, you'll soon discover that the Cessna 182 is a real performance machine compared to the Camel. While the Cessna climbs at about 80 kts, the Camel is around 20 kts slower.

One feature of the Camel is missing from Flight Simulator, and it's something you won't miss—namely the torque effects of the rotary engine. Torque, as you may know, is twisting force. Combine that with Newton's third law (every action has an equal and opposite reaction), and you get a phenomenon that affects, to some degree, any single-propeller aircraft. The Camel's low weight and short wingspan allow it to roll very easily, so the torque of the engine has a greater influence on the Sopwith. The real Camel was treacherous during takeoff, often sending the unwary or novice pilot spinning into the ground. A popular joke among pilots (the same joke circulated during World War II about Chance-Vought Corsair pilots) was that you could always tell a Camel pilot because his left leg was twice the size of the right. A

bit of overstatement, perhaps, but it was true that the Camel usually needed a little left rudder in order to fly straight.

We took off to the west southwest, or 250 degrees true. Once we've gained a bit of altitude—1500 feet or so—begin a gentle climbing turn to the right, to a heading of 315 degrees. Our flight plan is to head northwest for about 45 nautical miles until we pick up the Somme River. As we're flying with the most basic of Visual Flight Rules, we'll use dead reckoning (or deduced reckoning) to establish just when we should reach the Somme. Continue climbing until we reach 3000 feet (any higher and we might not see the river under the clouds), level off, and then throttle back to about 2000 rpm. This should give us an airspeed of 80-85 kts with calm conditions. At that airspeed we should reach the Somme in about 40 minutes.

We're headed for the Somme River so that we can follow it westward for a few miles to Amiens. The river is famous in aviation mostly because on April 21, 1918, Manfred von Richtofen met his death somewhere over the Somme, supposedly from the guns of Canadian pilot Roy Brown's Sopwith Camel. "Supposedly," because to this day there are a few who maintain that von Richtofen was actually killed by Australian army ground fire when he flew too low.

From Amiens, we'll head northeast to the area around Cambrai, where the nascent Royal Air Force had some of its greatest victories in the closing months of the war. We'll land, at Niergnies Airport, our journey completed, and just in time for a cup of coffee and a tale-swapping session with the local pilots.

Unlike some of its RAF brethren, the Camel is not an easy plane to fly for long distances. There is, of course, the torque from the engine that's always present, but there are other factors to make the little plane less than ideal for longer flights. The engine, for all its smoothness compared to the radial and in-line engines of the day, was still a headache for most pilots, mainly because of its tendency to throw oil. Both the oil and the fuel were fed to the engine by centrifugal force, and as the nine cylinders spun around (and they spun at the same rpm as the propeller), the oil would leak from the cylinder heads and be thrown back by the prop wash into the pilot's face.

Beyond that, the Camel's basic design made it less than rock-steady in the air. The aircraft was very short compared to other designs, and this close-coupled quality made it rather "squirrely" in all flight axes. The kicker is that this "squirreliness" was what made the Camel such an outstanding dogfighter. Rather than having to fight a very stable plane, the Camel pilot had only to flick

The Somme River.

the controls, and the Camel would dart away...to the right, at least. Engine torque made left turns something to be avoided if possible. German pilots quickly learned this about the Camel, and most anticipated that an attacked Camel pilot would use a snap turn to the right for evasion. That foreknowledge didn't help as much as you might think—the Sopwith turned so quickly that a pilot could still usually get away.

You've been cruising for a while, and once you've wiped the castor oil from your goggles, you should check below to see if you've found the river. In the real Camel this usually meant leaning over the cockpit coaming or banking the plane a bit to get a better view, but you can just hit W on the keyboard and get rid of that instrument panel for a few moments.

Now that you've found the Somme, make a gradual left turn and pick up the course of the river as it flows to the west for its rendezvous with the English Channel, just south of the Pas de Calais (or the Straits of Dover, if you will). It's a twisting river, but not that difficult to follow if you stay around 2500 to 3000 feet. You may want to fly a bit lower to enjoy the scenery. Remember: for your purposes this is 1918 again, so don't worry about the odd charter flight.

The trip to Amiens is another 45 nautical miles, so while we have the river for a reference point to keep us on course, let's try a few maneuvers, starting with a common loop. If you've already tried aerobatics with the Extra 300S, be prepared to do things a little differently in the Camel. While the two planes are fairly close in size and weight, the Camel has only a bit more than a third the

Looping the Sopwith Camel.

horsepower of the Extra. (The final versions of the Camel did sport 200 hp Bentley engines.) It's also penalized by its lack of aerodynamic refinement, to be kind about it. A blunt nose, bulky landing gear, and all the various struts and wires crisscrossing the wing hardly make for an efficient flying machine. Even in its own time, the Camel compared poorly in aerodynamics to some of its peers. But then, it didn't have to be sleek and fast—it was designed expressly to turn and dive quickly in order to best insert .30-caliber bullets where they would do the most harm to planes sporting black Maltese crosses.

But to the loop. As we said, you don't have a lot of power, so there's none of this "throttle down to 140 kts before beginning the maneuver." The Camel pilot would be lucky to see 140 kts just before he hit the ground at the end of a terminal dive. (That would, quite naturally, be the full extent of his good luck.) No, to loop the Camel we're going to have to build up some speed, and of course the best way to accomplish that is to put the plane into a shallow dive. Ideally you'll want to get your airspeed up to at least 90 kts, but don't try too steep a dive to get there. Under normal conditions, 90—or even 100—should be easily attained, but don't push your luck.

Once you've found the airspeed, apply back pressure to the stick, firmly but smoothly. Pull it all the way back and check out the side of the plane to make sure your wingtips are describing a circle on the horizon. It's usually better to use the upper wing to sight on. Because the airspeed going into the maneuver is much lower, and because you don't have 300 horsepower to pull you through

the maneuver, this loop will be of much smaller diameter than one you'd perform in the Extra 300S. The plane should stay vertical only for a second as it continues the loop to the inverted position. Don't even think about extending your stay at vertical any longer, or the only maneuver you'll be perfecting will be a tailslide (not one of the Camel's complement of maneuvers, by the way—the stress would probably tear the fabric covering off the elevator and rudder, unless it just rips off the entire tail assembly instead).

And never forget torque. Watch out for the effects of engine torque during the loop (keep an eye on the horizon off to the side), especially after the plane is inverted and nosing over into the downward part of the loop. With the propeller now unloaded, the engine revolutions will increase quickly, making it all the more likely that the plane will try to roll. Again, the experienced pilot could use this to his or her advantage, letting the plane roll out of the loop in something of a modified Immelmann.

We'll continue with the loop, however, letting the plane carry through the maneuver, centering the stick just before regaining level flight. If you've performed the loop correctly, you should be nose on with the Somme once again.

From this position, let's try a quick maneuver that's well suited to the Camel's unique flying characteristics. The Split-S could have been designed by a Camel pilot. Although it's often thought of as useful when you're evading a pursuing aircraft, the reverse was more often true, especially if the plane being evaded could turn more tightly. But

Performing a Split-S.

The Immelmann.

the Camel could, in most situations, use the Split-S for evasion since the Fokker Triplane was the only German plane that could match it in a turn. Most pilots, however, used the maneuver quickly to change directions in order to get on the tail of an oncoming enemy aircraft.

Note also that in keeping with the real Camel's idiosyncratic handling, it will be a Split-S with a roll to the right. Flying level, sight on the river as a reference, advance the throttle to about 2100 rpm, and push the stick firmly to the right to roll the plane over. As the plane reaches full inverted flight, take a quick look over the nose to reacquire your reference line (the river.) As you center the stick to stop the roll, reduce the throttle a bit, and then pull the stick back to put the plane into a dive. Continue back pressure and the plane will recover to level flight, just as in the exit of a loop. These steps should all be performed seamlessly for a smooth maneuver.

To get back to our original course and altitude, we'll do the Immelmann, the reverse of the Split-S. Max Immelmann, the German ace known affectionately to his comrades as the "Eagle of the Lille," may not have invented the maneuver that bears his name, but he certainly used it to rack up 15 victories in his very short life. Because he died in 1915, two years before the Sopwith Camel entered service, we can only imagine how he might have yearned to try out the nimble fighter.

We'll need some speed to perform the Immelmann properly, so put the plane into a shallow dive again, letting airspeed build to around 90 kts (100 if you can manage it). Sight once again on the river for reference, and then pull

the stick back firmly, as if you were doing another loop. Hold that back pressure until just before the plane reaches level inverted flight (check your reference again), and then center the stick longitudinally (front to rear) as you push it over to the left. We're rolling to the left in the Immelmann because of the real Camel's tendency for the nose to rise in a left turn. (This effect is not present with the Flight Simulator Camel.) Center the stick just as the wings level out. If all went well, you should sight the Somme once again.

Sighting Amiens.

By now we've reached Amiens. If you want to check your position to make sure you've actually reached the town, go to World Set Exact Location menu and check the readings there. The coordinates for Amiens' Glisy Airport are 49 degrees, 52 minutes North, and 2 degrees, 23 minutes East. Take a new heading of 59 degrees, and we'll begin the final leg to Cambrai. It should be noted that, under normal flight conditions, there is almost always some wind. This should be factored in to any dead reckoning to allow for drift away from the flight path. In our case, that degree of navigation specificity wasn't required for the leg of our flight from Reims to the Somme River because we could have varied by several miles either way and still picked up the river. Once at the river, we followed its course to Amiens, so, yet again, there was no need to correct for wind. Our last leg, from Amiens to Cambrai, is only about 30 nautical miles, so the effects of wind drift will be minimal. Had we flown a longer leg, however, we'd want to take the wind into account. With a plane as light as the Camel and in a straight crosswind, you should probably figure on correcting about one degree for every 10 kts of wind.

Check out this photo in full color—along with details on the aircraft's performance envelope—in Pilot's Help.

Niergnies Airport, Cambrai, France.

It's a short flight to Cambrai, scene of some of the RAF's (it was actually still the RFC— Royal Flying Corps— until April of 1918) greatest successes during World War I. Here, in March of 1918, a great air battle was waged, and Sopwith Camels played a pivotal role. In addition to their job as England's front-line fighter, they were also called on to perform as bombers— albeit very light bombers—carrying a maximum payload of four 20-pound bombs. But its reputation as a fighter was only enhanced because Camels accounted for the great majority of enemy planes downed in the battle. One Camel pilot, captain J. L. Trollope, managed the astounding feat of shooting down six planes in one day.

Cambrai's Niergnies Airport (50 degrees, 8 minutes North; 3 degrees, 15 minutes East) has

several runways, although only the two longest show up in Flight Simulator. Take either one, and bring the plane in at about 60 kts (1000 rpm). Runway elevation is 312 feet, so take that into account for the landing. Runway 33 is the longest and should give you plenty of room to set the Camel down. Fully retard the throttle as you cross the runway threshold. Don't forget to flare the plane just before touchdown. But be careful not to rotate the nose too much, or the tailskid will hit the ground first, and that's not even close to textbook technique. Brake gently to a stop, and then switch the magnetos off. Now how about that cup of coffee?

SELECTED AIRPORT CHARTS, USA

At first glance an aeronautical navigation chart can seem a hopeless jumble of information, packed too closely together to be of any use. The trick to reading a chart is to learn to filter out information you don't need, focusing only on what you *do* need. For the purposes of the basic radio navigation we use in Flight Simulator, the main things you're looking for are 1) the various VOR transmitter sites, and 2) the VOR radial overlay that usually accompanies a primary VOR site.

Reading Navigation Charts

Reading the VOR transmitter site data is easy—the information is almost always enclosed in a small rectangle, with the type of transmitter (VOR, VOR-DME or VORTAC) at the top of the box. There are several bits of info inside the box, including primary COMM channels, but the data you need is the VOR frequency, which is the first set of numbers underneath the location of the station.

The other part of the chart that we need to use is the VOR radial overlay itself. As we mentioned in the chapter on radio navigation, all VOR stations are aligned to magnetic north, and so are all aligned with one another. Therefore flying out on, for example, the 90-degree radial to a station exactly due east will have you flying along the second station's 270 radial (although, as we've hit you over the head with several times, you use the reciprocal of the radial your flying into—in this case the 90-degree radial).

You might also note that, on detailed maps such as this one, major airport runway orientations are shown, as well as primary airways. Take, for example, the 22-degree radial out of the Santa Catalina Island VOR. This is a common path to take when flying across the San Pedro Channel to the Los Alamitos Air Station east of Long Beach.

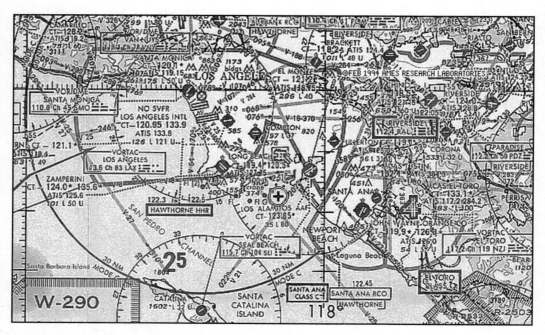

A VOR Chart Showing the Greater Los Angeles Area.

Note that, all runways on the charts have numbers, with some numbers accompanied by an "R" or an "L." The numbers refer to the orientation of the runway relative to magnetic north. To decipher a number, multiply it by ten. The answer is the centerline direction of that runway. For example, a runway labeled O3 would be oriented to the East Northeast at a heading of approximately 30 degrees as measured from magnetic north. If that same runway were labeled 03L, it would denote the left runway of two parallel runways. By the way, runways are labeled from both directions, so an approach from the opposite end would mean the same runway would be on the right side, named 21R (approximately 210 degrees, the reciprocal of 030 degrees).

All aeronautical charts displayed in Flight Simulator for Windows 95: Inside Moves are captured from the AmesMaps moving map CD-ROM and are printed here with their gracious permission. (Ames Navigation Maps copyright 1993-1996, Ames Maps LLC.) The moving-map technology utilized in this package allows point-and-click seamless movement around both U.S. Sectional

Charts and World Aeronautical Charts. A Global navigation map is included on the same CD. Jeppesen Navigation Data® provides airport and communication frequency information. Designed for optional use with a PCMCIA GPS (Global Positioning System) receiver, AmesMaps can be run on a pilot's laptop and track current position on a seamless, scrolling, real-time map. Although we couldn't test this feature in Flight Simulator, we could—and did—exhaustively use the scrolling maps feature to create this special preview series of maps for the Microsoft Southern California Expansion Pack. The current version of the AmesMaps software runs under MS-DOS. Note that our black and white images don't do the software full justice: the CD-maps appear in 256 colors. For more information on the AmesMaps software system, contact them at the address here, or e-mail them at: 102102.457@CompuServe.

Airport runway diagrams and selected navigational data are compiled from various FAA resources. (See Internet Resources, Appendix D.) The Flight Simulator help and data files were also a source of useful information.

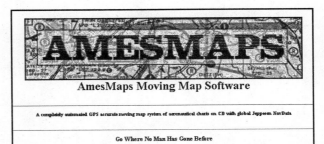

AmesMaps Moving Map Software

A completely automated GPS accurate moving map system of aeronautical charts on CD with global Jeppesen NavData

Go Where No Man Has Gone Before

http://ourworld.compuserve.com/homepages/amesmaps

AMES Research Laboratories

tel: (541)924-9849

fax: (541)924-9884

Oregon Research & Development

1895 16th St. SE

Salem, OR 97302-1436

tel: 1-800-345-0809

THE MOST ADVANCED GPS NAVIGATION SYSTEMS

The AmesMaps scrolling-map feature allowed the seamless capture of adjacent navchart overlays in Appendix B.

Albuquerque International Airport (ABQ)

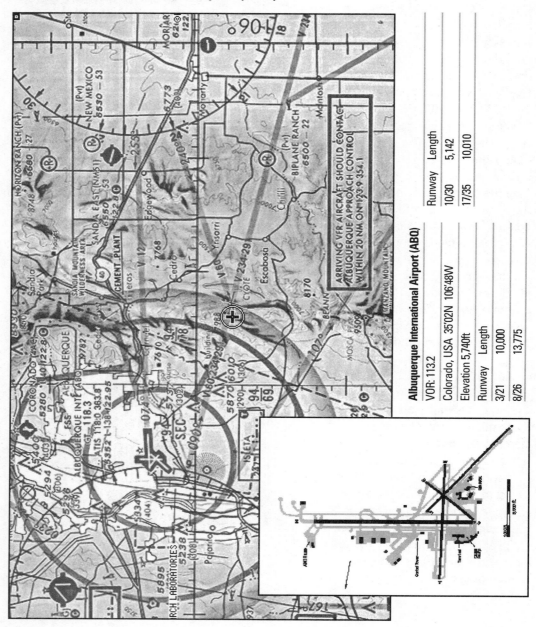

Albuquerque International Airport (ABQ)

VOR: 113.2	
Colorado, USA 3502N 106'48W	
Elevation 5,740ft	

Runway	Length
3/21	10,000
8/26	13,775

Runway	Length
10/30	5,142
17/35	10,010

ARRIVING VFR AIRCRAFT SHOULD CONTACT ALBUQUERQUE APPROACH CONTROL WITHIN 20 NM ON 139.9 354.1

Atlanta Hartsfield International Airport (ATL)

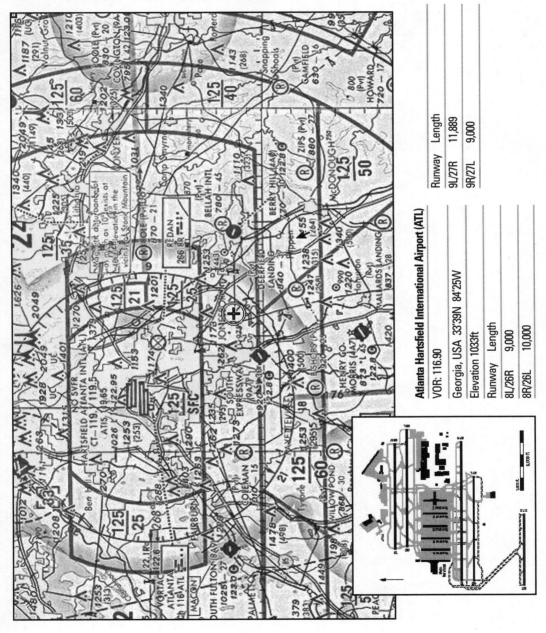

Atlanta Hartsfield International Airport (ATL)

VOR: 116.90

Georgia, USA 33°39N 84°25W

Elevation 1033ft

Runway	Length
8L/26R	9,000
8R/26L	10,000

Runway	Length
9L/27R	11,889
9R/27L	9,000

Boston Logan (BOS)

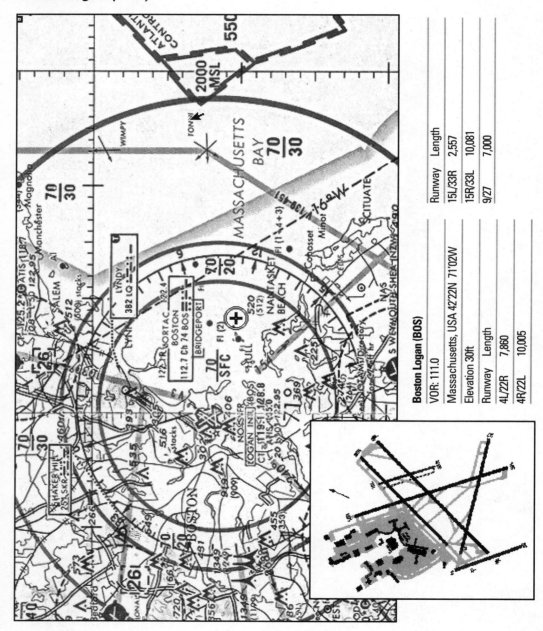

Boston Logan (BOS)

VOR: 111.0

Massachusetts, USA 42°22N 71°02W

Elevation 30ft

Runway	Length
4L/22R	7,860
4R/22L	10,005

Runway	Length
15L/33R	2,557
15R/33L	10,081
9/27	7,000

Chicago Midway Airport (MDW)

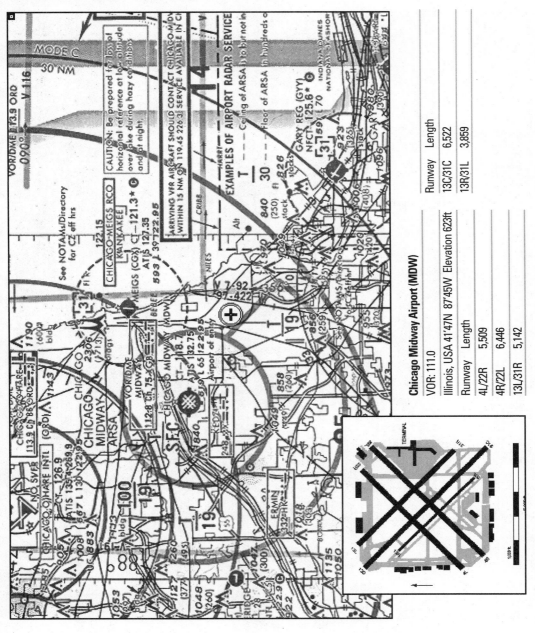

Chicago Midway Airport (MDW)

VOR: 111.0

Illinois, USA 41°47N 87°45W Elevation 623ft

Runway	Length
4L/22R	5,509
4R/22L	6,446
13L/31R	5,142

Runway	Length
13C/31C	6,522
13R/31L	3,859

Chicago O'Hare International Airport (ORD)

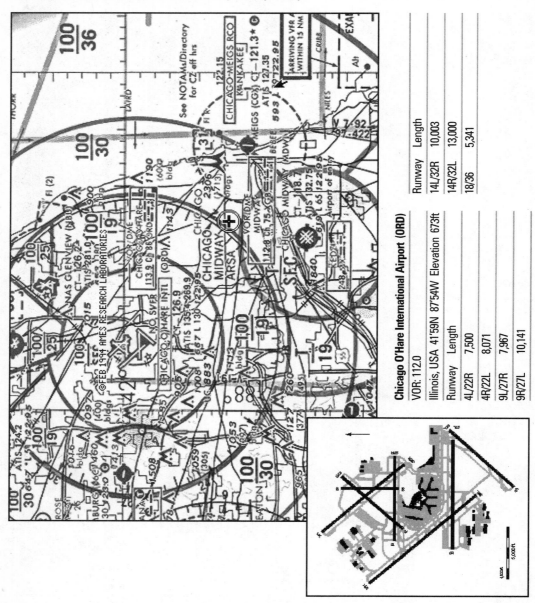

Chicago O'Hare International Airport (ORD)

VOR: 112.0

Illinois, USA 41°59N 87°54W Elevation 673ft

Runway	Length
4L/22R	7,500
4R/22L	8,071
9L/27R	7,967
9R/27L	10,141

Runway	Length
14L/32R	10,003
14R/32L	13,000
18/36	5,341

Dallas Love Field (DAL)

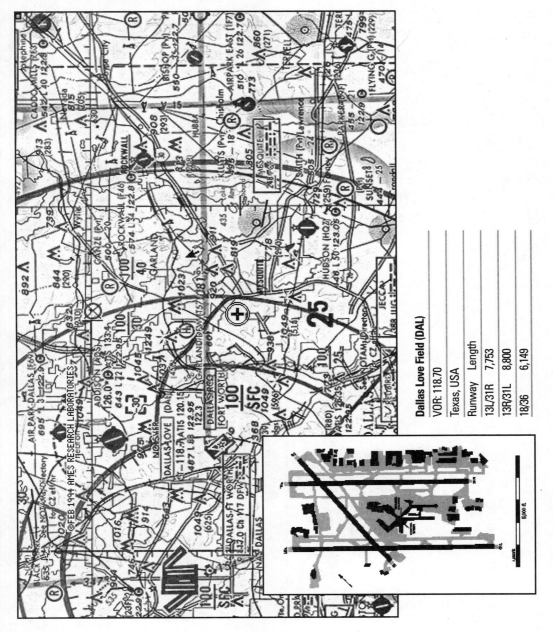

Dallas Love Field (DAL)

VOR: 118.70	
Texas, USA	

Runway	Length
13L/31R	7,753
13R/31L	8,800
18/36	6,149

5,000 ft.

Dallas-Fort Worth International Airport (DFW)

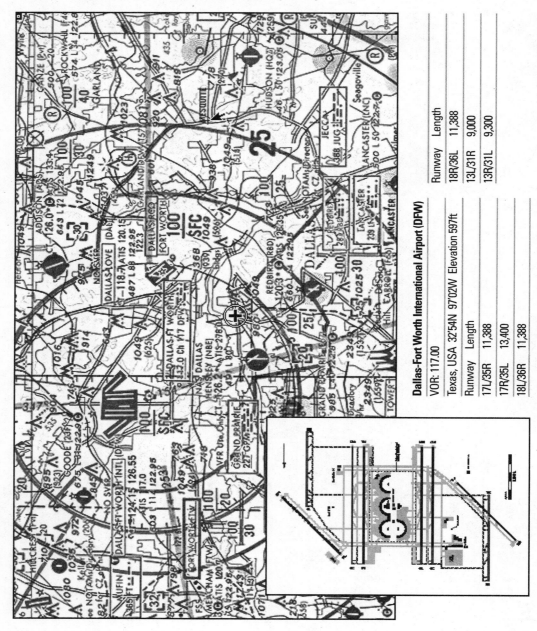

Dallas-Fort Worth International Airport (DFW)

VOR: 117.00

Texas, USA 32°54N 97°02W Elevation 597ft

Runway	Length
17L/35R	11,388
17R/35L	13,400
18L/36R	11,388

Runway	Length
18R/36L	11,388
13L/31R	9,000
13R/31L	9,300

Denver International / Denver Stapleton International Airport (DEN)

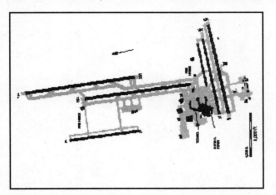

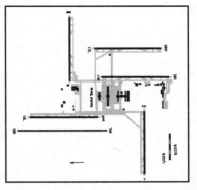

(Although Denver Stapleton has closed with the opening of Denver International Airport, it lives on in Flight Simulator.)

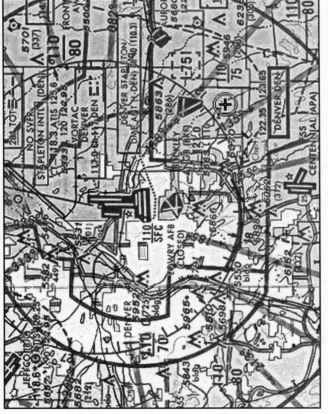

Denver International Airport (DEN)

VOR: 117.90

Colorado, USA 39°48N 104°39W

Elevation 5,440ft

Runway	Length
16R/34L	12,000
16L/34R	12,000
17R/35L	12,000
17L/35R	12,000
7/25	12,000
8/26	12,000

Denver Stapleton International Airport (DEN)

VOR: 117.0

Colorado, USA 39°48N 104°53W   Elevation 5,334ft

Runway	Length
8L/26R	8,599
8R/26L	10,004
17L/35R	12,000
17R/35L	11,500
7/25	4,871
18/36	7,750

Detroit Metropolitan Wayne County Airport (DTW)

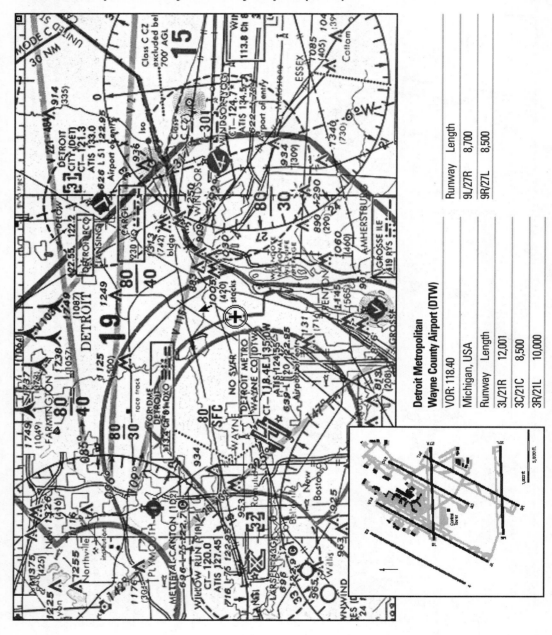

Detroit Metropolitan
Wayne County Airport (DTW)

VOR: 118.40

Michigan, USA

Runway	Length
9L/27R	8,700
9R/27L	8,500

Runway	Length
31/21R	12,001
3C/21C	8,500
3R/21L	10,000

Indianapolis International Airport (IND)

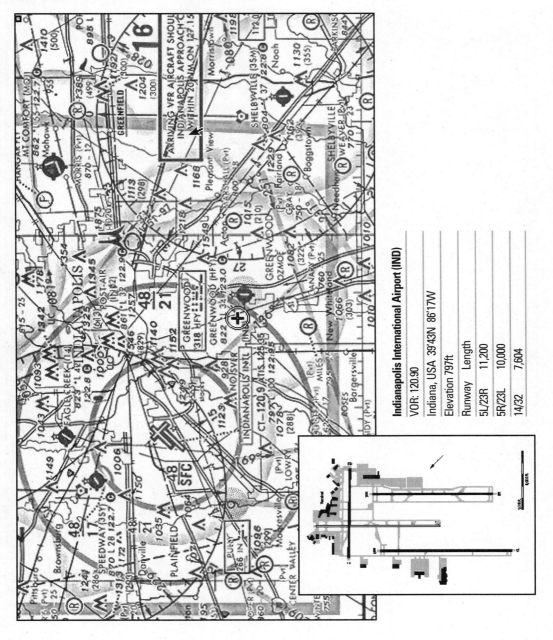

Indianapolis International Airport (IND)

VOR: 120.90

Indiana, USA 39°43'N 86°17'W

Elevation 797ft

Runway	Length
5L/23R	11,200
5R/23L	10,000
14/32	7,604

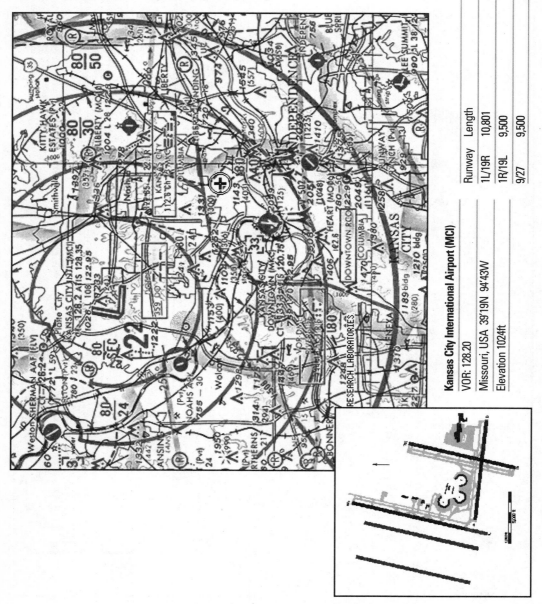

Kansas City International Airport (MCI)

Kansas City International Airport (MCI)

VOR: 128.20	
Missouri, USA	39'19N 9443W
Elevation 1024ft	

Runway	Length
1L/19R	10,801
1R/19L	9,500
9/27	9,500

Las Vegas McCarran International Airport (LAS)

Las Vegas McCarran International Airport (LAS)

VOR: 116.90

Nevada, USA 36°05'N 115°10'W Elevation 2178ft

Runway	Length
7L/25R	14,512
7R/25L	10,600
1L/19R	5,002

Runway	Length
1R/19L	9,776

Miami International Airport (MIA)

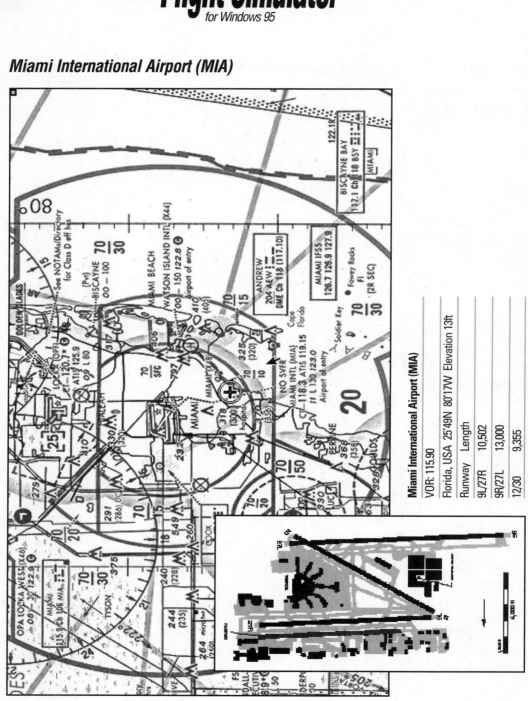

Miami International Airport (MIA)

VOR: 115.90

Florida, USA 25°49N 80°17W Elevation 13ft

Runway	Length
9L/27R	10,502
9R/27L	13,000
12/30	9,355

Minneapolis-St. Paul International Airport (MSP)

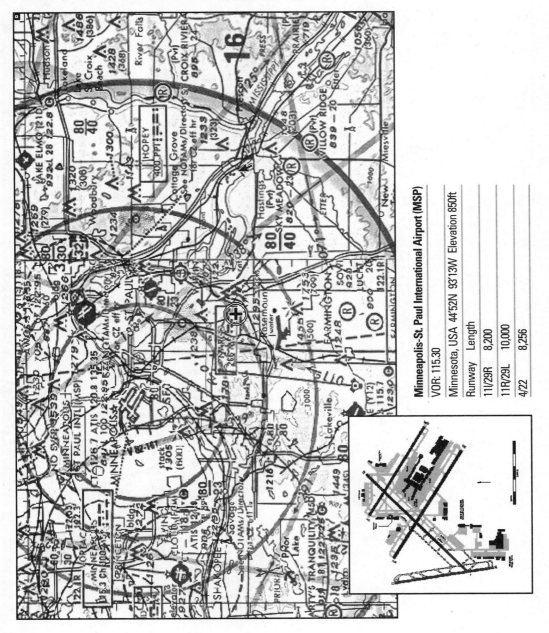

Minneapolis-St. Paul International Airport (MSP)

VOR: 115.30

Minnesota, USA 44°52N 93°13W Elevation 850ft

Runway	Length
11/29R	8,200
11R/29L	10,000
4/22	8,256

Nashville International Airport (BNA)

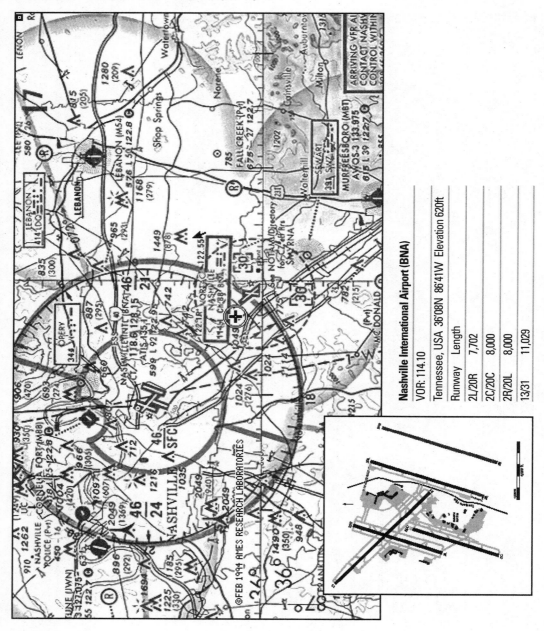

Nashville International Airport (BNA)

VOR: 114.10

Tennessee, USA 36°08N 86°41W Elevation 620ft

Runway	Length
2L/20R	7,702
2C/20C	8,000
2R/20L	8,000
13/31	11,029

New Orleans International Airport (MSY)

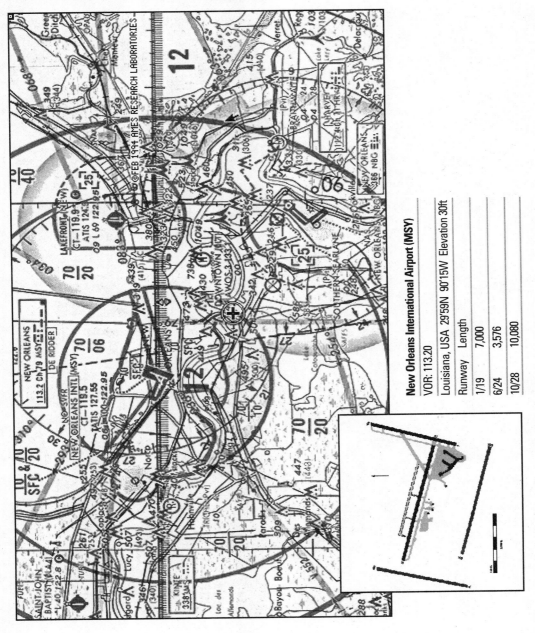

New Orleans International Airport (MSY)

VOR: 113.20

Louisiana, USA 29°59N 90°15W Elevation 30ft

Runway	Length
1/19	7,000
6/24	3,576
10/28	10,080

Newark International Airport (EWR)

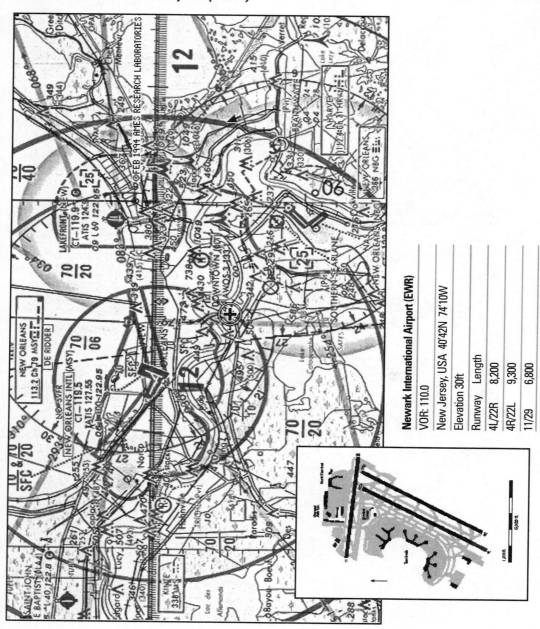

Newark International Airport (EWR)

VOR: 110.0

New Jersey, USA 40'42N 74'10W

Elevation 30ft

Runway	Length
4L/22R	8,200
4R/22L	9,300
11/29	6,800

New York John F. Kennedy International Airport (JFK)

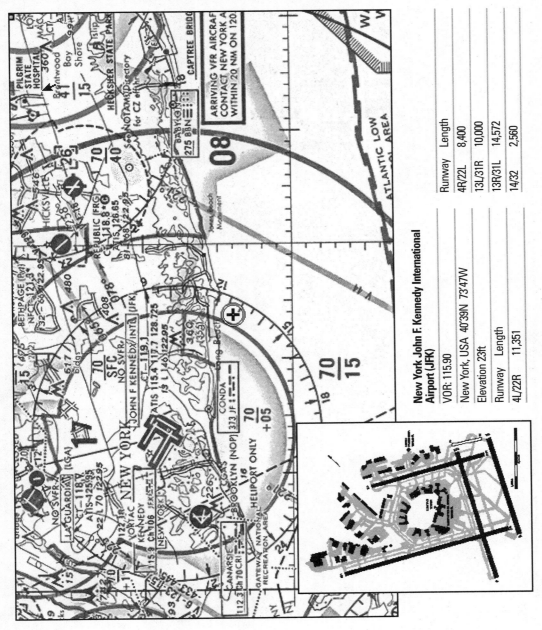

New York John F. Kennedy International Airport (JFK)

VOR: 115.90	
New York, USA 40°39N 73°47W	
Elevation 23ft	

Runway	Length
4L/22R	11,351

Runway	Length
4R/22L	8,400
13L/31R	10,000
13R/31L	14,572
14/32	2,560

New York La Guardia (LGA)

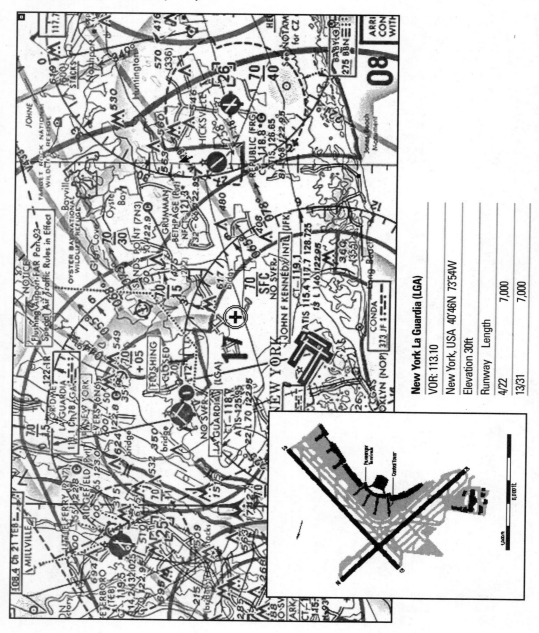

New York La Guardia (LGA)

VOR: 113.10	
New York, USA 40°46N 73°54W	
Elevation 30ft	
Runway	Length
4/22	7,000
13/31	7,000

Oakland International Airport (OAK)

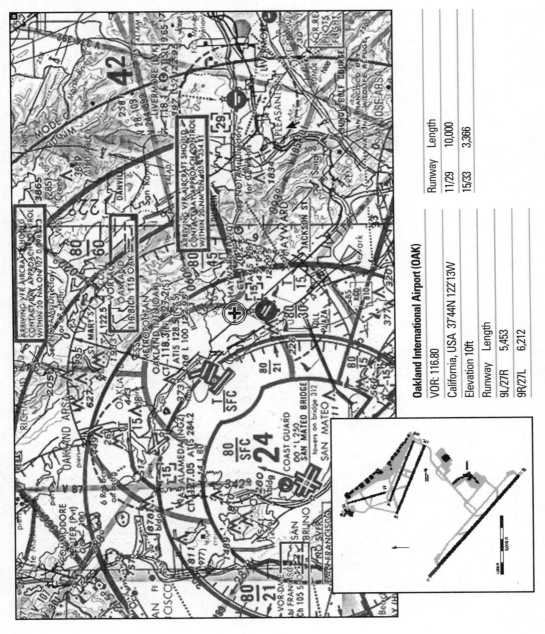

Oakland International Airport (OAK)

VOR: 116.80
California, USA 37'44N 122'13W
Elevation 10ft

Runway	Length
9L/27R	5,453
9R/27L	6,212

Runway	Length
11/29	10,000
15/33	3,366

Pittsburgh International Airport (PIT)

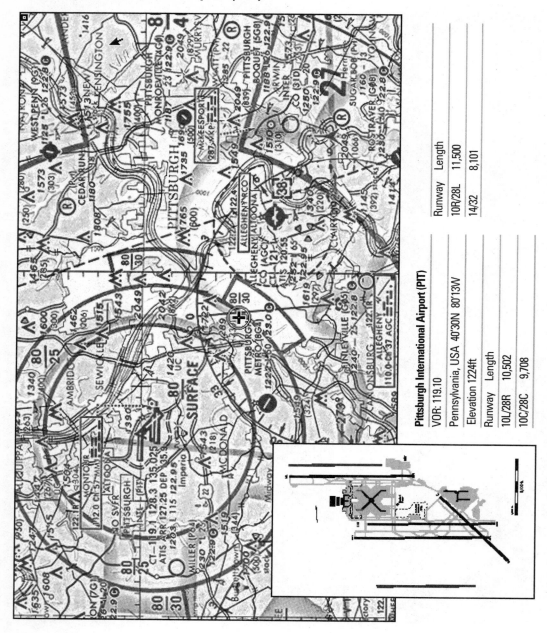

Pittsburgh International Airport (PIT)

VOR: 119.10		
Pennsylvania, USA	40'30N	80'13W
Elevation 1224ft		

Runway	Length
10L/28R	10,502
10C/28C	9,708

Runway	Length
10R/28L	11,500
14/32	8,101

Sacramento Metropolitan Airport (SMF)

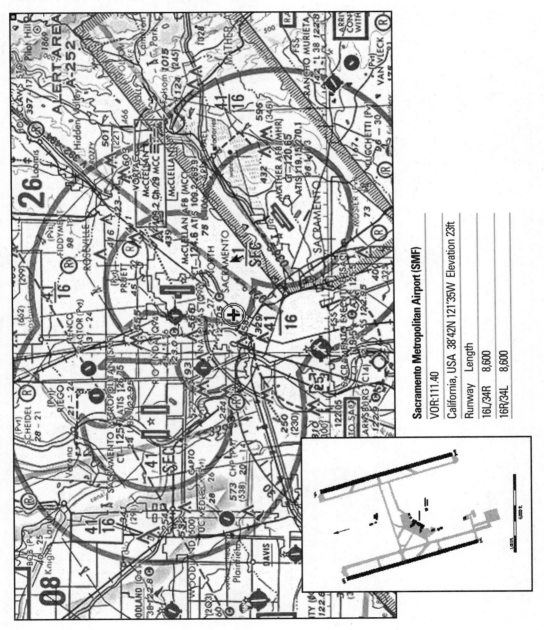

Sacramento Metropolitan Airport (SMF)

VOR:111.40

California, USA 38°42N 121°35W Elevation 23ft

Runway	Length
16L/34R	8,600
16R/34L	8,600

Salt Lake City (SLC)

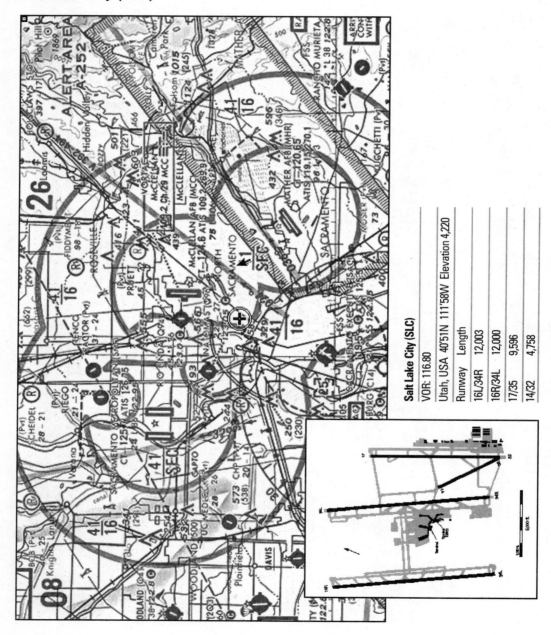

Salt Lake City (SLC)

VOR: 116.80

Utah, USA 40°51'N 111°58'W Elevation 4,220

Runway	Length
16L/34R	12,003
16R/34L	12,000
17/35	9,596
14/32	4,758

San Francisco (SFO)

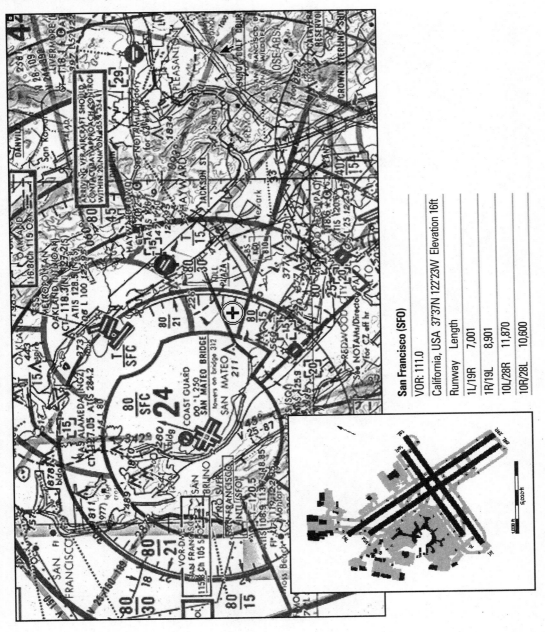

San Francisco (SFO)

VOR: 111.0

California, USA 37°37'N 122°23'W Elevation 16ft

Runway	Length
1L/19R	7,001
1R/19L	8,901
10L/28R	11,870
10R/28L	10,600

San Jose International Airport (SJC)

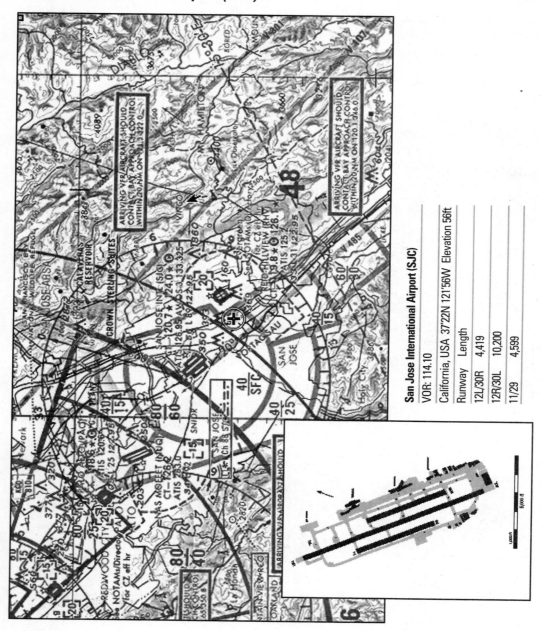

San Jose International Airport (SJC)

VOR: 114.10

California, USA 37°22N 121°56W Elevation 56ft

Runway	Length
12L/30R	4,419
12R/30L	10,200
11/29	4,599

Seattle-Tacoma International Airport (SEA)

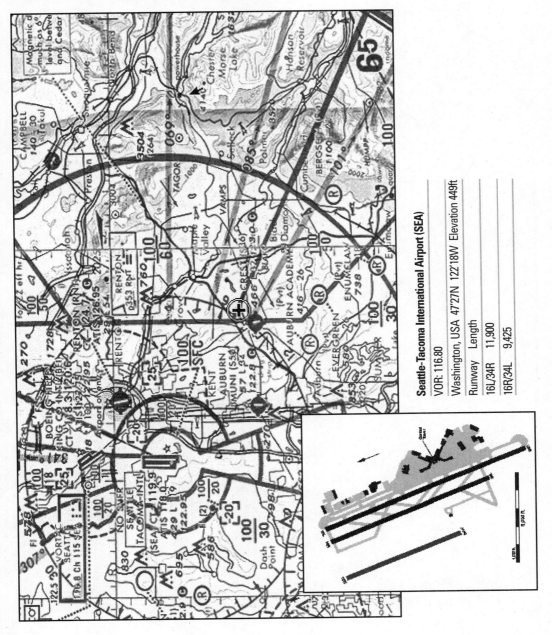

Seattle-Tacoma International Airport (SEA)

VOR: 116.80

Washington, USA 47°27'N 122°18'W Elevation 449ft

Runway	Length
16L/34R	11,900
16R/34L	9,425

St. Louis International Airport (STL)

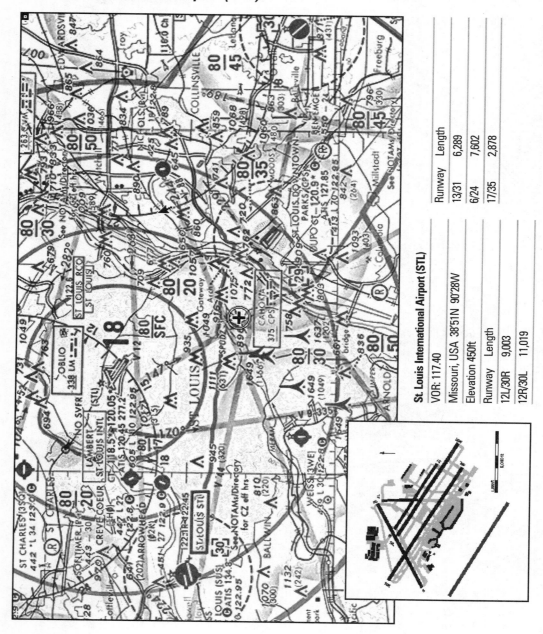

St. Louis International Airport (STL)

VOR: 117.40	
Missouri, USA 38°51′N 90°28′W	
Elevation 450ft	

Runway	Length
12L/30R	9,003
12R/30L	11,019

Runway	Length
13/31	6,289
6/24	7,602
17/35	2,878

Washington Dulles International Airport (IAD)

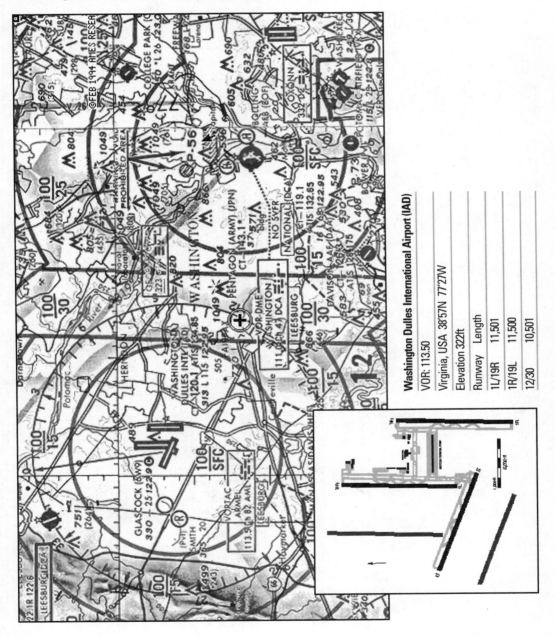

Washington Dulles International Airport (IAD)

VOR: 113.50

Virginia, USA 38°57N 77°27W

Elevation 322ft

Runway	Length
1L/19R	11,501
1R/19L	11,500
12/30	10,501

Washington National Airport (DCA)

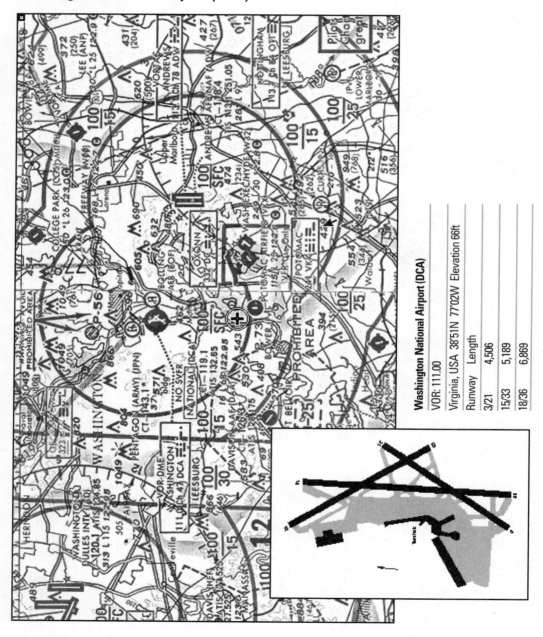

Washington National Airport (DCA)

VOR: 111.00

Virginia, USA 38°51'N 77°02'W Elevation 66ft

Runway	Length
3/21	4,506
15/33	5,189
18/36	6,869

Appendix B

Southern California Expansion Pack

The southern california Expansion Pack is the first scenery product for Microsoft Flight Simulator for Windows 95. Although this product was still under development while we were completing this book, we were able to get enough pre-release information to provide this chart-pack. The Expansion Pack is designed to provide new levels of realistic accuracy and visual quality. The charts included here cover the entire area available for exploration in the Expansion Pack. We've also included selected airport layouts to help you navigate the adventures included in the scenery pack.

Airport Information for Southern California, USA

ID	Name	NAV	Lat		Lon		Type	Notes
AVE	AVENAL	117.10	35	38.8	19	58.7	DME	H-VORTAC [CA] BAKERSFIELD FSS (BFL)
BFL	BAKERSFIELD	111. 20	35	25.	119	2.8	UNK	[CA] BAKERSFIELD FSS (BFL)
CMA	CAMARILLO	115.	34	12.	119	5.7	DME	L-VORW/DME [CA] SANTA BARBARA FSS (SBA)
CPM	COMPTON	378	33	53. 1	18	14.	NDB	MHW [CA] HAWTHORNE FSS (HHR)
DAG	DAGGETT	113.	34	57.	116	34.	DME	L-VORTAC [CA] RIVERSIDE FSS (RAL)
EDW	EDWARDS	116.	34	58.	117	44.	DME	L-VORTAC [CA] RIVERSIDE FSS (RAL)
EHF	SHAFTER	115.	35	29.	119	5.8	DME	H-VORTAC [CA] BAKERSFIELD FSS (BFL)
EKG	ESCONDIDO	374	33	9.4	117	5.1	NDB	MHW [CA] SAN DIEGO FSS (SAN)
EMT	EL MONTE	359	34	5.3	118	1.9	NDB	MHW [CA] RIVERSIDE FSS (RAL)
FIM	FILLMORE	112.	34	21.	118	52.	DME	L-ABVORTAC [CA] HAWTHORNE FSS (HHR)
FLW	FELLOWS	117.	35	5.6 1	19	51.	DME	L-VORTAC [CA] BAKERSFIELD (BFL)
FUL	FULLERTON	110.	33	52. 1	17	59.	UNK	VOT [CA] HAWTHORNE FSS (HHR)

Airport Information for Southern California, USA, continued

ID	Name	NAV	Lat		Lon		Type	Notes
GLJ	GUADALUPE	111.	34	57. 1	20	31.	VOR	T-ABVOR [CA] SANTA BARBARA FSS (SBA)
GMN	GORMAN	116.	34	48.	118	51.	DME	L-VORTAC [CA] BAKERSFIELDFSS (BFL)
GVO	GAVIOTA	113.	34	31.	120	5.5	DME	L-VORTACW [CA] SANTA BARBARA FSS (SBA)
GWF	GEN WILLIAM	282	34	44.	118	13.	NDB	MHW [CA] RIVERSIDE FSS FOX (RAL)
HDF	HOMELAND	113.	33	46.	117	11.	VOR	L-VOR [CA] RIVERSIDE FSS (RAL)
HEC	HECTOR	112.	34	47.	116	27.	DME	H-VORTAC [CA] RIVERSIDE FSS (RAL)
HGT	HUNTER LIGGETT	209	35	56.	121	9.7	NDB	MHW [CA] SALINAS FSS (SNS)
IZA	SANTA YNEZ	394	34	36.	120	4.6	NDB	MHW [CA] SANTA BARBARA FSS (SBA)
JLI	JULIAN	114.	33	8.4	116	35.	DME	L-VORTACW [CA] SAN DIEGOFSS (SAN)
LAX	LOS ANGELES	113.	33	56.	118	25.	DME	H-VORTACW [CA] HAWTHORNE FSS (HHR)
LAX	SAN PEDRO HILL	113.	33	44. 1	18	20.	UNK	VOT [CA] HAWTHORNE FSS (HHR)
LHS	LAKE HUGHES	108.	34	41.	118	34.	DME	L-VORTACW [CA] HAWTHORNE FSS (HHR)
LKA	SWAN LAKE	257	33	58.	17	33.	NDB	MHW [CA] RIVERSIDE FSS (RAL)
LPC	LOMPOC	223	34	39.	120	27.	NDB	MHW [CA] SANTA BARBARA FSS (SBA)
MQO	MORRO BAY	112.	35	15.	120	45.	DME	L-VORTAC [CA] HAWTHORNE FSS (HHR)
MZB	MISSION BAY	117.	32	46.	117	13.	DME	H-VORTAC [CA] SAN DIEGO FS (SAN)
NFG	CAMP PENDLETON		33	18.	117	21.	TAC	T-TACAN [CA] SAN DIEGO FSS (SAN)
NID	CHINA LAKE	348	35	41.	117	41.	NDB	HW [CA] RIVERSIDE FSS (RAL) (NAVY)
NID	CHINA LAKE		35	41.	117	41.	TAC	L-TACAN [CA] RIVERSIDE FSS (NAVY) (RAL)
NKX	MIRAMAR (NAVY)	280.	32	52.	117	8.4	UHF NDB	H-SAB [CA] SAN DIEGO FSS (SAN)
NKX	MIRAMAR (NAVY)		32	52.	117	9.3	TAC	L-TACAN [CA] SAN DIEGO FSS (SAN)
NRS	IMPERIAL BEACH		32	33.9	117	6.6	TAC	L-TACAN [CA] SAN DIEGO FSS (NAVY) (SAN)
NSI	SAN NICOLAS	203	33	14.	119	27.	NDB	MH [CA] HAWTHORNE FSS (HHR) (NAVY)
NSI	SAN NICOLAS		33	14.	119	27.	TAC	L-TACAN [CA] HAWTHORNE FSS(NAVY) (HHR)
NTD FSS	POINT MUGU		34	7.4	119	7.3	TAC	L-TACAN [CA] SANTA BARBARA (NAVY) (SBA)
NTK	TUSTIN		33	42.	117	49.	TAC	L-TACAN [CA] HAWTHORNE FSS (HHR)
NUC	SAN CLEMENTE	350	33	1.6	118	34.	NDB	H [CA] HAWTHORNE FSS (HHR) (NAVY)
NUC	SAN CLEMENTE		33	1.6	118	34.	TAC	L-TACAN [CA] HAWTHORNE FSS (NAVY) (HHR)
NXP	COYOTE		34	17.	116	9.6	TAC	L-TACAN [CA] RIVERSIDE FSS (RAL)
NZJ	EL TORO	117.	33	40.	117	43.	DME	L-VORTAC [CA] HAWTHORNE FSS (HHR)

Airport Information for Southern California, USA, continued

ID	Name	NAV	Lat		Lon		Type	Notes
NZJ	EL TORO	284.	33	40.	117	43.	UHF NDB	MH [CA] HAWTHORNE FSS (HHR)
NZJ	EL TORO	410	33	40.	117	43.	NDB	HW [CA] HAWTHORNE FSS (HHR)
NZY	NORTH ISLAND		32	42.	117	13.	TAC	L-TACAN [CA] SAN DIEGO FSS (NAVY) (SAN)
OCN	OCEANSIDE	115.	33	14.	117	25.	DME	H-VORTAC [CA] SAN DIEGO FSS (SAN)
PAI	PACOIMA	370	34	15.	118	24.	NDB	MHW [CA] HAWTHORNE FSS (HHR)
PDZ	PARADISE	112.	33	55.	117	31.	DME	H-VORTAC [CA] RIVERSIDE FSS (RAL)
PGY	POGGI	109.	32	36.	116	58.	DME	L-VORTACW [CA] SAN DIEGO FSS (SAN)
PMD	PALMDALE	114.	34	37.	118	3.8	DME	H-VORTAC [CA] RIVERSIDE FSS (RAL)
POM	POMONA	110.	34	4.7	117	47.	DME	L-ABVORTACW [CA] RIVERSIDE FSS (RAL)
PRB	PASO ROBLES	114.	35	40.	120	37.	DME	L-VORTACW [CA] HAWTHORNE FSS (HHR)
PSP	PALM SPRINGS	115.	33	52.	116	25.	DME	L-VORTAC [CA]RIVERSIDE FSS (RAL)
PTV	PORTERVILLE	109.	35	54.	119	1.2	DME	L-VOR/DME [CA] FRESNO FSS (FAT)
RAL	RIVERSIDE	112.	33	57.	117	27.	VOR	T-VOR [CA] RIVERSIDE FSS (RAL)
RIV	MARCH		33	54.	117	16.	TAC	L-TACAN [CA] RIVERSIDE FSS (RAL)
RZS	SAN MARCUS	114.	34	30.	119	46.	DME	H-VORTAC [CA] HAWTHORNE FSS (HHR)
SAN	ENCAT		32	42.	117	5.5	FAN	LFM [CA] SAN DIEGO FSS MARKER (SAN)
SAN	MOUNT SOLEDAD	109.	32	50.	17	15.	UNK	VOT [CA]SAN DIEGO FSS (SAN)
SB	PETIS	397	34	3.4	117	22.	NDB	HW/LOM [CA] RIVERSIDE FSS (RAL)
SBD	NORTON		34	6.0	117	14.	TAC	L-TACAN [CA] RIVERSIDE FSS (RAL)
SEE	GILLESPIE FIELD	110.	32	49.	116	58.	UNK	VOT [CA] SAN DIEGO FSS (SAN)
SJY	SAN JACINTO	227	33	47.	116	60.	NDB	MHW [CA] RIVERSIDE FSS (RAL)
SLI	SEAL BEACH	115.	33	47.	118	3.3	DME	L-VORTACW [CA] HAWTHORNE FSS (HHR)
SMO	SANTA MONICA	110.	34	0.6	118	27.	DME	L-VORW/DME [CA] HAWTHORNE FSS (HHR)
SNA	SANTA ANA	110.	33	40.	117	52.	UNK	VOT [CA] HAWTHORNE FSS (HHR)
SXC	SANTA CATALINA	111.	33	22.	118	25.	DME	L-VORTACW [CA] HAWTHORNE FSS (HHR)
TIJ	TIJUANA	116.	32	32.	116	57.	DME	L-VORW/DME
TRM	THERMAL	116.	33	37.	116	9.6	DME	H-VORTAC [CA]RIVERSIDE FSS(RAL)
UN	TIJUANA	381	32	32.	117	2.0	NDB	HW
VBG	VANDENBERG		34	44.	120	35.	TAC	L-TACAN [CA] SANTA BARBARA FSS (SBA)
VCV	GEORGE		34	35.	117	23.	TAC	L-TACAN [CA] RIVERSIDE FSS(RAL)
VNY	VAN NUYS	13.	34	13.	118	29.	DME	L-VORW/DME [CA] HAWTHORNE FSS (HHR)
VTU	VENTURA	108.	34	6.91	19	3.0	DME	L-VORTACW [CA]SANTA BARBARA FSS (SBA)

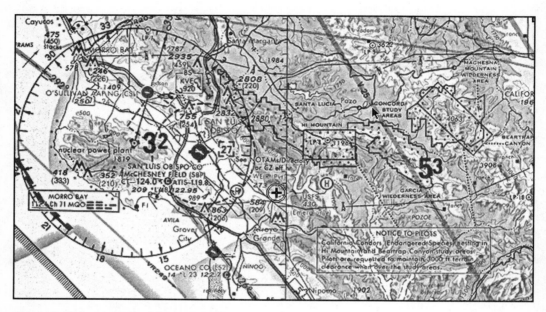

San Luis Obispo, north of Santa Barbara.

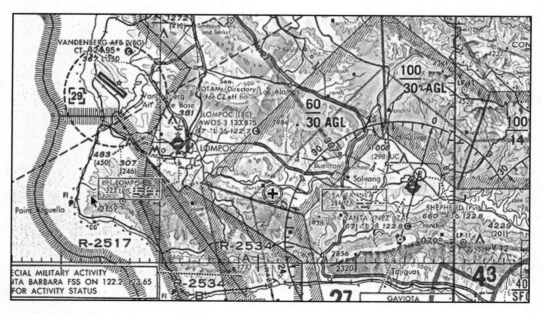

Vandenberg AFB, northeast of Santa Barbara.

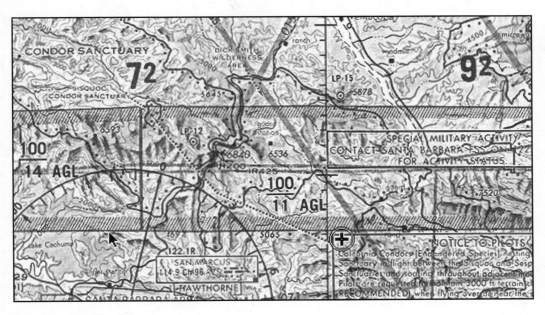

Santa Barbara/San Marcus.

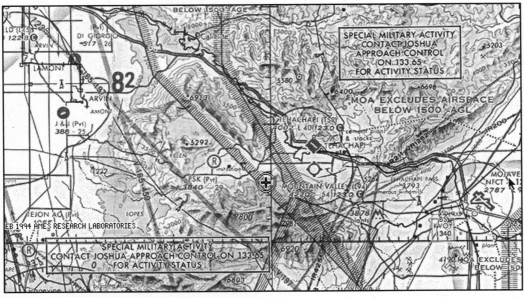

Lamont/Tehachapi/Mojave area.

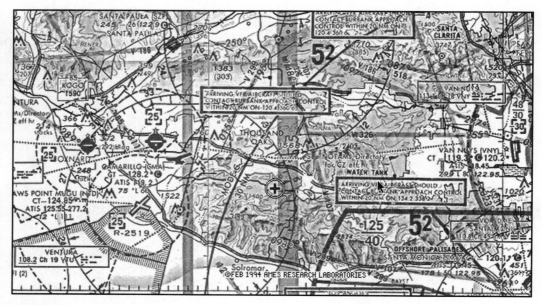

Camarillo, northwest of Los Angeles.

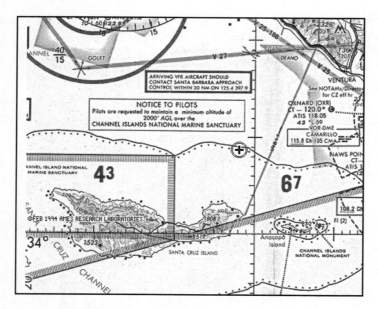

Santa Cruz Island, west of Camarillo.

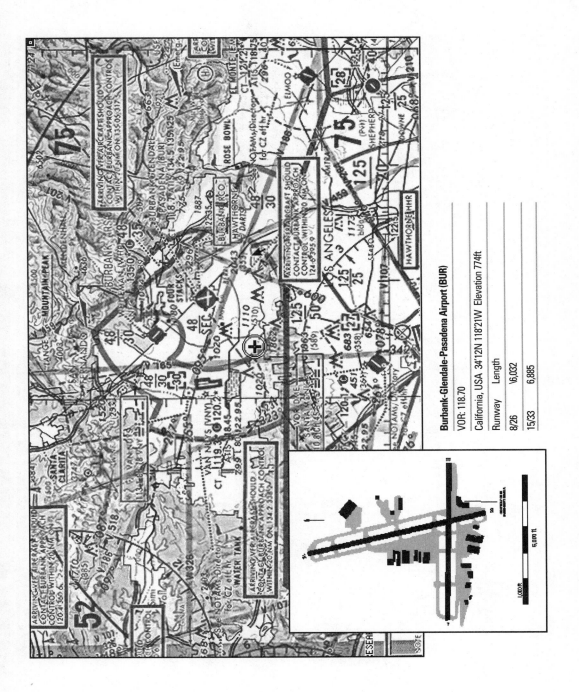

Burbank-Glendale-Pasadena Airport (BUR)

VOR: 118.70

California, USA 34°12N 118°21W Elevation 774ft

Runway	Length
8/26	6,032
15/33	6,885

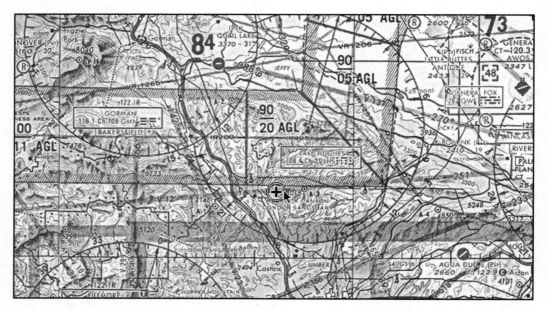

Lake Hughes/Bakersfield/Gorman.

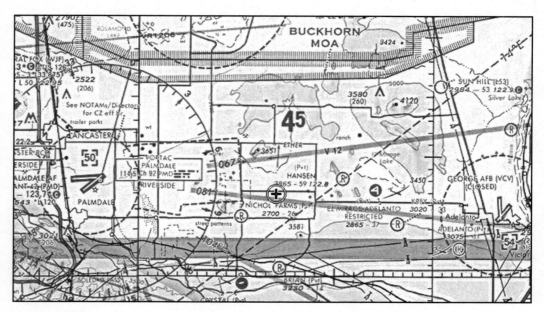

Palmdale/Lancaster, northeast of Los Angeles.

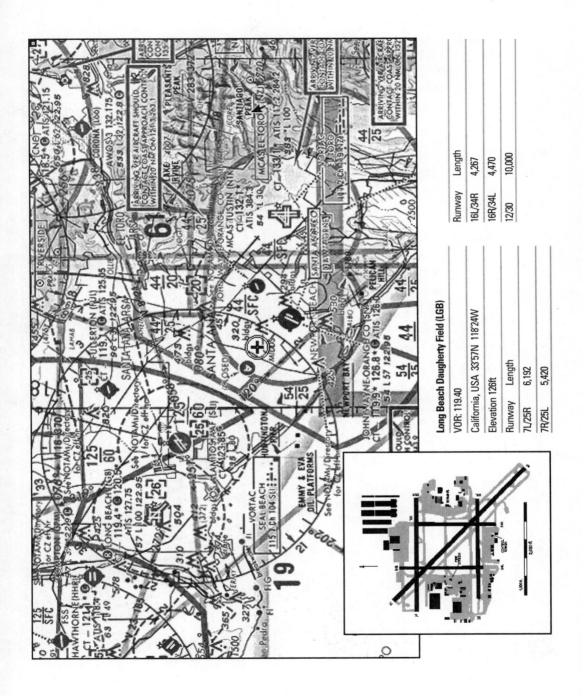

Long Beach Daugherty Field (LGB)

VOR: 119.40	
California, USA 33°57N 118°24W	
Elevation 126ft	

Runway	Length
7L/25R	6,192
7R/25L	5,420

Runway	Length
16L/34R	4,267
16R/34L	4,470
12/30	10,000

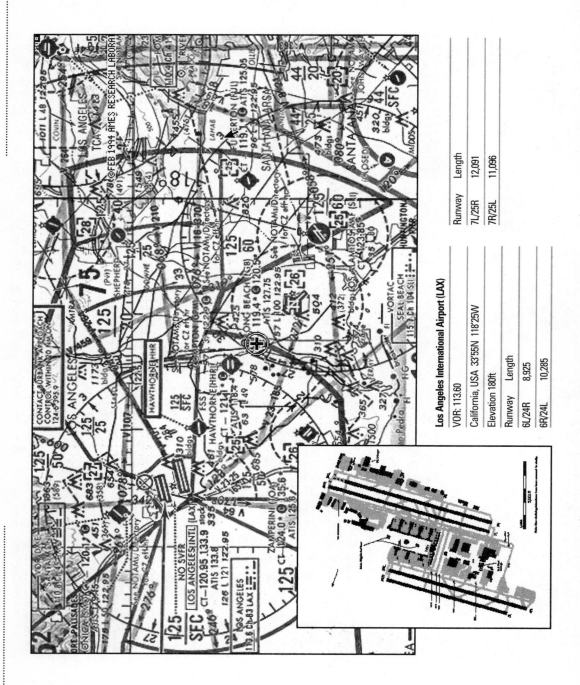

Los Angeles International Airport (LAX)

VOR: 113.60
California, USA 3355N 11825W
Elevation 180ft

Runway	Length
6L/24R	8,925
6R/24L	10,285

Runway	Length
7L/25R	12,091
7R/25L	11,096

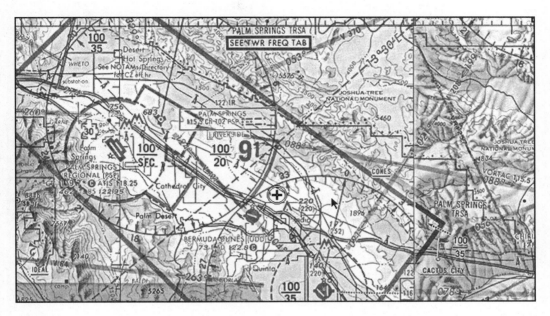

Palm Springs.

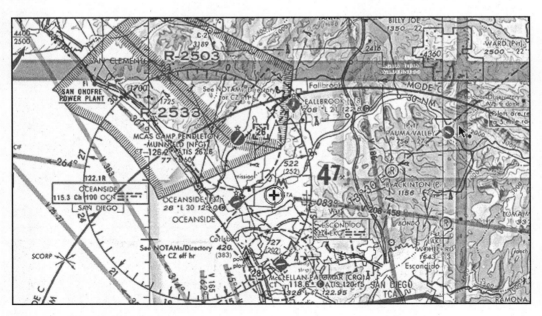

Camp Pendleton/San Clemente.

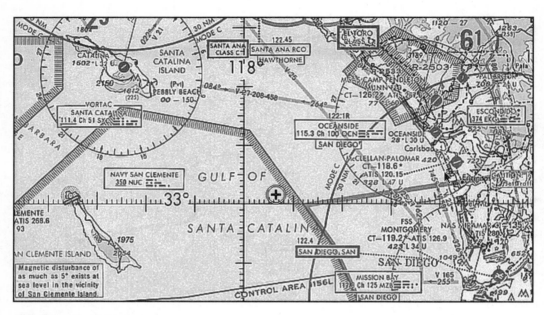

Santa Catalina Island.

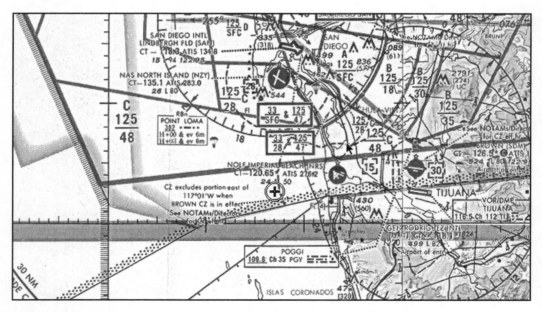

San Diego/Tijuana.

San Diego International Lindberg Field (SAN)

VOR: 118.30

California, USA 32°44N 117°10W

Elevation 30ft

Runway	Length
6/27	9,400

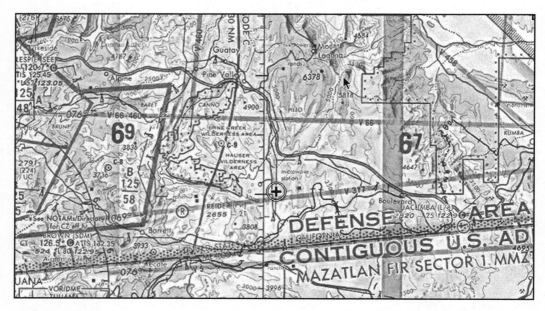

East of San Diego.

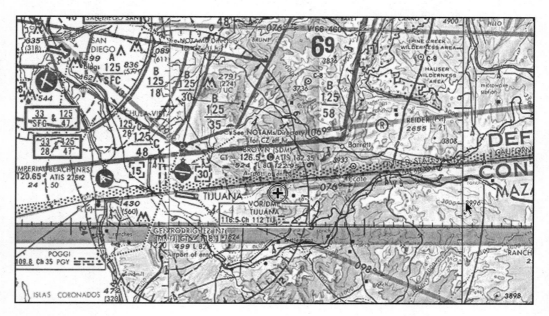

Tijuana.

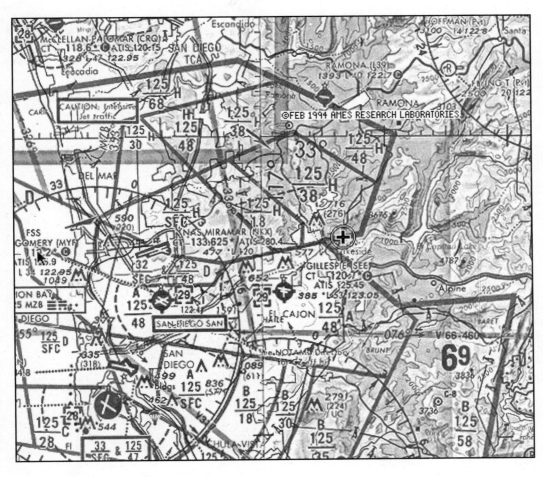

Detail of San Diego area and northeast.

WORLD VOR LISTINGS

The tables that follow list selected VOR stations throughout the world. The list is arranged by continent, and then within each continent by country. Identifier codes, the two or three letter codes unique to each airport, are included to aid in locating these stations on standard navigation charts. The latitude and longitude data are rounds off to the closest minute of degree.

Location/Name	Ident	Freq	Lat	Long
Africa				
Canary Islands				
Fuerteventura	FTV	114.10	N28°26'	W13°51'
Gran Canaria	GDV	112.90	N28°04'	W15°25'
Lanzarote	LT	113.70	N28°56'	W13°36'
Lanzarote	LZR	115.20	N29°09'	W13°30'
Tenerife	TFN	112.50	N28°32'	W16°16'
Tenerife-South	TFS	116.40	N28°00'	W16°41'
Egypt				
Cairo	CAI	112.50	N30°09'	E31°25'
Cairo	CVO	115.20	N30°05'	E31°23'
Fayoum	FYM	117.30	N29°25'	E30°21'
Kenya				
Anthi River	TV	115.50	S01°30'	E37°01'
Lodwar	LOV	114.50	N03°07'	E35°37'
Nairobi	NI	113.10	S01°17'	E36°57'
Nakuru	NAK	115.10	S00°18'	E36°09'
Ngong	GV	115.90	S01°23'	E36°38'

Location/Name	Ident	Freq	Lat	Long
Ivory Coast				
Abidjan	AD	114.30	N05°16'	W03°56'
Libya				
Djanet	DJA	114.10	N24°16'	E09°26'
Madagascar				
Antananarivo	TVN	114.50	S18°48'	E47°31'
Toamasina	MT	113.10	S18°07'	E49°23'
Morocco				
Casablanca	CBA	116.90	N33°31'	W07°40'
Casablanca-Mohamed	BRC	114.00	N33°17'	W07°33'
Rabat-Sale	RBT	116.50	N34°03'	W06°44'
Nigeria				
Cotonou	TYE	113.30	N06°21'	E02°23'
Ibadan	IB	112.10	N07°20'	E03°58'
Lagos	LG	113.70	N06°42'	E03°19'
Seychelles Islands				
Praslin	PRA	115.70	S04°18'	E55°42'
Seychelles	SEY	113.10	S04°40'	E55°32'

Location/Name	Ident	Freq	Lat	Long
South Africa				
Cape Town	CTV	115.70	S33°58'	E18°36'
Grasmere	GAV	115.50	S26°30'	E27°40'
Hartebeespoortdam	HBV	112.10	S25°40'	E27°50'
Heidelberg	HGV	116.70	S26°41'	E28°17'
Jan Smuts	JSV	115.20	S26°09'	E28°13'
Lanseria	LAV	114.50	S25°56'	E27°55'
Witbank	WIV	113.30	S25°49'	E29°11'
Sudan				
Khartoum	KTM	112.10	N15°35'	E32°33'
Merowe	MRW	116.00	N18°24'	E31°49'
Zaire				
Brazzaville	BZ	113.10	S04°14'	E15°15'
Kinshasa	KSA	115.00	S04°24'	E15°25'
Zimbabwe				
Fydle	VFY	114.90	S18°10'	E29°59'
Harare	VSB	113.10	S17°54'	E31°07'
Asia				
Hong Kong				
Cheung Chau	CH	112.30	N22°13'	E114°01'
Tathong Point	TH	115.50	N22°14'	E114°17'
Tung Lung	TD	116.10	N22°15'	E114°17'
India				
Aurangabad	AAU	116.30	N19°51'	E75°23'
Bombay	BBB	116.60	N19°05'	E72°52'
Calcutta	CEA	112.50	N22°38'	E88°27'
Daman	DMN	113.30	N20°26'	E72°51'
Jamshedpur	JJS	115.40	N22°48'	E86°10'
Rajshahi	RAJ	114.60	N24°26'	E88°37'
Japan				
Ami	TLE	116.00	N36°01'	E140°12'
Choshi	CVC	113.60	N35°43'	E140°48'
Hammatsu	LHE	110.00	N34°44'	E137°41'
Haneda	HME	109.40	N35°32'	E139°46'

Location/Name	Ident	Freq	Lat	Long
Japan, continued				
Kisarazu	KZE	114.50	N35°23'	E139°54'
Kohtoh	KWE	115.00	N35°36'	E139°49'
Kushiro	KSE	112.50	N43°01'	E144°12'
Memanbetsu	TBE	110.85	N43°52'	E144°10'
Monbetsu	MVE	110.00	N44°15'	E143°31'
Moriya	SNE	114.00	N35°55'	E139°59'
Nakashibetsu	NSE	115.60	N43°34'	E144°57'
Obihiro	OBE	109.65	N42°43'	E143°13'
Onjuku	OJC	115.70	N35°10'	E140°22'
Sakuri	TYE	112.70	N35°46'	E140°16'
Sekiyado	SYE	117.00	N36°00'	E139°50'
Tateyama	PQE	112.50	N34°56'	E139°53'
Yokosuka	HYE	116.20	N35°15'	E139°35'
Korea				
Anyang	SEL	115.10	N37°24'	E126°55'
Kimpo	KIP	113.60	N37°33'	E126°47'
Osan	OSN	114.70	N37°05'	E127°01'
Pyongtaek	PTK	108.20	N36°58'	E127°01'
Seoul	KSM	113.00	N37°26'	E127°06'
Indonesia				
Bali	BLI	116.20	S08°45'	E115°09'
Maldives				
Male	MLE	114.70	N04°11'	E73°32'
Pakistan				
Karachi	KC	112.10	N24°54'	E67°10'
Nawabshah	NH	112.90	N26°13'	E68°23'
Phillipines				
Cabanatuan	CAB	112.70	N15°27'	E120°58'
Jomalig	JOM	116.70	N14°43'	E122°24'
Lipa	LIP	115.10	N13°57'	E121°07'
Manila	MIA	113.80	N14°30'	E121°01'
Russia				
Bratsk	BRT	113.60	N56°22'	E101°41'
Sheremetyevo	MR	114.60	N55°57'	E37°20'

Location/Name	Ident	Freq	Lat	Long
Singapore				
Batum	BTM	116.00	N01°08′	E104°07′
Johor Bahru	VJR	112.70	N01°43′	E103°37′
Papa Uniform	PU	115.10	N01°25′	E103°56′
Sinjon	SJ	113.50	N01°13′	E103°51′
Tekong	VTK	116.50	N01°24′	E104°01′
Sri Lanka				
Batticaloa	BAT	114.60	N07°42′	E81°40′
Columbo Katunayake				
	KAT	112.70	N07°09′	E79°52′
Columbo Ratmalana	RML	116.70	N06°49′	E79°53′
Taiwan				
Green I	GID	116.90	N22°40′	E121°28′
Hengchun	HCN	113.70	N21°55′	E120°50′
Shikang	TNN	113.30	N23°08′	E120°11′
Thailand				
Bangkok	BKK	115.90	N13°59′	E100°39′
Korat	KRT	113.70	N14°55′	E102°07′
U-Taphao	BUT	110.80	N12°39′	E101°00′

Australia

Location/Name	Ident	Freq	Lat	Long
Australia				
Alice Springs	AS	115.90	S23°47′	E133°52′
Avalon	AV	116.10	S38°03′	E144°27′
Ballidu	BIU	114.30	S30°35′	E116°46′
Bindook	BIK	116.80	S34°10′	E150°06′
Brisbane	BN	113.20	S27°22′	E153°08′
Christmas Island	XMX	112.40	S10°25′	E105°41′
Coolangatta	CG	112.30	S28°10′	E153°30′
Cowes	CWS	117.60	S38°30′	E145°12′
Darwin	DN	112.40	S12°24′	E130°51′
Darwin	DAR	113.70	S12°24′	E130°52′
Eildon Weir	ELW	112.30	S37°12′	E145°50′
Fentons Hill	FTH	115.30	S37°30′	E144°48′

Location/Name	Ident	Freq	Lat	Long
Australia, continued				
Jacobs Well	JCW	116.50	S27°45′	E153°20′
Laravale	LAV	117.80	S28°05′	E152°55′
Maroochydore	MC	114.20	S26°36′	E153°05′
Melbourne	ML	114.10	S37°39′	E144°50′
Mt Mcquoid	MQD	117.30	S33°06′	E151°08′
Perth	PH	113.70	S31°56′	E115°57′
Sydney	SY	115.40	S33°56′	E151°10′
Tennant Creek	TNK	112.90	S19°38′	E134°10′
West Maitland	WMD	114.60	S32°45′	E151°31′
Wonthaggi	WON	115.90	S38°28′	E145°37′
Yarrowee	YWE	114.30	S37°44′	E143°45′
Fiji Island				
Nadi	NN	112.50	S17°39′	E177°23′
Nausori	NA	112.20	S18°02′	E178°33′
Guam				
Nimitz	UNZ	115.30	N13°27′	E144°43′
Johnston Island				
Johnston Island	JON	111.80	N16°44′	W169°32′
New Zealand				
Auckland	AA	114.80	S37°00′	E174°48′
Hamilton	HN	113.30	S37°51′	E175°19′
Invercargill	NV	112.90	S46°24′	E168°19′
Palmerston North	PM	113.40	S40°19′	E175°36′
Slope Hill	SH	113.60	S44°59′	E168°47′
Tory	TR	114.60	S41°11′	E174°21′
Wellington	WN	112.30	S41°20′	E174°49′
Whenuapai	WP	108.80	S36°47′	E174°37′
Papua New Guinea				
Girua	GUA	116.50	S08°44′	E148°15′
Port Moresby	PY	117.00	S09°27′	E147°12′
Wake Island				
Wake Island	AWK	113.50	N19°17′	E166°37′

Location/Name	Ident	Freq	Lat	Long
Central America				
Antigua				
V C Bird	ANU	114.50	N17°07'	W61°47'
Aruba				
Aruba	ABA	112.50	N12°30'	W69°56'
Bahamas				
Bimini	ZBV	116.70	N25°42'	W79°17'
Eleuthera I	ZGV	112.50	N25°15'	W76°18'
Nassau	ZQA	112.70	N25°01'	W77°27'
Treasure Cay	ZTC	112.90	N26°44'	W77°22'
Barbados				
Adams	BGI	112.70	N13°04'	W59°29'
Belize				
Belize	BZE	114.30	N17°32'	W08°18'
Bermuda				
Bermuda	BDA	113.90	N32°21'	W64°41'
Cayman Islands				
France	FTD	109.00	N09°21'	W79°51'
Cuba				
Manzanillo	UMZ	116.00	N20°18'	W77°06'
Navy Guantanamo Bay	NBW	114.60	N19°54'	W75°11'
Nuevas	UNV	116.30	N21°23'	W77°13'
Santiago De Cuba	UCU	113.30	N20°04'	W75°09'
Costa Rica				
El Coco	TIO	115.70	N09°59'	W84°14'
Liberia	LIB	112.80	N10°35'	W85°32'
Limon	LIO	116.30	N09°57'	W83°01'
Dominican Republic				
Cabo Rojo	CRO	114.30	N17°56'	W71°38'
Puerto Plata	PTA	115.10	N19°45'	W70°34'
Punta Cana	PNA	112.70	N18°33'	W68°21'
Punta Caucedo	CDO	114.70	N18°25'	W69°40'

Location/Name	Ident	Freq	Lat	Long
El Salvador				
El Salvador	CAT	117.50	N13°26'	W89°02'
Ilopango	YSV	114.70	N13°41'	W89°07'
La Aurora	AUR	114.50	N14°35'	W90°31'
La Mesa	LMS	113.10	N15°28'	W87°54'
Guadeloupe				
Pointe A Pitre	PPR	115.10	N16°16'	W61°30'
Guatemala				
La Aurora	AUR	114.50	N14°35'	W90°31'
Rabinal	RAB	116.10	N15°00'	W90°28'
San Jose	SJO	114.10	N13°56'	W90°51'
Haiti				
Cap Haitien	HCN	113.90	N19°43'	W72°11'
Obleon	OBN	113.20	N18°26'	W72°16'
Port Au Prince	PAP	115.30	N18°34'	W72°18'
Jamacia				
Kingston	KIN	115.90	N17°58'	W16°53'
Montego Bay	MBJ	115.70	N18°29'	W77°55'
Martinique				
Fort De France	FOF	113.30	N14°35'	W60°59'
Mexico				
Apan	APN	114.80	N19°38'	W98°23'
Chihuahua	CUU	114.10	N28°48'	W105°57'
Ciudad Juarez	CJS	116.70	N31°38'	W106°25'
Colima	COL	117.70	N19°16'	W103°34'
Cozumel	CZM	112.60	N20°28'	W86°57'
Cuautla	CUA	116.30	N18°47'	W98°54'
Del Norte	ADN	115.40	N25°51'	W100°14'
Del Norte	ADN	115.40	N25°51'	W100°14'
Guadalajara	GDL	117.30	N20°31'	W103°18'
Hermosillo	HMO	112.80	N29°05'	W111°02'
Lucia	SLM	116.60	N19°44'	W99°01'
Manzanillo	ZLO	116.80	N19°09'	W104°34'

Location/Name	Ident	Freq	Lat	Long
Mexico, continued				
Matamoros	MAM	114.30	N25°46'	W97°31'
Mateo	SMO	112.10	N19°33'	W99°13'
Merida	MID	117.70	N20°54'	W89°38'
Mexico City	MEX	115.60	N19°26'	W99°04'
Monterrey	MTY	114.70	N25°46'	W100°06'
Nautla	NAU	112.30	N20°11'	W96°44'
Nuevo Laredo	NLD	112.60	N27°26'	W99°33'
Otumba	OTU	115.00	N19°41'	W98°46'
Pachuca	PCA	112.70	N20°07'	W98°41'
Pasteje	PTJ	114.50	N19°38'	W99°47'
Poza Rica	PAZ	111.50	N20°36'	W97°28'
Puebla	PBC	115.20	N19°09'	W98°22'
Reynosa	REX	112.40	N26°00'	W98°13'
Tampico	TAM	117.50	N22°17'	W97°51'
Tequis	TEQ	113.10	N18°41'	W99°15'
Tijuana	TIJ	116.50	N32°32'	W116°57'
Toluca	TLC	114.30	N19°21'	W99°34'
Uruapan	UPN	114.20	N19°23'	W102°02'
Zihuatanejo	ZIH	113.80	N17°36'	W101°28'
Netherland Antilles				
Curacao	PJG	116.70	N12°12'	W69°00'
St Maarten	PJM	113.00	N18°02'	W63°07'
Panama				
David	DAV	114.30	N08°23'	W82°26'
France	FTD	109.00	N09°21'	W79°51'
Santiago	STG	114.50	N08°05'	W80°56'
Taboga Island	TBG	110.00	N08°47'	W79°33'
Tocumen	TUM	117.10	N09°03'	W79°24'
Puerto Rico				
Borinquen	BQN	113.50	N18°29'	W67°06'
Mayaguez	MAZ	110.60	N18°15'	W67°09'
Ponce	PSE	109.00	N17°59'	W66°31'
San Juan	SJU	114.00	N18°26'	W65°59'
Trinidad				
Piarco	POS	116.90	N10°27'	W61°23'

Location/Name	Ident	Freq	Lat	Long
Turks Islands				
Grand Turk	GTK	114.20	N21°26'	W71°08'
Virgin Islands				
St Croix	COY	108.20	N17°44'	W64°42'
St Thomas	STT	108.60	N18°21'	W65°01'
Canada				
Alberta				
Calgary	YYC	116.70	N51°06'	W113°52'
Edmonton	VEG	117.60	N53°11'	W113°52'
Empress	YEA	115.90	N50°55'	W109°59'
Grande Prairie	YQU	113.10	N55°10'	W119°01'
High Level	YOJ	113.30	N58°33'	W117°05'
Lethbridge	YQL	115.70	N49°38'	W112°40'
Medicine Hat	YXH	116.50	N49°57'	W110°48'
Peace River	YPE	117.20	N56°12'	W117°30'
Rocky Mountain	YRM	114.30	N52°30'	W115°19'
Spring Bank	YBW	108.60	N51°06'	W114°22'
Wainwright	YWV	114.50	N52°58'	W110°50'
Whitecourt	YZU	112.50	N54°08'	W115°47'
British Columbia				
Cranbrook	YXC	112.10	N49°33'	W116°05'
Enderby	YNY	115.20	N50°40'	W118°56'
Fort Nelson	YYE	112.90	N58°53'	W123°00'
Fort Saint John	YXJ	114.20	N56°17'	W120°53'
Port Hardy	YZT	112.00	N50°41'	W127°21'
Prince George	YXS	112.30	N53°53'	W122°27'
Princeton	YDC	113.90	N49°22'	W120°22
Sandspit	YZP	114.10	N53°15'	W131°48'
Vancouver	YVR	115.90	N49°04'	W123°09'
Victoria	YYJ	113.70	N48°43'	W123°29'
Williams Lake	YWL	113.60	N52°14'	W122°10'
Manitoba				
Brandon	YBR	113.80	N49°54'	W99°56'
Churchill	YYQ	114.10	N58°44'	W94°08'
Dauphin	YDN	116.10	N51°06'	W100°03'

Location/Name	Ident	Freq	Lat	Long
Manitoba, continued				
Langruth	VLR	112.20	N50°25'	W98°43'
Lynn Lake	YYL	112.60	N56°51'	W101°04'
Portage	YPG	114.60	N49°53'	W98°16'
The Pas	YQD	113.60	N53°58'	W101°06'
Winnipeg	YWG	115.50	N49°55'	W97°14'
Northwest Territories				
Baker Lake	YBK	114.50	N64°19'	W96°06'
Cambridge Bay	YCB	112.70	N69°07'	W105°10'
Fort Good Hope	YGH	112.30	N66°14'	W128°37'
Fort Simpson	YFS	117.90	N61°46'	W121°17'
Hall Beach	YUX	117.30	N68°46'	W81°14'
Norman Wells	YVQ	112.70	N65°15'	W126°43'
Wrigley	YWY	113.10	N63°11'	W123°21'
Yellowknife	YZF	115.50	N62°27'	W114°26'
New Bruswick				
Fredericton	YFC	113.00	N45°53'	W66°25'
Moncton	YQM	117.30	N46°11'	W64°34'
Saint John	YSJ	113.50	N45°24'	W65°52'
Newfoundland				
Deer Lake	YDF	113.30	N49°14'	W57°12'
Gander	YQX	112.70	N48°54'	W54°32'
Goose	YYR	117.30	N53°19'	W60°17'
St Johns	UYT	108.60	N47°37'	W52°44'
Stephenville	YJT	113.10	N48°34'	W58°40'
Torbay	YYT	113.50	N47°29'	W52°51'
Nova Scotia				
Halifax	YHZ	115.10	N44°55'	W63°24'
Sydney	YQY	114.90	N46°09'	W60°03'
Ontario				
Ameson	YAN	112.40	N49°46'	W84°35'
Coehill	VIE	115.10	N44°39'	W77°53'
Geraldton	YGQ	114.20	N49°46'	W86°59'
Killaloe	YXI	115.60	N45°39'	W77°36'
London	YXU	117.20	N43°02'	W81°08

Location/Name	Ident	Freq	Lat	Long
Ontario, continued				
Mans	YMS	114.50	N44°08'	W80°08'
Marathon	YSP	115.90	N48°44'	W86°19'
Midland	YEE	112.80	N44°34'	W79°47'
Moosenee	YMO	112.90	N51°17'	W80°36'
North Bay	YYB	115.40	N46°21'	W79°26'
Ottawa	YOW	114.60	N45°26'	W75°53'
Red Lake	YRL	114.00	N51°04'	W93°45'
Simcoe	YSO	117.35	N44°14'	W79°10'
Sioux Narrows	VBI	115.20	N49°28'	W94°02'
Stirling	VQC	113.50	N44°23'	W77°43'
Sudbury	YSB	112.30	N46°37'	W80°47'
Thunder Bay	YQT	114.10	N48°15'	W89°26'
Timmins	YTS	113.00	N48°34'	W81°22'
Toronto	YYZ	113.30	N43°40'	W79°38'
Waterloo	YWT	115.00	N43°27'	W80°22'
Wawa	YXZ	112.70	N47°57'	W84°49'
Wiarton	YVV	117.70	N44°44'	W81°06'
Windsor	YQG	113.80	N42°14'	W82°49'
Prince Edward Island				
Charlottetown	YYG	114.10	N46°12'	W62°58'
Quebec				
Bagotville	XBG	111.80	N48°19'	W70°59'
Baie-Comeau	YBC	117.70	N49°08'	W68°13'
Beauce	VLV	117.20	N45°55'	W70°50'
Gaspe	YGP	115.40	N48°45'	W64°24'
Grindstone	YGR	112.00	N47°25'	W61°46'
Mirabel	YMX	116.70	N45°53'	W74°22'
Mont Joli	YYY	115.90	N48°36'	W68°12'
Montreal	YUL	116.30	N45°36'	W73°58'
Quebec	YQB	112.80	N46°42'	W71°37'
Riviere Du Loup	YRI	113.90	N47°45'	W69°35'
Saguenay	VBS	114.20	N48°01'	W71°15'
Sept-Iles	YZV	114.50	N50°13'	W66°16'
Sherbrooke	YSC	113.20	N45°18'	W71°47'

Location/Name	Ident	Freq	Lat	Long
Quebec, continued				
St Jean	YJN	115.80	N45°15'	W73°19'
Val-D'or	YVO	113.70	N48°10'	W77°49'
Saskatchewan				
Broadview	YDR	117.50	N50°21'	W102°32'
Lumsden	VLN	114.20	N50°40'	W104°53'
Prince Albert	YPA	113.00	N53°12'	W105°39'
Saskatoon	YXE	116.20	N52°10'	W106°43'
Swift Current	YYN	117.40	N50°17'	W107°41'
Yorkton	YQV	115.80	N51°15'	W102°28'
Yukon Territory				
Watson Lake	YQH	114.90	N60°05'	W128°51'
Whitehorse	YXY	116.60	N60°37'	W135°08'

Europe

Location/Name	Ident	Freq	Lat	Long
Austria				
Eurach	EUR	115.20	N47°44'	E11°15'
Fischamend	FMD	110.40	N48°06'	E16°37'
Kempten	KPT	109.60	N47°44'	E10°21'
Linz	LNZ	116.60	N48°13'	E14°06'
Munich	MUN	112.30	N48°10'	E11°49'
Roding	RDG	114.70	N49°02'	E12°31'
Salzburg	SBG	113.80	N48°00'	E12°53'
Souenau	SNU	115.50	N47°52'	E16°17'
Stockerau	STO	113.00	N48°25'	E16°01'
Villach	VIW	112.90	N46°41'	E13°54'
Wagram	WGM	112.20	N48°19'	E16°29'
Belgium				
Affligem	AFI	114.90	N50°54'	E4°08'
Bruno	BUN	110.60	N51°04'	E4°46'
Brussels	BUB	114.60	N50°54'	E4°32'
Chievers	CIV	113.20	N50°34'	E3°49'
Costa	COA	111.80	N51°20'	E3°21'
Diekirch	DIK	114.40	N49°51'	E6°07'
Haamstede	HSD	115.50	N51°43'	E3°51'

Location/Name	Ident	Freq	Lat	Long
Belgium, continued				
Huldenberg	HUL	117.55	N50°45'	E4°38'
Koksy	KOK	114.50	N51°05'	E2°39'
Luxembourg	DIK	114.40	N49°51'	E6°07'
Nicky	NIK	117.40	N51°10'	E4°11'
Olno	LNO	112.80	N50°35'	E5°42'
Spirmont	SPI	113.10	N50°30'	E5°37'
Czech Republic				
Cheb	OKG	115.70	N50°03'	E12°24'
Hermsdorf	HDO	115.00	N50°55'	E14°22'
Neratovice	NER	108.60	N50°18'	E14°23'
Prague	OKL	112.60	N50°06'	E14°13'
Roudnice	RCE	117.60	N50°27'	E14°12'
Vlasim	VLM	114.30	N49°42'	E15°04'
Vozice	VOZ	116.30	N49°32'	E14°52'
Denmark				
Alma	ALM	116.40	N55°24'	E13°33'
Astor	AOR	113.90	N56°07'	E12°57'
Codan	CDA	114.90	N55°00'	E12°22'
Kastrup	KAS	112.50	N55°35'	E12°36'
Korsa	KOR	112.80	N55°26'	E11°38'
Nora	NOA	112.60	N56°06'	E12°14'
Odin	ODN	115.50	N55°34'	E10°39'
Sevda	SVD	116.20	N56°10'	E12°34'
Sturup	SUP	113.00	N55°32'	E13°22'
Trano	TNO	117.40	N55°46'	E11°26'
Finland				
Anton	ANT	113.70	N60°51'	E25°07'
Helsinki	HEL	114.20	N60°20'	E24°57'
Utti	UTT	114.60	N60°53'	E26°56'
Vihti	VTI	117.00	N60°27'	E24°14'
France				
Abberville	ABB	116.60	N50°08'	E1°51'
Amboise	AMB	113.70	N47°25'	E1°03'
Angers	ANG	113.00	N47°32'	W00°51'

Location/Name	Ident	Freq	Lat	Long
France, continued				
Beauvais	BVS	115.90	N49°26'	E2°09'
Boursonne	BSN	112.50	N49°11'	E3°03'
Bray	BRY	114.10	N48°24'	E3°17'
Caen	CAN	115.40	N49°10'	W00°27'
Cambrai	CMB	112.60	N50°13'	E3°09'
Charles-De-Gaulle (Paris)				
	CGN	115.35	N49°01'	E2°30'
Charles-De-Gaulle (Paris)				
	PGS	117.05	N49°00'	E2°37'
Chartres	CHW	115.20	N48°28'	E00°59'
Chateaudun	CDN	116.10	N48°03'	E1°23'
Chatillon	CTL	117.60	N49°08'	E3°34'
Coulommiers	CLM	112.90	N48°50'	E3°00'
Creil	CRL	109.20	N49°15'	E2°31'
Deauville	DVL	110.20	N49°18'	E00°18'
Dieppe	DPE	115.80	N49°55'	E1°10'
Dijion	DIJ	113.50	N47°16'	E5°05'
Dijion	DIJ	113.50	N47°16'	E5°05'
Epernon	EPR	115.65	N48°37'	E1°39'
Evreux	EVX	112.40	N49°01'	E1°13'
L'aigle	LGL	115.00	N48°47'	E00°32'
Le Bourget (Paris)	BT	108.80	N48°58'	E2°27'
Melun	MEL	109.80	N48°27'	E2°48'
Montdidier	MTD	113.65	N49°33'	E2°29'
Moulins	MOU	116.70	N46°42'	E3°38'
Nevers	NEV	113.40	N47°09'	E2°55'
Orly (Paris)	OL	111.20	N48°43'	E2°23'
Pithiviers	PTV	116.50	N48°09'	E2°15'
Pontoise	PON	111.60	N49°05'	E2°02'
Rambouillet	RBT	114.70	N48°39'	E1°59'
Reims	REM	112.30	N49°18'	E4°02'
Rolampont	RLP	117.30	N47°54'	E5°15'
Rouen	ROU	116.80	N49°27'	E1°16'
Toussus	TSU	108.25	N48°45'	E2°06'

Location/Name	Ident	Freq	Lat	Long
France, continued				
Troyes	TRO	116.00	N48°15'	E3°57'
Allersberg	ALB	111.20	N49°12'	E11°13'
Alsie	ALS	114.70	N54°54'	E9°59'
Alster	ALF	115.80	N53°38'	E9°59'
Ausburg	AUG	115.90	N48°25'	E10°56'
Brunkendorf	BKD	117.70	N53°02'	E11°32'
Dinkelsbuhl	DKB	117.80	N49°08'	E10°14'
Elbe	LBE	115.10	N52°39'	E9°35'
Erding	ERD	113.60	N48°19'	E11°57'
Erlangen	ERL	114.90	N49°39'	E11°09'
Eurach	EUR	115.20	N47°44'	E11°15'
Hamburg	HAM	113.10	N53°41'	E10°12'
Hehlingen	HLZ	117.30	N52°21'	E10°47'
Helgoland	DHE	116.30	N54°11'	E7°54'
Karlspuhe	KRH	115.95	N48°59'	E8°35'
Kempten	KPT	109.60	N47°44'	E10°21'
Klagenfurt	KFT	113.10	N46°35'	E14°33'
Leine	DLE	115.20	N52°15'	E9°53'
Germany				
Lubeck	LUB	110.60	N53°56'	E10°40'
Luburg	LBU	109.20	N48°54'	E9°20'
Maisach	MAH	108.40	N48°15'	E11°18'
Michaelsdorf	MIC	112.10	N54°18'	E11°00'
Milldorf	MDF	117.00	N48°14'	E12°20'
Moosburg	MBG	117.15	N48°34'	E12°15'
Munich	MUN	112.30	N48°10'	E11°49'
Munich	DMN	116.00	N48°22'	E11°47'
Munich	DMS	108.60	N48°20'	E11°46'
Nienburg	NIE	116.50	N52°37'	E9°22'
Roding	RDG	114.70	N49°02'	E12°31'
Tango	TGO	112.50	N48°37'	E9°15'
Transasdingen	TRA	114.30	N47°41'	E8°26'
Villach	VIW	112.90	N46°41'	E13°54'

Location/Name	Ident	Freq	Lat	Long
Germany, continued				
Walda	WLD	112.80	N48°34'	E11°07'
Warburg	WRB	113.70	N51°30'	E9°06'
Weser	WSR	112.90	N53°21'	E8°52'
Wurzburg	WUR	116.35	N49°43'	E9°56'
Zurich	ZUE	110.50	N47°35'	E8°49'
Greece				
Athens	ATH	114.40	N37°54'	E23°43'
Didimon	DDM	117.20	N37°28'	E23°13'
Kea	KEA	115.00	N37°33'	E24°18'
Milos	MIL	113.50	N36°44'	E24°31'
Tripolis	TRL	116.20	N37°24'	E22°20'
Hungary				
Gyor	GYR	115.10	N47°39'	E17°43'
Iceland				
Ingo	ING	112.40	N63°48'	W16°38'
Keflavik	KEF	112.00	N63°59'	W2°36'
Ireland				
Baldonnel	BAL	115.80	N53°18'	W6°26'
Connaught	CON	117.40	N53°54'	W8°49'
Dublin	DUB	114.90	N53°30'	W6°18'
Isle Of Man	IOM	112.20	N54°04'	W4°45'
Shannon	SHA	113.30	N52°43'	W8°53'
Italy				
Ajaccio	AJO	114.80	N41°46'	E8°46'
Alghero	ALG	113.80	N40°27'	E8°14'
Bastia	BTA	114.15	N42°34'	E9°28'
Bolsena	BOL	114.40	N42°37'	E12°02'
Campagnano	CMP	111.40	N42°07'	E12°22'
Carbonara	CAR	115.10	N39°06'	E9°30'
Elba	ELB	114.70	N42°43'	E10°23'
Ostia	OST	114.90	N41°48'	E12°14'
Pescara	PES	115.90	N42°26'	E14°11'
Pisa	PIS	112.10	N43°40'	E10°23'
Ponza	PNZ	114.60	N40°54'	E12°57'

Location/Name	Ident	Freq	Lat	Long
Italy, continued				
Sorrento	SOR	112.20	N40°34'	E14°20'
Tarquinia	TAQ	111.80	N42°12'	E11°44'
Teano	TEA	112.90	N41°17'	E13°58'
Norway				
Flesland	FLE	114.50	N60°18'	E5°12'
Vollo	VOO	114.85	N60°32'	E5°07'
Poland				
Karnice	KRN	117.80	N51°56'	E20°26'
Lodz	LDZ	112.40	N51°48'	E19°39'
Piaseczno	PNO	112.90	N52°03'	E21°03'
Siedlce	SIE	114.70	N52°09'	E22°12'
Warsaw	OKE	113.40	N52°10'	E20°57'
Zaborowek	WAR	114.90	N52°15'	E20°39'
Portugal				
Beja	BEJ	115.80	N38°07'	W7°55'
Espichel	ESP	112.50	N38°25'	W9°11'
Fatima	FTM	113.50	N39°39'	W8°29'
Lisbon	LIS	114.80	N38°53'	W9°09'
Sintra	SRA	112.10	N38°49'	W9°20'
Spain				
Bagur	BGR	112.20	N41°56'	E3°12'
Barahona	BAN	112.80	N41°19'	W2°37'
Barcelona	QUV	114.30	N41°17'	E2°05'
Campo Real	CPL	114.50	N40°19'	W3°22'
Castejon	CJN	115.60	N40°22'	W2°32'
Colmenar Viejo	CNR	117.30	N40°38'	W3°44'
Domingo	DGO	112.60	N42°27'	W2°52'
Maella	MLA	112.10	N41°07'	E00°10'
Reus	RES	114.20	N41°09'	E1°10'
Toledo	TLD	113.20	N39°58'	W4°20'
Torrejon	TJZ	115.10	N40°28'	W3°28'
Villatobas	VTB	112.70	N39°46'	W3°27'

Location/Name	Ident	Freq	Lat	Long
Sweden				
Mantor	MNT	114.00	N58°23'	E15°17'
Trosa	TRS	114.30	N58°56'	E17°30'
Switzerland				
Chambery	CBY	115.40	N45°53'	E5°45'
Epinal	EPL	113.00	N48°19'	E6°03'
Fribourg	FRI	110.85	N46°46'	E7°13'
Geneva	GVA	114.60	N46°15'	E6°08'
Hochwald	HOC	113.20	N47°28'	E7°40'
Martigues	MTG	117.30	N43°23'	E5°05'
Nice	NIZ	112.40	N43°46'	E7°15'
Passeiry	PAS	116.60	N46°09'	E6°00'
Rolampont	RLP	117.30	N47°54'	E5°15'
Saronno	SRN	113.70	N45°38'	E9°01'
Satolas	LSA	114.75	N45°43'	E5°05'
St Prex	SPR	113.90	N46°28'	E6°26'
Tour Du Pin	TDP	110.60	N45°29'	E5°26'
United Kingdom				
Barkway	BKY	116.25	N51°59'	E00°03'
Biggin	BIG	115.10	N51°19'	E00°02'
Blackbushe	BLC	116.20	N51°19'	W00°50'
Boulogne	BNE	113.80	N50°37'	E1°54'
Bovingdon	BNN	113.75	N51°43'	W00°32'
Brookmans Park	BPK	117.50	N51°44'	W00°06'
Burnham	BUR	117.10	N51°31'	W00°40'
Clacton	CLN	114.55	N51°50'	E1°09'
Compton	CPT	114.35	N51°29'	W1°13'
Daventry	DTY	116.40	N52°10'	W1°06'
Deancross	DCS	115.20	N54°43'	W3°20'
Fairoaks	FRK	109.85	N51°20'	W00°33'
Glasgow	GOW	115.40	N55°52'	W4°26'
Lambourne	LAM	115.60	N51°38'	E00°09'
London	LON	113.60	N51°29'	W00°27'
Lydd	LYD	114.05	N50°59'	E00°52'

Location/Name	Ident	Freq	Lat	Long
United Kingdom, continued				
Manchester	MCT	113.55	N53°21'	W2°15'
Mayfield	MAY	117.90	N51°00'	E00°07'
Midhurst	MID	114.00	N51°03'	W00°37'
Ockham	OCK	115.30	N51°18'	W00°26'
Odiham	ODH	109.60	N51°13'	W00°56'
Perth	PTH	110.40	N56°26'	W3°22'
Pole Hill	POL	112.10	N53°44'	W2°06'
Saint Abbs	SAB	112.50	N55°54'	W2°12'
Seaford	SFD	117.00	N50°45'	E00°07'
Southampton	SAM	113.35	N50°57'	W1°20'
Talla	TLA	113.80	N55°30'	W3°21'
Turnberry	TRN	117.50	N55°18'	W4°47'

Middle East

Location/Name	Ident	Freq	Lat	Long
Israel				
Bengurion	BGN	115.40	N32°00'	E34°52'
Metzada	MZD	115.00	N31°19'	E35°23'
Natania	NAT	112.40	N32°20'	E34°58'
Kuwait				
Kuwait	KUA	115.50	N29°13'	E47°58'
Ras Al Mishab	RAS	116.40	N28°04'	E48°36'
Wafra	KFR	112.00	N28°37'	E47°57'
Saudi Arabia				
Al Ahsa	HSA	116.60	N25°16'	E49°29'
Al Kharj	AKJ	117.30	N24°04'	E47°24'
King Khalid	KIA	113.30	N24°53'	E46°45'
Magala	MGA	116.30	N26°13'	E47°16'
Riyadh	RIY	114.50	N24°43'	E46°43'
Thumamah	TIH	113.80	N25°09'	E46°33'
Turkey				
Beykoz	BKZ	117.30	N41°07'	E29°08'
Istanbul	IST	112.50	N40°58'	E28°48'
Tekirdag	EKI	116.30	N40°57'	E27°25'

Location/Name	Ident	Freq	Lat	Long
Turkey, continued				
Yalova	YAA	117.70	N40°34'	E29°22'
Yemen				
Aden	KRA	112.50	N12°49'	E45°01'
Taiz	TAZ	113.60	N13°42'	E44°08'
South America				
Argentina				
Ezeiza	EZE	116.50	S34°49'	W58°32'
General Belgrando	GBE	115.60	S35°45'	W58°27'
La Plata	PTA	113.70	S34°58'	W57°53'
Lobos	BOS	114.60	S35°12'	W59°08'
Moriano Moreno	ENO	112.90	S34°33'	W58°47'
San Fernando	FDO	114.40	S34°27'	W58°35'
Ascension Island				
Ascension Aux	ASI	112.20	S07°58'	W14°23'
Azores				
Lajes	LM	112.30	N38°47'	W27°06'
Lajes	LAJ	110.80	N38°42'	W27°07'
Santa Maria	VSM	113.70	N36°57'	W25°10'
Boliva				
Arica	ARI	116.50	S18°21'	W70°20'
Cochabamba	CBA	112.10	S17°25'	W66°10'
La Paz	PAZ	115.70	S16°30'	W68°13'
San Borja	BOR	117.50	S14°55'	W66°44'
Brazil				
Anapolis	ANP	115.40	S16°15'	W48°59'
Brasilia	BRS	115.90	S15°52'	W48°01'
Caxias	CAX	113.00	S22°46'	W43°20'
Goiania	GOI	112.70	S16°37'	W49°12'
Marica	MRC	114.00	S22°58'	W42°53'
Mossoro	MSS	112.40	S05°11'	W37°21'
Natal	NTL	114.30	S05°54'	W35°14'
Pirai	PAI	115.00	S22°27'	W43°50'
Porto	PCX	114.60	S22°42'	W42°51'
Santa Cruz	SCR	113.60	S22°57'	W43°43'

Location/Name	Ident	Freq	Lat	Long
Chile				
Los Cerrillos	SCL	112.30	S33°29'	W70°42'
Quintero	ERO	113.30	S32°47'	W71°30'
Santiago	AMB	116.10	S33°25'	W70°47'
Santo Domingo	SNO	113.70	S33°39'	W71°36'
Tabon	TBN	113.90	S32°55'	W70°50'
Columbia				
Bogota	BOG	114.70	N04°50'	W74°19'
Girardot	GIR	117.30	N04°11'	W74°52'
Mariquita	MQU	116.10	N05°12'	W74°55'
Villavicencio	VVC	116.70	N04°04'	W73°23'
Ecuador				
Ambato	AMV	112.70	S01°16'	W78°32'
Condorcocha	QIT	115.30	S00°02'	W78°30'
Ipiales	IPI	113.60	N00°51'	W77°40'
Monjas Sur	QMS	115.00	S00°13'	W78°28'
French Guiana				
Rochambeau	CYR	115.10	N04°48'	W52°22'
Parauay				
Asuncion	VAS	115.90	S25°08'	W57°29'
Formosa	FSA	115.60	S26°12'	W58°13'
Peru				
Asia	ASI	115.00	S12°45'	W76°36'
Chimbote	BTE	112.50	S09°08'	W78°31'
Lima	LIM	114.50	S12°00'	W77°07'
Pisco	SCO	114.10	S13°44'	W76°12'
Salinas	SLS	114.70	S11°17'	W77°34'

INTERNET RESOURCES

There's a strong, and very active, aviation community on the World Wide Web. In this section, we've tried to present many of the better resources available to interested and aspiring pilots and Flight Simulator users. This list, while broad, is not complete. We apologize if we've missed anyone that should have been included here.

An excellent resource for selected domestic US airport data is at http://asc-www.hq.faa.gov/welcome.html.

This site features one of the most user-friendly and accessible web interfaces we've found, and has a generous supply of well-designed downloadable data and software.

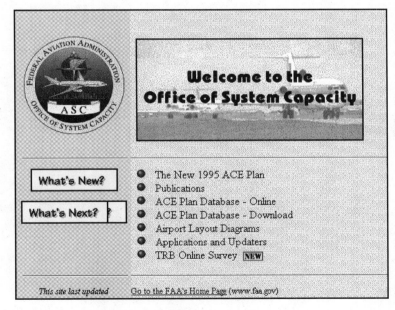

http://www.cc.gatech.edu/db1/fly/

Visits since Sep 18, 1995:
If this page doesn't look good on your screen or doesn't work, click HERE.

AirNav

the pilot's window into the world of aviation information

AirNav was updated with current data on August 31, 1996!
The current data set is what was published by the FAA as of 08/15/1996.

Now go ahead and send me that postcard, will you? Click Here

AirNav provides free access to FAA data on airports and navigational aids. We offer some fast database s
allowing the pilot to retrieve information which may assist in flight planning. It's also useful for some hangar flying
when the weather or the checkbook keep you on the ground.

The AirNav page is a relatively new site that's fly of useful flight data for real and simulated piloting.

http://www.cc.ga tech.edu/db1/fly/

Significant Obstructions within 10 nautical miles of the Airport

What	Where	ft MSL (AGL)
Building in San Diego	1.5 nm SE	497 (469)
Building in San Diego	1.5 nm SE	478 (448)
Building in San Diego	1.6 nm ENE	481 (180)
Building in San Diego	1.7 nm NE	494 (196)
Building in San Diego	1.8 nm SE	500 (485)
Building in San Diego	1.6 nm ESE	430 (359)

Getting ready to fly into San Diego? Paulo's page can help prepare you for the maze.

http://www.cc.gatech.edu/fly/cgi-bin/airport-info?id=lga

Radio aids to navigate to the Airport

VOR radial/distance	VOR name	Freq	Var
LGA at field	LA GUARDIA VOR/DME	113.10	12W
TEBr127/9.6	TETERBORO VOR/DME	108.40	11W
JFKr344/9.8	KENNEDY VORTAC	115.90	12W
CRIr017/9.9	CANARSIE VOR/DME	112.30	11W
DPKr280/25.9	DEER PARK VORTAC	117.70	12W
COLr036/30.9	COLTS NECK VOR/DME	115.40	11W
CMKr216/32.9	CARMEL VORTAC	116.60	12W
SAXr131/34.8	SPARTA VORTAC	115.70	11W

NDB name	Hdg/Dist	Freq	Var	ID	
PALISADES PARK	136/5.6	233	12W	PPK	.--. .--. -.-
CONDA	356/11.9	373	12W	JF	.--- ..-.
BRIDGE	014/12.6	414	12W	OGY	--- --. .--
PATERSON	141/16.2	347	12W	PNJ	.--. -. .---
BETHPAGE	285/19.4	248	12W	BPA	-... .--. .-
BABYLON	300/23.1	275	14W	BBN	-... -... -.
CHATHAM	096/25.4	254	11W	CAT	-.-. .- -

Need naviads for a particular US airport? Here's another nice feature of Paulo Santos' pages at Georgia Tech.

Another node on http://www.cc.gatech.edu/fly allows you to locate a specific navaid, complete with full FAA data for that location.

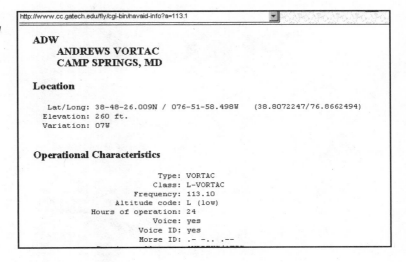

```
http://www.cc.gatech.edu/fly/cgi-bin/navaid-info?a=113.1

ADW
     ANDREWS VORTAC
     CAMP SPRINGS, MD

Location

   Lat/Long: 38-48-26.009N / 076-51-58.498W    (38.8072247/76.8662494)
   Elevation: 260 ft.
   Variation: 07W


Operational Characteristics

                 Type: VORTAC
                Class: L-VORTAC
            Frequency: 113.10
        Altitude code: L (low)
    Hours of operation: 24
                Voice: yes
             Voice ID: yes
             Morse ID: .- -.. .--
```

Landings is a good resource with numerous links to other aviation pages.

```
http://www.landings.com/aviation.html
```

LANDINGS   *Aviation's busiest cyber-hub*   www.landings.com

- Overview
- Search
- Directory
- Add Link
- Contact

- Flight Planning
- Pilot Training
- Hangar Talk
- Weather
- NEWS

- Companies
- What's New
- Market-Place
- Classifieds
- SITES

BECOME VISIBLE

Web Sites starting at $4.16/mo
graphics. Secure Order Forms.
Unlimited Updates.

Welcome To The Busiest Aviation Hub in Cyberspace

The Tiger mapping project through the Census Bureau won't generate nav aids for you, but can give you a bird's eye view of the neighborhood.

http://tiger.census.gov

```
http://www.microwings.com/mwaptnav.html
```

- To view information about an Apt/Nav/Fix, enter the facility's Identifier (ex. DFW for Dallas/Ft. Worth Int'l)
- To see a map of an area, enter the Lat/Lon coordinates for the area in the form of deg dec
- Click here to return to our home page

Airport identifier: [   ]   **Get Apt Info**

NavAid identifier: [   ]   **Get Nav Info**

Fix identifier: [   ]   **Get Fix Info**

Enter the lat/lon coordinates in decimal degrees (ex. for DFW, Lat:32.90, Lon: -97.05)...

Latitude: [41.46]   Longitude: [-73.52]   **Get Map (may take a few minutes)**

Microsoft
Flight Simulator
for Windows 95

Aerolink is an interesting
and news-filled page.

http://www.aerolink.com

One of the nice features
of flightdata is the
ability to search for
nearby airports.
*http://www.flightdata.co
m/avlink/airportsearch.h
tml*

Among the international web pages with good resource links is the Aviation Resource Center.

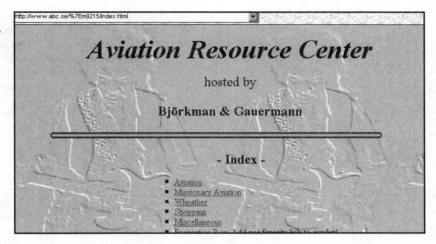

Aviation Resource Center

hosted by

Björkman & Gauermann

- Index -

- Aviation
- Missionary Aviation
- Wheather
- Shopping
- Miscellaneous

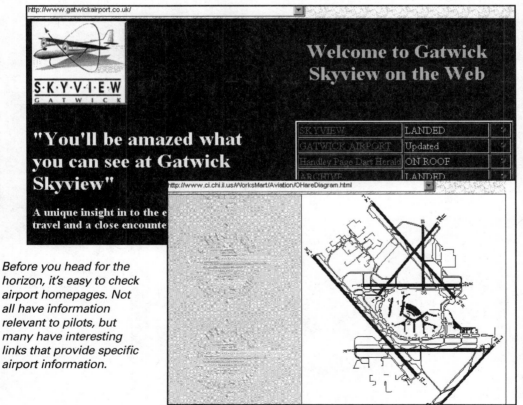

http://www.gatwickairport.co.uk/

S·K·Y·V·I·E·W
GATWICK

Welcome to Gatwick Skyview on the Web

"You'll be amazed what you can see at Gatwick Skyview"

A unique insight in to the e...
travel and a close encounte...

SKYVIEW	LANDED	
GATWICK AIRPORT	Updated	
Handley Page Dart Herald	ON ROOF	
ARCHIVE	LANDED	

http://www.ci.chi.il.us/WorksMart/Aviation/OHareDiagram.html

Before you head for the horizon, it's easy to check airport homepages. Not all have information relevant to pilots, but many have interesting links that provide specific airport information.

Microsoft

Flight Simulator

for Windows 95

http://macwww.db.erau.edu/www_virtual_lib/aviation.html

World Wide Web Virtual Library

Aviation

*This resource is used by over **30,000 people** each month.*

These pages maintained by *Embry-Riddle Aeronautical University*
and are current as of Tuesday, 03-Sep-96 22:32:47.

➤ **Universities**, specializing in Aviation ed

➤ **Aircraft**, aircraft home pages, manufac

➤ **Airlines, online reservations, etc.**

Among the general reference web sites, here are some of our favorites:
http://macwww.db.erau.edu/www_virtual_lib/aviation.html

Aviation Resources

- U.S. Federal Aviation Administration (FAA)
- Air Transport Association (ATA)
- Airlines on the Web UPDATED
- Airlines & Airports Page
- World Airport Database - 6600+ entries in 522 kb file!
- Airline Regulatory Filings NEW
- 1st Spotters Page - For aircraft spotter enthusiasts
- National Business Aircraft Association (NBAA)
- Aviation History
- Air Pix Aviation Photos
- Aircraft Picture Archive
- AeroLink NEW - The Global Aviation InfoSource
- U.S. Air Force Home Page
- U.S. Aircraft Registrations - Searchable!
- The Commercial Aviation Resource Center
- Air Affair's Aviation Web Hotlist
- Air & Space Magazine
- AIRFAX Online
- General Aviation WWW Server
- Aviation Enthusiast Corner
- General Aviation Information Page
- AviationWeb Links

also,
http://www.iglou.com/kj4vh/aviation.html

http://www.iquest.net/propilot/

The
Professional Aviator
The Resource Place for Pilots

The Professional Aviator page features a good link list.
http://www.iquest.net/propilot

Many of the commercial sites have useful images and links as well.
http://www.bekkoame.or.ip/~dynasty/

Airlines & Airports Hot Links

Dynasty's B747-400 at Tokyo Int'l Airport (Haneda)

MENU

Registration / Cargo Airlines--Links to World Airports--Other Aviation Links

Passenger Carriers TC1--Passenger Carriers TC2--Passenger Carriers TC3

International Airports in Japan--Domestic Airports in Japan

Another interesting aviation site: the Commercial Aviation Resource Center.
http://w3.one.net/~flypba

Welcome to...
The Commercial Aviation Resource Center

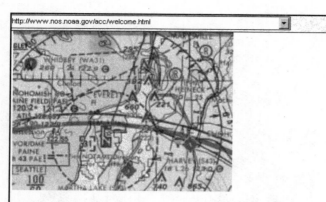

http://www.nos.noaa.gov/acc/welcome.html

The Office of Aeronautical Charting and Cartography

The Office of Aeronautical Charting and Cartography (AC&C) is responsible for p
charts to civil, military users, and controllers of the U. S. National Airspace System
and directs the construction; maintenance; reproduction; and distribution of aerona
of the United States and its territories to meet the requirements of civilian and milit

Keep up with US government efforts to go freely digital at sites like this. Some FAA and NOAA data is currently available to download; a smaller subset of that data is PC accessible, but don't give up. They're working on it.
Office of Aeronautical Charting and Cartography

http://www.nos.noaa.gov/aaa/wel come.html

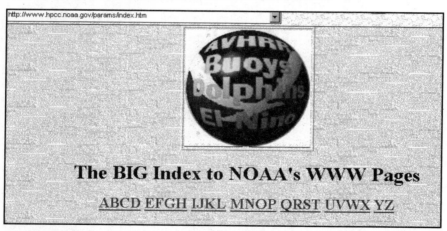

http://www.hpcc.noaa.gov/params/index.htm

The BIG Index to NOAA's WWW Pages

ABCD EFGH IJKL MNOP QRST UVWX YZ

http://www.ngs.noaa.gov/page3.html

NOAA Internet Information Servers

WEB SERVERS

National Oceanic and Atmospheric Administration(NOAA)

NOAA Directory Services

Tracking down sources of NOAA and FAA data can be an awesome task. Here are two servers that will help you get started.

MicroWINGS is probably the best known of the Flight Simulator pages, and is a valuable resource plus linker to other sites.

http://www.microwings.com/mwaptnav.html

http://www.microwings.com/mwaptnav.html

MicroWINGS

The International Association For Aerospace Simulations

Airport/NavAid/Fix Information and Maps

- To view information about an Apt/Nav/Fix, enter the facility's Identifier (ex. DFW for Dallas/Ft.Worth Int'l).
- To see a map of an area, enter the Lat/Lon coordinates for the area in the form of deg.dec
- Click here to return to our home page.

For GPS and mapping data, we recommend RDV's GIS List to the World. It is!

http://www.ecnet.net/users/murdv/wiu/more/gis.htm

http://www.ecnet.net/users/murdv/wiu/more/GIS.htm

RDV's GIS List to the World

Released 5/6/96

Ryan D. Vitek For New Posts

Page access: 2,624

What in the world is a GIS?
The GIS FAQlist

http://acro.harvard.edu/IAC/iac_homepg.html

International Aerobatic Club Home Page

Sport Aerobatic Magazine and the International Aerobatic Club were quite helpful to us in our discussion of aerobatic techniques. Here's where to find them:

International Aerobatic Club
EAA Aviation Center
P.O. Box 3086
Oshkosh, WI 54903-3086
414-426-4800
Membership: 1-800-843-3612

INTERNATIONAL
AEROBATIC
CLUB

Last Update: Wednesday, 04-Sep-96 12:06:22 EDT

Basic Aerodynamics

Standing near an aircraft on the ground, feeling so immediately its mass, it's hard not to agree with the term "heavier-than-air craft." But if a craft were truly heavier than air, it could never rise above the ground, could it? Actually, "heavier than air," as applied to airplanes, is every bit the misnomer "lighter than air" is when applied to the Goodyear blimp (the blimp's not lighter than air—the helium it encloses is). To be truly accurate, both types of aircraft should be called "weighs the same as air," when they're in flight, even if that phrase doesn't trip quite so lightly off the tongue.

Anything that floats, from Ivory soap to a 747, must be the same weight as the substance in which it is floating. Aircraft manage to weigh the same as the air around them with the help of that very same air. The wings of an airplane, moving through the air, produce the force, or lift, because air molecules are such petty little entities. No, let's be honest about this—air molecules are very competitive and simply cannot stand for any other air molecules to get ahead of them. Sort of the ultimate in "keeping up with the Jones," you might say.

That's a pretty fanciful way of stating it, but essentially a true one. Lift is the result of the air molecules rushing over the top of the curved wing faster than those flowing along the bottom of the wing. It's all based on a physical law called the Bernoulli Principle that describes how the molecules of a fluid (and for the physicist, air is every bit as much a fluid as is water) accelerate through a constriction. The constriction, in our

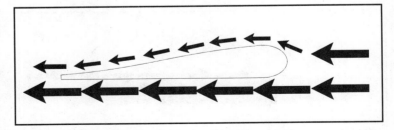

Airflow over a wing.

case, is produced by the curving of the wing. Air likes to flow in straight lines, but the curved wing prevents it from doing so. The little lines of air, called streamlines, have to bunch up to get around the wing's curve, and in doing so, become constricted. As we noted, constricted air flows more quickly, which leads us to another physical law that states the faster a fluid flows, the less pressure it exerts perpendicular to its flow.

Okay, let's see if we've got this: faster air over the top of the wing means less pressure pushing down on the wing, while the slower air beneath the wing—finding less resistance from above to its upward pushing— forces the wing up.

To go a step further, as the wing angle (the angle of attack) increases, the air on top has to take an even longer path, so it must travel a bit faster, decreasing its pressure a little more. Flaps and other aerodynamic devices along the wing can also change the wing's shape, resulting in even greater lift. But why does the air feel this overwhelming need to travel along the surface of the wing? The rather involved mechanics of this phenomenon (called laminar flow) describe an interaction between the molecules at the interface between the wing surface and the air that creates a very low pressure area (or near-vacuum) which literally holds the air streamlines against the wing.

As the angle of attack increases, the air molecules continue in this laminar flow, but there's a limit to their blind obedience. Somewhere in the area of 15-18 degrees positive angle (depending on wing shape), the laminar effect is no longer strong enough to keep the air streamlined against the wing surface— the airflow suddenly breaks away and becomes very turbulent. This has the effect of killing lift completely, and the plane experiences a stall.

Flight, however, is more than just lift. It's actually a delicate balancing act of four forces—lift, weight, thrust, and drag. Lift and weight go up against one another, while thrust and drag do battle. When the lifting force equals the weight of the aircraft, and the propulsive force (thrust) counterbalances the friction-produced drag,

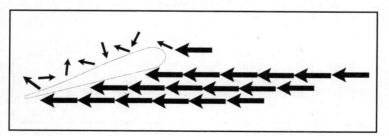

As airflow breaks up, a stall occurs.

you have flight. True flight—turning, banking, diving, cruising along at twice the speed of sound, etc.—is the alteration of this balancing act.

Modifications of the balancing act along the three axes of flight are effected by the control surfaces—elevator, ailerons, and rudder. The force of moving air against an obstruction changes an aircraft's attitude. Applying right rudder, for example, causes the rudder, a hinged flap attached to the trailing edge of the vertical stabilizer at the tail, to deflect, or move to the right, into the airflow. The air pushing against this newly created obstacle forces the tail of the aircraft to the left, and as the plane rotates along its center of gravity, the nose goes right. The same principle is in effect with all the control surfaces.

Powerplants

Aviation pioneers had actually figured out a great deal of the theory of flight well before the Wright Brothers. It is often said that the Wrights were not so much innovators as refiners, that they took the lessons of earlier experimenters and built upon them. To state this as the *complete* truth would be seriously underrating the contributions the Wrights made to aviation, but there is some verity to it. Certainly, both Orville and Wilbur would admit that, had it not been for the efforts of men like Otto Lilienthal and Octave Chanute, they would not have flown as soon as they did.

People were, indeed, flying well before the Wrights. The daring Lilienthal alone made well over 2,000 glider flights before crashing to his death in 1896. But powered flight—now there was the sticking point. The aerodynamics were there, but no one had been able to couple a flyable aircraft with a suitable engine. Dr. Samuel Langley came close to beating the Wrights into the air by a couple of months when he and his assistant, Charles Manly, were able to develop a powerful and relatively compact 52-horsepower engine. Unfortunately, Langley's ungainly aircraft, the Aerodrome, wasn't up to the task.

But Manly's engine design proved successful in that it set the design standard for the radial engine, one of the three basic types of piston-engines. The radial, as its name suggests, has its cylinders radiating out from a central crankcase. Manly's first model had only five cylinders, but it wasn't too long before radial engines sported as many as nine. To make even more powerful engines, manufacturers took to stacking radial engines together, so that in some

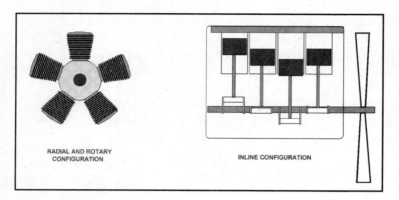

RADIAL AND ROTARY
CONFIGURATION

INLINE CONFIGURATION

The rotary, radial and in-line engines.

cases an engine might have as many as 36 cylinders. Even though many aircraft still use radial engines today, none of the planes in Flight Simulator uses one.

From outward appearances the rotary engine appears identical to the radial. Both have their cylinders arranged in a circle around the crankcase, but that's where the similarity ends. Start a rotary engine, and you'll be amazed to see that the engine cylinders spin along with the propeller. This provided excellent cooling for the cylinders, and resulted in a relatively simple engine that was quite powerful for its weight. The downside, however, was that the spinning cylinders made carburetion difficult. The spinning also created a great amount of torque which could adversely affect a light airplane such as the Sopwith Camel or the Fokker Triplane. Rotary engines were not used much beyond World War I. By the way, both rotary and radial engines are almost invariably air-cooled.

The third type of engine, and perhaps the most common—at least since World War II—is the in-line engine. The engine in your car (unless you own a Mazda RX-7) is an in-line engine, with the cylinders placed one behind the other, sometimes in multiple banks. The transition from radial to in-line engines began in World War II, as aircraft designers, trying to streamline their aircraft began to see the overwhelming benefits of the in-line engine, which allowed a plane's nose to be much sleeker. The debate over the merits of radials and in-lines has always been a debate over reliability (the radial, being air-cooled, doesn't need the elaborate cooling system most in-line engines use) versus aerodynamics. It seems to be something of a draw, as evidenced by the Reno Air Races held each year. The usual entrants are World War II fighter planes, and although you might expect in a race for the edge to go to the streamlined in-line-powered planes such as the North American Mustang, as often as not a big, clunky radial-engined plane—such as the Grumman Bearcat—wins.

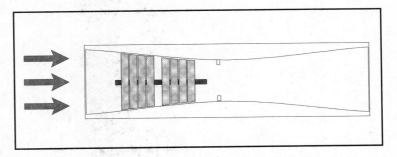

The turbojet engine.

Another transition that began in World War II was the transition from piston engines to jets. Due to the pioneering work of Frank Whittle (Great Britain) and Pabst von Ohain (Germany) prior to the war, both sides were able to put jet aircraft into the air before war's end. These were powered by turbojet engines, where air is introduced into a front intake, compressed with atomized fuel by a series of vaned compressors, and then ignited. The combustion can only

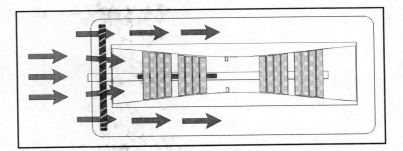

The turbofan engine.

go one way—out the tailpipe. Its frantic backward rush creates an equal force forward, and—voila!—you have thrust.

In the past 50 years the jet has developed in a number of ways. Most jet fighters still use some variation on the basic turbojet, albeit with a number of features (such as the afterburner) which increase either thrust or efficiency. Early on, when some aircraft designers were still wary of powering a plane with a pure jet engine, manufacturers used part of the thrust to turn a conventional propeller, resulting in the turboprop engine which powered many of the early jet airliners (and still powers many smaller commuter and business aircraft today). In fact, most of the by-pass engines used by modern airliners can be considered turboprops, since they use a portion of the engine's thrust to turn enclosed propellers, called fans (hence the name, turbofan). The Boeing 737-400 featured in Flight Simulator uses such an engine, while the Learjet 35A sticks with the basic turbojet.

Glossary

aileron: a movable control surface located on the wing's trailing edge, which, when deflected into the air stream, causes the wing either to rise or drop.

airbrake: any surface that extends into the slipstream to increase drag.

airfoil: the cross-sectional shape of a wing.

airway: a commonly used flight path defined by a VOR or other navigational aid.

angle of attack: the angle at which the wing meets the oncoming airflow.

aspect ratio: the ratio of the wing's span to its chord.

bearing: a directional notation as it relates to another direction.

by-pass engine: a jet turbine using auxiliary sets of blades to force air around the engine core and out the back for added thrust.

camber: the curve of an airfoil.

chord: the distance from a wing's leading edge to its trailing edge.

clean air turbulence: high altitude air turbulence occurring in otherwise clear conditions.

compressor: a series of turbine blades which compresses air for combustion in a turbojet engine.

control surface: any movable surface that modifies an aircraft's attitude when extended into the air flow.

drag: the resistance between air and any object moving through it.

drift: a lateral movement away from an aircraft's intended course, usually the result of a crosswind.

elevator: the movable surfaces on the trailing edge of the horizontal stabilizer which affects an airplanes pitch.

elevon: a control surface—usually on aircraft with delta wings—which functions both as an aileron and an elevator.

flair: raising the nose just prior to landing, providing a slight cushioning lift to the aircraft and allowing the plane to touch down on its main landing gear.

flap: an extendible section of the wing's trailing edge, used to change the effective shape of the wing and increase lift.

g-force: the force of gravity on an object.

glide path: a flight path with the proper heading and descent angle for a particular airfield.

gyrocompass: an inertial guidance system that uses a gyroscope to sense aircraft directional changes.

heading: the line of flight as it relates to the compass.

horizontal stabilizer: the (usually) fixed horizontal portion of the tail assembly or empennage.

IFR (Instrument Flight Rules): a set of procedures to be followed when navigating with methods other than visual.

ILS (Instrument Landing System): a system of radio transmitters that provides guidance to a pilot making a landing approach.

incidence: the angle of the wing when the airplane fuselage is level.

leading edge: the front edge of the wing.

lift: the force produced by the pressure drop of faster flowing air over the top of a wing's surface.

Mach number: a speed rating, named after physicist Ernst Mach, that expresses speed as a percentage of the speed of sound.

nautical mile: a distance measure equal to about 1.15 statute miles.

navaid: any aid to aeronautical navigation, including charts and radio beacons.

NDB (Non-Directional Beacon): a radio navigation beacon that transmits a single, nondirectional signal.

pitch: the angle of an aircraft's nose; also, the angle of attack for the blades of a propeller.

pitot: a small tube into which air is forced as a plane moves through the air. The airspeed indicator uses information from the pitot to calculate airspeed.

pitot-static: a system using forced air (pitot) and static air to send data to several aircraft instruments.

reciprocating engine: an engine in which the power is generated by pistons in cylinders, driven by repeating cycles of combustion.

roll: an aircraft's rotation along its longitudinal (fore to aft) axis.

rollout: the distance a plane travels after landing.

rotate: the lifting of an aircraft's nose just prior to takeoff, used to increase lift by changing the wing's angle of attack.

rudder: the movable surface—located on the trailing edge of the vertical stabilizer—which controls an aircraft's yaw.

slat: a section of the wing's leading edge that extends to provide extra lift.

spoiler: a section of the wing that extends into the air flow to produce drag, thus slowing the aircraft.

squawk: an ID code given to an aircraft to identify it to Air Traffic Control.

stall: a loss of lift, occurring when a too-high angle of attack causes the airflow over the top of the wing to become turbulent.

thrust: the energy produce in a jet by hot exhaust gases exiting the tail pipe.

torque: a mechanical twisting force.

touch and go: a landing followed by an immediate takeoff.

trailing edge: the rear edge of a wing.

trim: an aircraft's hands-off flight attitude. Small tabs on the control surfaces usually control trim.

turbine: any engine using enclosed rotating blades to compress and combust fuel.

turbofan: a jet turbine with extra fan blades for increased thrust. The blades force extra air around the outside of the engine core.

turbojet: a jet using rotating turbines to produce combustion, as opposed to a ramjet, which has no moving parts, and which relies on combustion to draw in more air.

V speed: a series of points along the speed continuum of an airplane's takeoff roll where critical decisions must be made.

vector: a directional measure, such as a bearing.

vertical stabilizer: the fixed vertical portion of the tail assembly to which the rudder is attached.

VFR (Visual Flight Rules): the set of procedures for navigating primarily by sighting visual cues.

VOR (Very high frequency Omnidirectional Range): a radio navigational beacon that broadcasts a signal divided into 360 radials.

yaw: the lateral movement of an aircraft's nose.

yoke: a type of control device, something of a cross between the traditional stick and a steering wheel.

Bibliography

Cacutt, Len, ed., *Great Aircraft of the World.* Secaucus, NJ: Chartwell Books, 1992.

Heppenheimer, T.A., *Turbulent Skies: The History of Commercial Aviation.* New York: John Wiley & Sons, 1995.

Mackworth-Praed, Ben, *Aviation: The Pioneer Years.* London: Studio Editions, Ltd., 1990.

Simpson, R.W., *Airlife's General Aviation.* Shrewsbury, England: Airlife Publishing Ltd., 1995.

Taylor, John W.R. and Kenneth Munson, *History of Aviation.* London: Octopus Books, Ltd., 1977.

Taylor, John W.R., ed., *The Lore of Flight.* Gothenburg, Sweden: AB Nordbok, 1990.

Wolters, Richard A., *The World of Silent Flight.* New York: McGraw-Hill Book Company, 1979.

Programs Used

Lorsche, Georges, *Final Approach.* Downloaded from the MicroWINGS web site. *Final Approach* shareware version by Georges Lorsche, who can be reached on-line at 100041.211@compuserve. Commercial version available from Colorado Technologies, Paris, France (colorado@club-internet.fr).

Index

rudder-only right turn, 83
Rules and Regulations. *See* Ground School
runway numbering, 203-204
runway orientation, 203

S

Sacramento Metropolitan Airport (SMF), 227
San Francisco International Airport (SFO), 115, *229*
San Jose International Airport (SJC), *230*
Save Flight, 3, 4.
Scenery Area, 191
Scenery Complexity, 15, *16*
Schweizer 2-32, 47, 59-61, *59, 61,* 167, 182, 183, 184, 190
Schweizer Aircraft Corporation, 61
Seattle-Tacoma International Airport (SEA), *231*
Set Exact Position option, 17
Simulation Rate, 4
simulators, airliner, 116
skidding, 22, 78, 84
Skyhawk, 50, 52
slat, 281
Slew Control, 17, 72
sliding, 22
slow roll, 147-150, *148*
Smoke System, 4, 6
Somme River, 193, 195, *195,* 199
Sopwith Camel, 22, 55, 62-65, *62, 64,* 137, 167, 190-201, *190, 191, 196, 200,* 276
Sound, 4, 10
Southern California Expansion Pack, 205
SPAD, 192
spin, 155-158, *156, 157*
Split-S, 162-165, *163, 164, 197*
spoilers, 115, 125, 127, 180, 181, 184, 187, 189, 281
spool up, 175
Spot Plane menu, 15, *31*
square loop, 142-144, *142, 143*
squawk, 173, 281
St. Louis International Airport (STL), 232
stall speed, 73, 75, 167, 187
stalls, 45, 81, 119, 156, 281
standard turn, 77-80
Straits of Dover, 195
Stewart, Betty, 132

T

tail-draggers, 89
takeoff roll, 57, 116, 117
Takeoff Stalls. *See* Lessons
TAS (True Airspeed), 21
TC (Turn Coordinator), 21, *21,* 70
thermals, 59, 62, 181, 182, 185, 186, *186,* 187, 188
    creating, 188
three-quarter loop, 160
Throttle Control, *22*
thrust, 113, 274, 281
thrust loss at high altitude, 174
Tiger mapping project web site, *265*
Time, 10
Time & Season. *See* Aircraft Controls
torque, 193, 276, 281
touch and go, 281
Tower View, 15, 31
towplane, 182
traffic pattern, 79
trailing edge, 281
Transponder, 10, 25, 96
trim, 281
trim indicator, 76
Trollope, Capt. J.L., 200
True Airspeed. *See* TAS
true magnetic heading, 95
T-tail, 183
turbine engines, 116, 117, 281
turbofan, 117, *277,* 281
turbojet engines, 277, *277,* 281
turboprop engine, 277
Turn and Bank Indicator, 21
Turn Coordinator. *See* TC

U

U.S. Sectional Charts, 204

V

V speeds, 116, 117, 281
variometer, 181
vector, 282
Vertical Speed Indicator. *See* VSI
vertical stabilizer, 22, 51, 275, 282
Very high frequency Omni-directional Range. *See* VOR
VHF Omni-directional Range, 98

The side with the best intelligence wins!

Outwit the enemy with CLOSE COMBAT: INSIDE MOVES.

Microsoft's World War II strategy game, Close Combat, requires that you master the strategies and tactics necessary to reach your objective. CLOSE COMBAT: INSIDE MOVES should be your battle planner as you play this exciting game because it explains both the historical context and the specific actions you need to take. The game is unique in its use of historical realism and war psychology—play is affected not only by your weapons and decisions but also by the mental and physical state of your troops and their units. Take command and win—with CLOSE COMBAT: INSIDE MOVES.

Close Combat
inside moves

Winning Tips and Strategies Straight from the Source

Microsoft **CLOSE COMBAT**

Microsoft Press   William R. Trotter

U.S.A.   **$16.95**
Canada $22.95
 [*Recommended*]
ISBN 1-57231-308-0

Microsoft®*Press*

Register Today!

Return this
Microsoft® Flight Simulator: Inside Moves
registration card for a
Microsoft Press® catalog

U.S. and Canada addresses only. Fill in information below and mail postage-free. Please mail only the bottom half of this page.

1-57231-362-5A   *MICROSOFT® FLIGHT SIMULATOR:*   *Owner Registration Card*
INSIDE MOVES

_____

NAME

_____

INSTITUTION OR COMPANY NAME

_____

ADDRESS

_____

_____

CITY   STATE   ZIP

Microsoft®*Press*
Quality Computer Books

**For a free catalog of
Microsoft Press® products, call
1-800-MSPRESS**

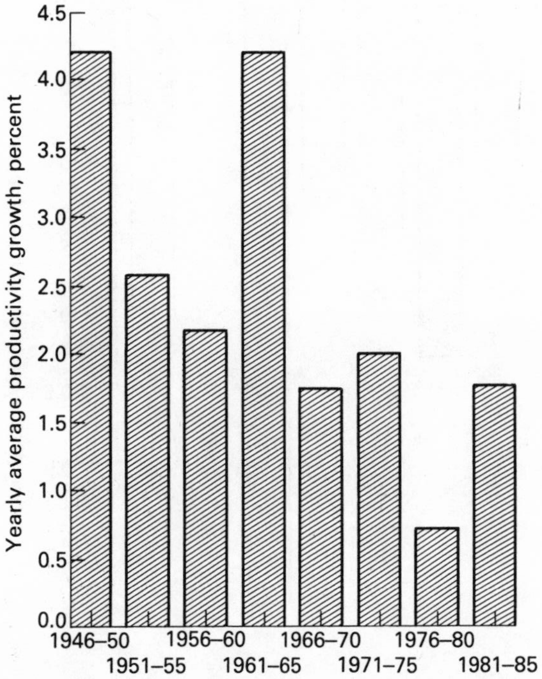

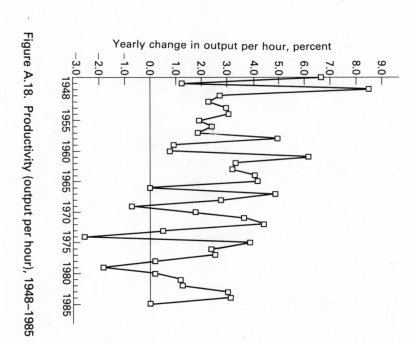

Figure A.17. Productivity growth, 1946–1985

Figure A.18. Productivity (output per hour), 1948–1985

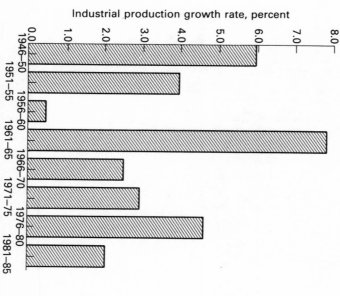

Figure A.19. Industrial production growth rates, 1946–1985
(yearly averages during period)

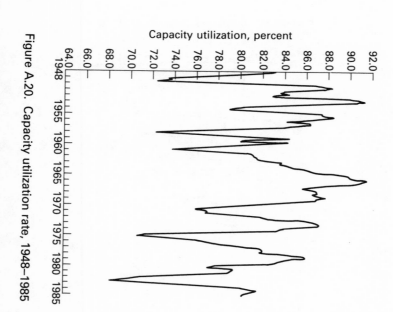

Figure A.20. Capacity utilization rate, 1948–1985

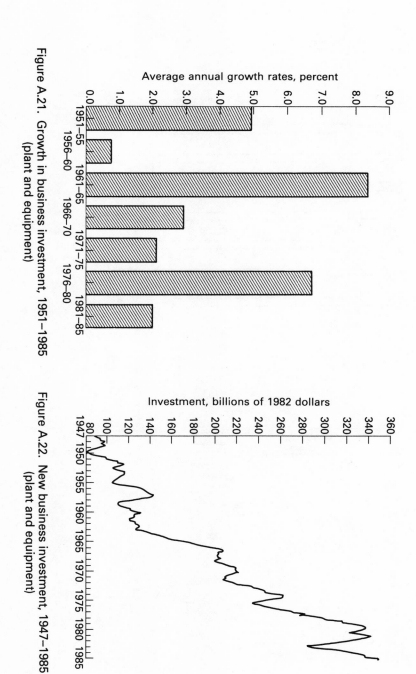

Average annual growth rates, percent

Figure A.21. Growth in business investment, 1951–1985
(plant and equipment)

Investment, billions of 1982 dollars

Figure A.22. New business investment, 1947–1985
(plant and equipment)

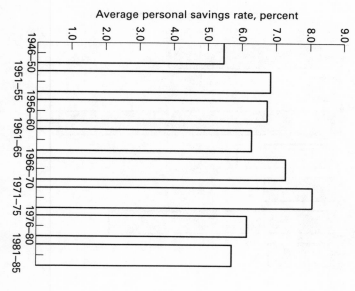

Figure A.23. Average personal savings rate, 1946–1985

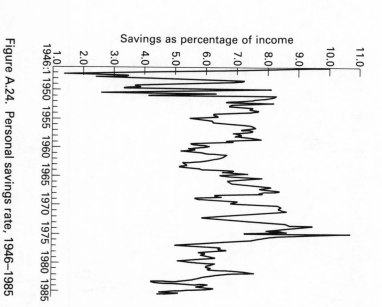

Figure A.24. Personal savings rate, 1946–1985

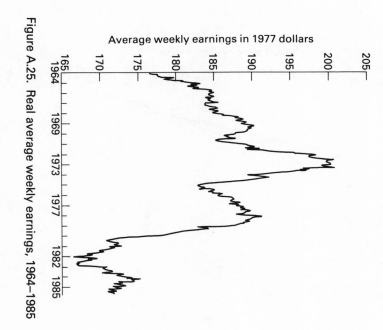

Figure A.25. Real average weekly earnings, 1964–1985

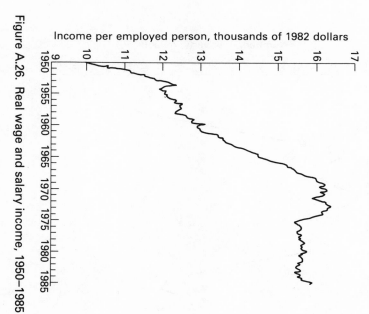

Figure A.26. Real wage and salary income, 1950–1985

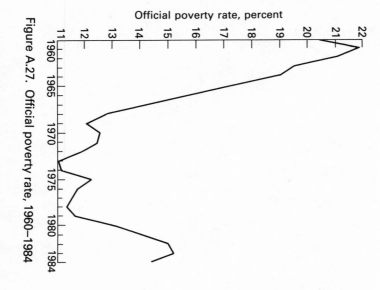

Official poverty rate, percent

Figure A.27. Official poverty rate, 1960–1984

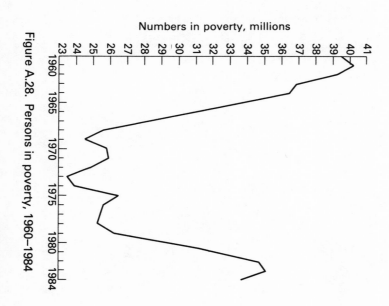

Numbers in poverty, millions

Figure A.28. Persons in poverty, 1960–1984

Index